# Successfully
# Navigating
# the Downturn

# Successfully Navigating the Downturn

**Donald Todrin**

Publisher: Jere Calmes
Cover Design: Andrew Welyczko, CWL Publishing Enterprises, Inc.
Editorial and Production Services: CWL Publishing Enterprises, Inc., Madison, Wisconsin, www.cwlpub.com

This publication is designed to provide accurate and authoritative information in regard to the subject matter covered. It is sold with the understanding that the publisher is not engaged in rendering legal, accounting, or other professional services. If legal advice or other expert assistance is required, the services of a competent professional person should be sought.
> —From a Declaration of Principles jointly adopted by a
> Committee of the American Bar Association and
> a Committee of Publishers and Associations

ISBN 13: 978-1-59918-419-7
10: 1-59918-419-2

Every effort has been made to ensure that the information in this book is accurate and current at the time of publication. However, laws, regulations, policies, contact information, and so on may be changed without notice. This book is not a substitute for individual advice rendered by a professional who is able to work with you one-on-one.

## To my wife Diane Todrin

After 32 years of peaks and valleys, opening and operating over 56 distinct businesses, most of them ultimately successful, my wife has stood by me through thick and thin, rich and poor, good and not-so-good times. I am eternally grateful to her for supporting my doing whatever I wanted in my business arena. She is a saint. I dedicate this work to her. She has earned it.

# Contents

 # Preface

## Ready for Battle

If you haven't noticed, it's a war out there. In any economy, building a small business is a challenge. When revenues shrink, the fight for customers and their dollars can be the ultimate fight for survival. Yet if you blame the economy or come up with any other excuse why your business is not flourishing, then you aren't fighting for your company.

Here is the most frequent excuse I hear from owners with an underperforming business: "The economy is bad."

You make or break your own business. Take responsibility. Look around and you will see there are businesses doing very well. Why, you ask? Because they are not concerned about excuses, only action plans and good business practices that result in growing sales and profits.

There are successful businesses opening and operating in every economy, every day, every season, every year, that are located next door to failures. If we truly believe success or failure is a function of external forces, we are doomed, as external forces always happen and are typically out of our control. Since we cannot control these factors but can control our own business practices, we must direct our energies toward that which we can control as we chart our business course to reflect necessary and appropriate changes.

This book is not an A–Z textbook on running a small business; there are shelves full of them, mostly in college bookstores. This book homes in on the essentials for operating a successful small business in this fast-changing battle zone.

There are numerous books that focus on one aspect of running a business, such as branding, sales, or finance. It's not uncommon to have a pile of must-read books gathering dust at the bedside while more pressing demands fill the precious time allotted for reading. This book reports from the trenches with advice you can only learn by trial and error, from tying into what is working in the marketplace and what is not.

While most books are written to be read from beginning to end, you can pick this one up and thumb through the table of contents to find topics to help you solve your most difficult business problems or to help you grow a more profitable business. Each topic is short and succinct, and so you can read the book in short increments and implement strategies as you go.

I encourage you, however, to read even those sections that you think you're good at, because it's easy to forget what's important after living in an economy where revenue flowed freely. So jump in anywhere and read as much as you can, when you can; then implement.

It is a wonderful spirit we nurture in this country, where anybody can dream, open a business, and succeed. Success will come when you have a plan and business skills, and only if you adapt and keep up to date with the needs of the changing world around you.

## Acknowledgments

Claudia Gere: my editor and publishing consultant. In a word, she is the best. She is patient, very knowledgeable, tireless, and she translated my material from some foreign unknown language into a quality presentation. It would never have happened had she not been my leader.

Don Parsons: my first mentor. He taught me the concept of standards and how to live up to them. He showed me the value of doing the right thing . . . no matter what. He is a great man.

Fred Seibert: a third mentor, who taught me the value of people. He showed me how to live, as well as how to do business. I count him as a friend and a mentor. I am fortunate to have his influence in my life.

The Magnificent 7: my men's group, with Ed Hunt as one of its leaders. These men helped me learn what it means to be the man I want to be and helped me get there. Their influence is beyond description.

Bernard and Annette Todrin: my parents. My father taught me how to be the business man I am. He taught me this by my watching how he lived and worked. There could be no better a role model. I am very fortunate. My mother taught me wisdom. She is a very wise woman and has always given me what I needed. I am a very lucky man to have such terrific parents as role models.

Richard and David: my brothers, who have been huge influences in my life.

My daughter Elizabeth and my son Aaron. My best and most important work. I measure my wealth by my family's happiness; they are happy, therefore I am successful.

To the men in the trenches at Second Wind, the men in the front lines doing the hand-to-hand small business combat, saving families, one business at a time: Norm Schell, Peter Tur, Adam Duso, Adam Gleason, Harry Greenhouse, Greg Wales, Richard McGravey, and Joe Conforto. These men get it, know what's at risk, and refuse to lose . . . They are my inspiration. Kenny Butler: Leading me to places I did not even know existed. Dave Tomolillo: Teaching me that the brutal truth is a gift.

To every small business in America, the engine of growth, the source of most jobs, and the backbone of the country.

## Disclaimer

The advice given in this book should not be construed as legal advice or tax advice. Consult your lawyer or tax consultant as appropriate prior to implementing changes.

 # Surviving the Downturn

## No Business Will Escape . . . Prepare

**E**very business will be affected by this economic meltdown. There is no escaping. Those that think they will escape are fooling themselves.

The root causes are universal and will impact every business, in a kind of domino effect, with profits tumbling one after the other. I spoke with my insurance agent, and she reported revenues down over 30 percent. "Why?" I asked, "It makes little sense. People are not yet taking their cars off the road, are they?"

"No," she responded, "but they are not buying new cars, so the insurance premiums are less, and also people are reducing their coverage to lower their bills. All in all, it amounts to an overall 30 percent decline." Then she added, "And defaults are up for nonpayment." Her hours were cut, as were her staff's.

A produce delivery business I represent, which I assumed would be relatively immune to the downturn, is likewise experiencing a deep reduction in revenues. People are not eating out as much, the small business owner reports. Thus, consumption at restaurants is down, reducing his revenues by 30 to 40 percent. He is making fewer and smaller deliveries.

We need not discuss the auto industry, the housing market, and the trades and businesses that are supported by these markets. Can you even imagine the depth and width of their tremor? Of course, the financial markets lost tens of thousands of jobs nationally. New York City alone experienced a 20 percent decline in its revenue flow as a direct result of the reduction in the financial market.

The unemployment statistics are sobering. Depending on whose numbers you are looking at, unemployment is at least 10 percent, and another 5 percent of the population is no longer looking for jobs and, thus, not counted.

Even Microsoft has laid off 5,000 people.

It's the ripple effect that will undo us all. Fewer people working, more foreclosures, less purchasing power. It affects every business. The reason gas prices have declined so much is a direct result of less demand for fuel. Factories, trucks, and, yes, cars are using less fuel. Can you imagine the amount of reduced demand required to reduce gas consumption as much as it has gone down? It must be huge.

> **It's the ripple effect that will undo us all. Fewer people working, more foreclosures, less purchasing power. It affects every business.**

Of course, this is also a global issue: Imports and exports are declining, providing additional momentum to the downturn.

I hear some small business owners saying that they believe the bottom is near, that they are surviving, that they are OK, and that they expect to persevere throughout the recession with modest adjustments. These small business owners are kidding themselves. The bottom has not been reached, and it will be a long slide until it does. We are in for a five- to 10-year disaster. Everyone will be affected; every business will be reduced.

Plan, adjust, and prepare. Failure to do this will be at your own peril. There is no escape. Downsize; do your preemptive workouts. Market effectively and not only can you survive, but you can maintain profitability.

Failure to adjust will end in a slow death ... or maybe a rapid one.

## Learning from the Greatest Entrepreneur of All

I recently read the book *1776* by award-winning author David McCullough. If you are not familiar with it, it is the story of the first year of the American Revolution. During that year, the Continental

Congress commissioned Washington as the Commander in Chief of the Continental Army. In and of itself, his appointment was a leap of faith, as Washington had limited battle experience and none in small-skirmish or large-scale war strategy.

Worse yet, he had few experienced leaders capable of handling the men in the field. His troops were completely untrained and were equipped with few arms and little ammunition. The men came and went as they pleased, depending on weather and family needs at home. Sickness often disabled as many as one-third of his men at any given time.

Even worse, they were confronting the greatest army and navy in the world at that time, well trained and well armed. The British navy comprised 400 ships armed with hundreds of guns. The Revolutionary forces had no navy and few guns and were badly outnumbered by a ratio of 10 to 1.

In the winter, the Revolutionary forces had no tents and insufficient clothing and shoes to keep them dry and warm. It was, in a word, pathetic to consider this ragtag band of farmers, hunters, and a few aristocrats an army. It was an undisciplined, untrained, unarmed, unequipped band of passionate men who fought among themselves and had no idea how to conduct warfare.

Washington's strategies were most often wrong. His lack of experience led him into one defeat after another, and yet he persevered. That is the quality of an entrepreneur. The one characteristic used most often in reaching the desired goals—not experience, intelligence, or skill, but perseverance. An entrepreneur refuses to lose, rejects defeat, insists on reaching the goal no matter how slim the odds or likelihood of victory.

The Revolutionary leaders bet everything they owned, including their lives. They gave up their families, power, wealth, and comfort to battle against the most formidable force in the world, knowing that should they lose the war and survive, they would all surely hang. Yet, against the most impossible odds imaginable, they persevered.

This is the true hallmark of an entrepreneur, perseverance, and George Washington demonstrated this trait to the greatest degree. When the going gets tough, we can all take a lesson from Washington as the ultimate entrepreneur. He gave birth to the most amazing business the world has ever seen against the most severe odds any entrepreneur ever bet against, and he won, giving life to America.

When your situation seems grim, and the challenge is seemingly impossible, too difficult to go another day, remember George Washington and his perseverance. Then do it. Persevere. He won so we could enjoy the freedom to fight our own battles safely and securely. We can never give up, or we will be dishonoring his entrepreneurial victory.

## How Long Will This Recession Last?

There are many conflicting opinions regarding the length and depth of this so-called recession and the difficulty it will cause us all. The world financial markets will have a huge impact on our recovery, as they too have a tremendous impact on what happens in our financial markets. Academics and the economists hedge their bets, some suggesting that this recession will last at least through 2012, but they say this also depends on what actions our government takes to shorten it. Others say it is a 10-year trough, with small incremental growth after we eventually bottom out.

> Academics and economists hedge their bets, some suggesting that this recession will last at least through 2012, but they say this also depends on what actions our government takes to shorten it.

Unfortunately, I agree with the second opinion about a long-term change in the economy for the following reasons. Unemployment will continue to rise as more and more jobs will be eliminated. According to a CNN Money news report,[1] "The hemorrhaging of American jobs accelerated at a record pace at the end of 2008, bringing the year's total job losses to 2.6 million or the highest level in more than six decades." And there is much more shrinkage coming. Once gone, rebuilding the workforce to reflect the previous economy either will take a long time to accomplish or, in all likelihood, will never happen. Once gone, gone forever. Different people will be filling different jobs during the recovery, and this will take time. I believe the financial downspin can be reversed in a few years, but it will take five to 10 years to rebuild to where we were at the first point of decline.

Further, the second influence, which will help determine the duration of the recession, is the recovery of the world's financial markets.

This influence is substantial in both directions: our influence on the world and the world's collective influence on us. If every country succeeds in stemming its economic decline as fast as possible, we could be out in two years, but this will not happen. There are likely to be mixed recovery results among the countries with the most influence. Some will be more successful than others. Some will do a lot worse. Thus, the overall impact will be an accumulation and average of all the various degrees of success and failure. So the recovery period for the world, including the United States, will stretch further than some are projecting.

Of course, there is also the question of what our government does to reverse our economic downspin. If we implement the correct strategies, we all win and will end the decline sooner. If we guess wrong, and it is a guess, we stay in recessionary economics for many more years.

Given that wager, I will bet our government leaders will not make the best moves all the time, which will extend the economic downturn and slow the recovery period for a long while.

To successfully exit this recession requires fixing some of the other major issues in our economy, which will take time, effort, and investment, as well as political leadership and success. This includes defining and implementing a viable energy policy, defining and implementing a workable health care strategy, and overcoming the political issues preventing resolution to date. We also need to repair our social security program, so our elderly will enjoy a respectful contribution to their retirement. We need to address the massive unemployment level and the destruction of the housing market along with the deflation of real estate values for the economy to rebound, or it will stall until these problems are resolved.

I say, you must prepare for a five- to 10-year cycle, which means we cannot look back. We must look at today's condition and understand that this is what we will be working with for the next five to 10 years as we slowly pull out and rebuild, with different economic engines, a different workforce, a different energy policy, a different health care system. Five to 10 years, folks, so start redefining your business model to accommodate the changes today.

We must recognize this as a huge change of direction, and everyone must use this to define a new way or be lost forever. Yes, this is not just a speed bump we can wait to pass; it's a change in the way we will be doing business for a long time.

My best advice for small business owners is to reevaluate your core business equations, force profitability immediately by making whatever changes are required, and downsize; then, reinvent your business by focusing on long-term permanent changes that develop profit, not gross revenue.

## Be Positive and Defeat the Downturn

After one of the biggest stock market drops in recent times, the morning's news used the word *panic* in describing the steady decline. Panic, fear driven, not based on fact but on emotion, has tremendous power, the power to change the direction of business.

We all have a choice. Do we follow the trend and give in to panic, throwing our hands in the air and accepting self-destruction, actually accelerating it, becoming a part of the panic, stimulating more?

Is there an alternative? Yes, of course there is. Change is an opportunity for advances, if you dare. We are definitely confronting change. The question is, are you going to take advantage of it or are you going to allow yourself to be buried by it? It's your choice.

There is much you can do to take advantage of the situation: create new marketing ideas; develop a positive outlook; exhibit a no-problem attitude; separate yourself from the crowd of competitors who are singing the blues and accepting defeat. Stand out. Take a positive stand. Market with positivity. Stimulate a positive response. People want to be positive. People want a reason to not panic, so give it to them. They will respond. Market with creativity and positivity and the clients will line up and take tickets to get in your front door. If you accept a doom-and-despair attitude, you will follow the crowds down the path to self-destruction.

> If you accept a doom-and-despair attitude, you will follow the crowds down the path to self-destruction.

Small business owners have choices, many. Make the right choices today and see the results tomorrow. It's not just about price—broadcast your differences, tell people why they should shop with you, provide them with added value, not price discount, and watch your business grow in a down market.

Be a leader, and the people will follow. Small business can lead us out of this financial crisis. Just as the small banks are healthy, small business is also healthy … if you choose to be. Buy into gloom and despair, and your premonition will be fulfilled.

Start with your employees, move to your vendors, and then support your customers and your market area. Announce the good news, and everyone will line up.

## The Quick-Response Strategy

I believe one of the most powerful aspects of small business is its ability to turn on a dime, make changes in an hour, a day, a week, and take advantage of changing circumstances, trends, and new ideas or adjust in response to profitability or losses.

While it may take large corporations months or even years to evaluate a situation, create new strategies, and then implement a new plan to effect a change, small business can do it overnight. That's powerful if a business does it.

I constantly see businesses that stagnate, doing the same thing every day irrespective of the results, and usually they are complaining, using the excuse that they lack adequate cash to make changes. Changes of strategy do not necessarily require huge investments of cash, just clear thinking and effective implementation.

In his book *Crazy Times Call for Crazy Organizations,* Tom Peters tells a story that illustrates an important point. Here's my summary: Paul Volker, past Federal Reserve chief, was talking with one of Japan's most successful foreign exchange traders. Volker asked the trader to name some of the factors he considered when evaluating possible trades. The trader answered by saying, "Many factors, sometimes very short term, some medium, and some long term." Volcker then asked what he meant by "long term." The trader thought for a moment and responded, "Probably ten minutes!"[2]

I wonder what short term was.

While it is true that most of us are not in a market so volatile that 10 minutes is considered long term, the point is well made. Business owners need to address their business as the above-mentioned trader does, with a current view.

If you are making money, figure out why and do more of whatever is most successful. If you are losing money, stop whatever you are doing and make changes immediately. Make a change today and see the results tomorrow. If it's good, do it again; if it's not, make another change. That's what small business can do that big business cannot. Unfortunately, most small business owners remain committed to the same actions and expect better results every day. It will not happen without change.

I see it all the time. Small businesses doing the same thing every day, every week, every month, not daring to utilize the most effective strategy available: change. Identify new ideas, new markets, new strategies; and implement them boldly and with commitment.

In some instances, we are talking about internal adjustments, which require monitoring your company's performance so trends can be spotted quickly and early, giving you the opportunity to make changes early in the cycle as opposed to after you have lost your way.

Other aspects of this quick-change strategy have more to do with directional changes that have greater impact: major marketing changes, major production changes, make-or-buy decisions, and so on.

Both are important, and both must be addressed as part of the business owner's strategy. Quick changes must be part of every small business owner's strategy for success.

This applies to personnel issues, as well. Small business owners hold onto ineffective employees too long. They fail to understand that a successful small business must closely monitor and adjust its employee base, always looking for the best possible team.

Pricing is also a frequently stalled evaluation, with small business owners failing to understand the need for profit and fearing that raising prices will result in lost sales, as opposed to understanding the value of their products and pricing them appropriately and profitably.

Be alert to marketing strategies that don't work and yet prevail, staying with brokers who fail to produce and yet are held onto forever, paying salespeople with a salary instead of using a reward-based commission program, not changing or expanding your target market. Be proactive, not stagnant.

The opportunity for change is limitless; the only real issue is the reluctance of the small business owner to leap into uncharted waters and dare to respond quickly and effectively, making changes. Do it.

# Change Strategies or Perish

In this economy you either adopt new strategies and skills or perish.

My wife went away with her parents and sister today for a long weekend to visit family. She asked me what am I going to do, and I thought for about a second and said … work, what else? To me and every other small business owner, work is not drudgery. It's what we do. It is how we become successful. We compete in the business arena, and success is our motivation. Money may be our reward, but success is our goal.

"So what," you say. "We all know this." Over the years, there is an important entrepreneurial skill you have developed and honed in response to shaky times. The knee-jerk reaction is to work harder, put in more time, and sacrifice yourself; to stay afloat, you take no paycheck, stop investing in your IRA, borrow against your insurance cash values, and max out your credit cards, finally moving on to absorb every other available dollar you can reach, from family, friends, anyone with cash.

It won't work. Instead, you will waste all the dollars you invest and put your family in harm's way. Your home mortgage will not get paid; cars will be repossessed; savings will be drained. Personal destruction will ensue, while the business fails to respond favorably.

Business owners must do things they abhor, but if they are to survive the current changing conditions of reduced revenues, increasing overhead, and choking debt, they must change their strategies rapidly to survive and emerge.

> **Downsize as deeply as possible. The most common mistake is to wait too long and not cut deeply enough.**

Downsize as deeply as possible. The most common mistake is to wait too long and not cut deeply enough. Reduce debt by working it out, going into default as soon as you see what is occurring. Stop paying on your credit cards and any other nonsurvival debt obligation. Reinvent your business model; emphasize profit, not revenue; and make major adjustments that will support your new mission.

Use Internet marketing and social networking; the time is here. Yes, social networking is new and hard to understand, but it will control your business future. Get on board.

Business owners don't want to take any of these actions, and so often we see them wait too long, absorbing unaffordable losses, preventing the reinvention, survival, and reemergence of a profitable business. The normal tendency under such pressures is to work harder and longer doing what you have always done, and this will not work in the current economy. The objective is to understand where you are and the changes you must make. It is not business as usual. It is upside down and backward to what you have always done. Unfortunately, failure to change as soon as necessary can be fatal.

## Rules to Survive the Downturn

I understand the reluctance of small business owners to make major changes before they are certain what is going to happen in an economy. When faced with a financial downturn, there are four pillars for successfully navigating the business world:

1. Downsize and tighten the systems. Controls are critical.
2. Reinvent yourself, consistent with the most profitable operation you can create with the least investment.
3. Do your debt workouts.
4. Use Internet marketing and social networking—figure it out.

Within those four pillars, here are 15 rules of engagement to successfully recast your business and succeed in the new economy:

1. Downsize immediately. Even if you think you're fine and immune from the changes in the economy, no businesses will escape unscathed. The market is suffering, unemployment is growing, people with jobs are not buying, real estate is crashing, and credit is scarce. This will have a ripple effect throughout the country. So if you're doing fine, downsize anyway. You can deliver the same amount—or more—with fewer people by increasing their productivity ... it's true. Downsize drastically. Force profitability by reducing your overhead and increasing productivity. It can be done!
2. You cannot wait another day! Install a key indicator system to track your business and have daily, weekly, and monthly financial reports issued. Follow profitability per job, per week, per client, per product. Make nothing that does not bring in a profit.
3. Evaluate and eliminate excessive debt, based on your downsized business model. Yes, this can be done through debt workouts.

4. Flatten your management system and add incentive-based rewards throughout the business.
5. Reduce inventories at any cost; create cash.
6. Reduce overhead wherever possible.
7. Train and cross-train everyone to be better, more skilled.
8. Review your marketing program and reduce the traditional approach. Use the Internet and focus on existing clients first; get more out of them. Internet marketing will save many companies; it's called the long tail theory. Read about it in Chris Anderson's blog (www.thelongtail.com) or in his book by the same name.
9. Resist profit-eating sales and discounting, giving away your profit for no good reason; instead, compete with service, quality, and uniqueness. Create a niche and have a competitive advantage. The big box stores cannot compete with you!
10. Emphasize service; it's the small business competitive advantage, its strong suit.
11. Reduce your focus to your most profitable products or services or joint venture for growth and development. It's cheaper and far more effective to do this. Faster, too.
12. Expand geographically if possible. Internet marketing can take you anywhere, especially if you can create an expertise or a unique specialty or a special item or service. Find what you do that is unique and do it as large as possible. Of course you can outcompete the big boxes; just be smarter and stop trying to compete on price alone.
13. Manage effectively. Flat incentives, key indicators, financial reports, productivity control, profitable sales, and effective marketing ... get smaller first and more profitable; then grow slowly and carefully.
14. It's all about quality; that's what wins in the long run. Never forsake this principle.
15. Consider vertical growth if you have the right product. If you make it or are prime, distribute it, wholesale it, and retail it, as well as going direct to the consumer through the Internet.

If you determine you cannot make the transition, stop, liquidate, and milk the company of its cash. Eliminate all but the critical employees and wind things down as quickly as possible.

The horse is out of the barn, but there is still time to close the door ... quickly. Get better, get smaller, get out, or be forced out. Your choice.

## Downsize

How does it make sense to downsize if you are still on the upward side of a growth curve or holding steady? There are a many examples of why downsizing is a good strategy in this economy. Mobil Oil even with 30 percent reduced revenue had a record-breaking, profitable year because it reduced its overhead and payroll to support the anticipated downturn. Like many Americans today, the business world is too fat. It needs to go on a diet.

Harvard University has the largest multibillion-dollar bankroll and endowment in the university world. Even having lost much on the stock market, it is still incredibly wealthy, and yet the university laid off professors and embarked on a belt-tightening austerity program. Why? Is it overresponding? No, it makes sense.

Increased overhead and excessive payroll are a recurring disease. It is always present and frequently peaks, showing its tenacity. Growing overhead, especially too much payroll, is easily overlooked while an organization is on an upward growth curve as revenues are abundant and profits significant, but those are the largest cost factors. Excessive spending must be avoided in good times and rooted out in bad times. It is waste that must be beaten back and controlled.

Inefficient business growth results in paying your employees overtime as well as adding employees required to handle the expansion ... but this is a low-productivity fix. Furthermore, there are other expenses such as additional computers, trucks, or machines; more vacation pay; and added insurance costs. A better response is to increase productivity and hold the addition of new employees and overtime to a minimum. Be like Mobil and Harvard. Reduce payroll, overtime, and expenses, and you will increase profit in times of decline as well as in times of growth.

This is a time of growth for some businesses, even though we are in a recession and most businesses are experiencing reduced revenues and lower profitability. We need to downsize, tighten procedures, control expenses, and hold on to profitability as best as we can. Still, some businesses are experiencing growth and seem immune to the recession. In fact, some industries are in higher demand because they are recession-proof. Used cars and auto mechanic shops are in greater demand as people are fixing or buying used rather than replacing with new vehicles.

Whether experiencing a decline or an increase, the idea is to take out the cleaver instead of the surgical knife and cut deep, deeper than the revenue reduction may require. Overcutting, some may claim, with unnecessary layoffs, is taking advantage of the downturn to lose excessive employees and reduce overhead—making the business leaner and meaner at the cost of employees. In reality, it is making up for years of unnecessary growth and development, cutting out the fat and leaving the meat.

Thus, no matter if you are losing ground, holding your own, or even expanding, a focus on training, incentives, and teamwork, all contributing to greater productivity without increased overhead and payroll, is the best answer. Cut cut your payroll, workforce, and overhead. I guarantee you have too much, and if your efforts are focused on getting better, not getting bigger, you will be around a lot longer, irrespective of the economic climate.

## The Six Biggest Downsizing Mistakes

Downsizing was not in the 2009–2010 year plan for most small business owners. No one predicted—or could prepare for—what is happening to our economy, and certainly no individual small business owners can be held responsible for their company's downturn in an economic situation outside their control.

However, failure to respond adequately and appropriately is an error you can avoid, as you can control your responses to the changing economy.

Here are half a dozen major stumbling blocks to consider in your downsizing plan.

### Mistake 1. Underestimating the Severity and Length of an Economic Downturn

Be stone-cold realistic. Acknowledge immediately that this is not a trend that will soon reverse itself. Our economy is severely damaged, and what we have now is what we are going to have for a long while—years—and then we will slowly grow. We will not see the burst of acceleration in values and growth and development that we experienced in the previous 10 years for a long while.

The point: Redesign your company based on a realistic evaluation of your worst case. Protect your core most profitable business, the parts that make up most of your volume and serve most of your customers.

Identify your top customers and make certain you are satisfying their needs. You must do your debt workouts or perish. It is that simple; there are no options here. Reduce your debt in the face of reduced revenues.

Not getting small enough quick enough is a short path to disaster. Do it all in one swipe: Redesign, reimplement, and off you go. Do it right, all the way, for the worst-case scenario using severe, bone-chilling cuts.

> Not getting small enough quick enough is a short path to disaster. Do it all in one swipe: Redesign, reimplement, and off you go.

### Mistake 2. Implementing Across-the-Board Cuts

Avoid making across-the-board cuts or reductions or shutting down entire divisions unnecessarily. Pinpoint the best way to downsize while maintaining your full capability. Cut your employee force in half; yet be able to perform the same functions. Letting go of the entire marketing department is not the way to downsize properly. Isolate and pinpoint reductions so your entire business can still perform.

### Mistake 3. Communicating Too Infrequently

It is important that you communicate with your employees early, often, and honestly; it's the right thing to do and will create great loyalty and support if done correctly. You must acknowledge the need to downsize in order to survive. You have to explain that the reasons are beyond anyone's control. Thus, there is no finger-pointing, only working together, digging in, and winning the war ... for everyone's best interest. Survival of the few at the expense of the many, but survival is critical or all will be lost for everyone.

Tell your employees you have the plan that will save the day and support your emergence. Demonstrate that you believe in your plan. If you are convincing, they will follow your lead, as that is how they will judge the situation, by your conviction and commitment to your plan. This is a key communication.

You must communicate your understanding and appreciation for the pain this is putting your people through and thank them for their support and sacrifice. The potential cost to everyone involved is huge. There may be no other jobs available for a long time.

### Mistake 4. Failing to Handle Layoffs with Caring

Go out of your way to demonstrate that you care about the employees being laid off. Create the best possible exit program you can, but most importantly, demonstrate that you really care. This will make this entire process much less painful and easier for all concerned. Also, the remaining employees are watching and assessing how you are handling this matter. If you do it with great care and concern, they know you will be kind to them as well.

These actions help teams come together. Employees will move into their discomfort zone and perform better than they think they can.

### Mistake 5. Hoarding Inventory

Do not hoard inventory; liquidate. Inventory is an expensive security blanket. Sell it and take the loss; access your locked-up capital. The cash is more valuable. Business owners feel more secure with inventory, and so they invest much too much money in it, then hate to part with it. In a downsizing, get rid of it!

> Do not hoard inventory; liquidate. Inventory is an expensive security blanket. Sell it and take the loss; access your locked-up capital.

### Mistake 6. Failing to Demonstrate How Cost-Cutting Hurts You More Than It Does Your Employees

If you ask for reductions in pay or benefits, somehow demonstrate how you, too, are sacrificing, and more than you are asking your employees to do. Do something dramatic and showy that demonstrates this sacrifice. Sell the Mercedes.

Cut deeper than you believe you should. Batten down the hatches and market like crazy. There will be a smaller pie to divide up, but you can get a larger share than you had even while downsizing.

## Renegotiate Anything and Everything

In this recession, revenues are plummeting and yet costs are high, based on yesterday's economy when it was boom time. Clearly, much focus for the individual business owner is aimed at internal adjustments: lowering overhead, reducing payroll, and cutting expenditures for marketing and other line items. This is appropriate and expected. However, to do the job thoroughly and effectively, you must look at every expense item, not just those that are easy to control. For example:

- **Payroll:** It's always a major expense line item.
- **Cost of goods:** Although typically viewed as untouchable, negotiate hard with your vendors or replace them; someone wants the business.
- **Leases:** Negotiate new deals for the equipment, cars, and so on that you lease for your place of business, even if the leases are presumably fixed, controlled by contract.
- **Service contracts:** Negotiate new deals for any service provided.

Everything you spend money on is now negotiable. The reason is obvious: everyone wants to keep the business flowing. Everyone is tied to the down economy one way or another and is now willing to renegotiate to preserve business. Something is better than nothing is the prevailing logic. Since the downturn affects us all, with everyone losing customers steadily and experiencing reduced revenue, it is now the "economy's fault," not your own problem.

> Everyone is tied to the down economy one way or another and is now willing to renegotiate to preserve business. Something is better than nothing is the prevailing logic.

This opens the door for renegotiating everything. Not negotiating means you do not understand the nature of the changes we are experiencing. The changes are not temporary; they are permanent. The economy we now have is what we will be experiencing for many years to come. At this writing, we have not yet hit bottom, so we have more decline ahead of us, more reduced revenues, more lost business.

The Christmas fourth quarter of 2010, so important to many businesses, was not good—or better stated, it was based on a new and different economy that is less powerful than what we were used to over the last 10 years. It's a permanent reduction of sales, revenue, and profitability, so your cost structure must be adjusted accordingly.

Call your landlord and negotiate a lease reduction or leave. Yes, you are breaking a contract, but this is a necessary cost of long-term survival.

Reduce payroll, add incentives for achieving greater productivity, and eliminate overtime.

Renegotiate your leases or return the equipment and either re-lease or purchase.

There are many ways to accomplish these goals. Make no assumptions. It's a new world and a new economy. Everything is negotiable; any contract can be broken safely, successfully, and cost efficiently. It's a matter of strategy.

It's not just about cutting some costs; it's about cutting all your costs. None are immune from this process if you want to survive in this new world.

## Beware, a Poor Economy Leads to Bad Decisions

It's a problem, and you need to be forewarned.

When under stress and drowning under feelings of desperation, people tend to make less carefully considered decisions. They also tend to make more emotional decisions, sometimes geared more at deflecting pain and supporting an ego, rather than making the right decisions, doing the right thing, and solving your problems, difficult as it may seem. Self-destruction is an all-too-frequent natural response to stress, uncertainty, pain, disappointment, and fear.

I cannot blame small business owners for making bad decisions in moments of extreme disarray. For unexplainable reasons beyond their control, the economy around them is melting, turning their previously successful business and life totally upside down. Unemployment is rising, revenue is dropping, overhead is increasing, real estate and retirement plans are worth far less, and the business that is holding up their world is failing. What can they do—or more to the point—what can you do?

You can answer this question by focusing on some of the common bad decisions that owners make under such circumstances. Proceed carefully; you are in a dangerous situation and are in jeopardy of making mistakes more harmful than the damage an economic meltdown can cause and the potential or actual failure of your business.

What am I talking about? Drugs, alcohol, and infidelity are the deadly three. Add gambling, and you have the complete picture.

Normally high-standard, family-loving community leaders, dedicated small business owners can fall from grace under the pressure of unpredicted financial disaster. In the Great Depression, people who could not face their business failures jumped out of windows. Today, they get addicted to prescription drugs, become dependent on alcohol, or commit adultery.

Whether it is to dull the pain, feel the rush of false exhilaration, or stroke the ego, engaging in those acts is a response to pressure and pain, self-doubt, and a need to feel positive about oneself. Being under such pressure can lead to poor decisions and mistakes, mistakes that will do more damage than financial destruction, that will destroy the fiber of the family and put everyone close to you at risk.

Think twice. Recognize you are under stress and accept the fact that your decision-making capability may be impaired. Gather your strength and dig deep, remember your standards, and hold on. Yes, it requires great strength and self-sacrifice, but we are all capable of making good decisions; we have demonstrated that skill repeatedly. Do not fail under duress, when the risks are so huge. Business owners are warriors, committed to standards and self-sacrifice. Do what is right.

Accept your responsibility with a "no-problem" attitude, ask for help if you need it, and find the way out. Do not sell out your family for a false sense of well-being. Accept your responsibility. You will be tested as never before. You must not allow business conditions to be excuses for bad behavior.

## Reinvent Your Business or Perish

I see, hear, and talk with small business owners every day, and they are frequently viewing their current situation as if they have a choice. We are confronting a changing business environment, and we all must make changes to survive. Holding the course, doing the same things we have always done, is not an option. Unless we all surrender to this clear mission, we are flirting with self-destruction. The new economy will tolerate no slackers.

So what does this mean?

Reinvent your business—what it does, how it does it, and what its sales revenue and profit can and will be—by:

- Downsizing immediately
- Tightening the operation

There will be decreased revenues. Thus overhead, payroll, expenses, and cost of goods must all be carefully controlled to maximize the profits available out of reduced revenues. Your business must be run as tightly as possible to survive these changes. Anything short of this two-step strategy is destined to fail. There is no such thing as a partial attempt here. It is all or nothing.

**Recognize the Need to Change.** The real first step is to acknowledge the intensity and danger of the situation. Then take action. You must surrender to the realities that a poor economy requires changes and that you have no option; then implement the changes.

The irony is that we all know what we should be doing, and we all know we ignore making these adjustments to tighten the operation for reasons that are excuses: "Tomorrow I will start to make adjustments," or "I am too busy today," or whatever your excuse may be. All that remains is doing the job.

**Work Out Debt.** Debt is the killer. Thus, there is no choice other than to work out the debt, reducing it so survival can continue. Debt cannot be ignored or absorbed in the context of smaller revenue. Debt taken on when projections of revenue were significantly larger cannot be serviced when revenues are decreasing rapidly. Reduce the debt, or the business will fail.

**Continue Marketing to Gain Market Share.** Marketing is usually the first line item to go, and that's a mistake. It's true that marketing strategies must change. But effective marketing is critical to survival and must be successfully implemented in a downturned economy. This is an opportunity to absorb a larger share of the declining market if marketing is appropriately implemented under the new and changing conditions. *Not* marketing is fatal.

Use the Internet; it is cost efficient and the way of the future. Get help if you need it, but this must be done.

> This is an opportunity to absorb a larger share of the declining market if marketing is appropriately implemented under the new and changing conditions. *Not* marketing is fatal.

## More Powerful Downturn Reinvention Strategies

Taking a general approach in today's business world, while historically successful, does not work well in today's marketplace. With decreasing sales revenue and increased competition fighting for consumers' dollars, it is time to create a specialty, an expertise, that will outdraw your competition, and then sell your customers all the other common products or services everyone else offers, as well.

The marketplace responds to the businesses with the widest and broadest selection, believing that this must mean they are the experts. Offer the most, and you become the best. Your business is the place to go. Identify a popular section of the market demand, and then expand inventory to offer the most of it.

A shoe store that specializes in sneakers, running shoes, wide sizes, large sizes, and so on, carves out a niche by having the largest selection and attracts not only an expanded sneaker business but whatever else the consumer requires when coming in to buy sneakers. Having the greatest variation of the theme is another way to specialize that every retail store can accomplish to create a real *expertise* and a competitive advantage. Your specialty does not have to be unique; merely expanding the breadth of your inventory to be the *largest* in the area will do the trick. Pick the product concept and then exploit it by providing every possible entry, including all the less popular items that do not sell much. It supports your expertise and attracts the audience.

Whatever product you are selling or manufacturing, whatever service you are offering, figure out where you can take a stand. Create a competitive advantage by developing a unique expertise, specialty, wider inventory of a general product or service line, anything that gives you an advantage over your competition. Attracting a larger audience than you would with the normal distribution of a product or services is an important way to hold on to your market share while competing in a down market.

> Create a competitive advantage by developing a unique expertise, specialty, wider inventory of a general product or service line, anything that gives you an advantage over your competition.

Any business can find some opportunity to specialize. For example, have the largest selection of wines or micro beers or foreign imports, but whatever you choose, have the most, and be the best. This is how to grow and prosper in a declining market. Find your specialty, invent one or claim one. Saying it makes it so and brings the customers in. Doing it delivers the results and supports success.

Create your own competitive advantage and promote it widely, and the business will follow. The unique business specialty will support growth and development and retain loyal customers as well as increase the geographical market you serve because of the willingness of consumers to go further to find your specialized business.

More is better; more attracts the audience. Even though customers will purchase the most popular, the market likes to have choices, and this becomes a competitive advantage worthy of exploitation.

## Dozens of Restaurants Close; One Has Waiting Lines

Even in a down market, a few business owners understand what it takes to capture a larger share of a declining market than their competitors. This restaurant story is a perfect example.

It's clear that a market downturn severely limits discretionary spending. Many people are out of work, or are in fear of losing their jobs. The stock market is down, and real estate is worth less than it was. In response, many are spending less money on luxuries.

Some industries are hurt more than others in a business recession. Restaurants are one of the industries feeling the pinch. On a visit to Florida, one of the hardest-hit states in the country, it is obvious how many restaurants have gone out of business or are teetering on disaster as a result of having fewer and fewer patrons. The good restaurants are working at a reduced capacity, and the average to poor ones are fighting for survival or going out of business.

Yet one local restaurant in the area I visited has the locals standing in line for over an hour to get a seat … every day of the week. How can it be, 20 local restaurants closing their doors in the immediate market area and one with long lines of people waiting to get in? What is this business doing right that others are not in the face of this recession?

> Quality sells well all the time. That is the message. Good quality at reasonable prices will always win out and bring the people in as well as back again and again.

The answer is predictable. It is because the restaurant serves a higher-quality product than others in the area and at a reasonable price. General, all-purpose American fare, priced above average but within reason.

Quality sells well all the time. That is the message. Good quality at reasonable prices will always win out and bring the people in, as well as back again and again. It's the repeat business that makes the restaurant a winner, as people know that they will get a high-quality product every time. Word of mouth spreads the success to others, and the lines never end.

There is a breakfast joint in Cape Cod, Massachusetts that is also like this. People flock there from miles around every day and spend more there than in most other breakfast spots. The product the restaurant serves is innovative and enticing, as well as of the highest quality. As a result, even at an above-average price point, the repeat business is consistent, and the new business grows from word-of-mouth advertising. There, too, people are standing in line to get in, while other breakfast eateries are practically empty.

Every day of the week, some win and some lose. Even in a down economy, competition continues, even more fiercely. Quality always wins out in the end in every kind of business, even during a recession.

## The Virtual Business Strategy

Subcontracting, strategic alliances, Internet sales, websites, blogs, podcasts, YouTube, e-mail, voice mail, other technologies, and partnerships make the virtual business model a serious consideration for any entrepreneur establishing a business or reconsidering the operational equation for an existing business.

Maybe a new format is the answer ... the virtual business.

What does this mean?

It's simple: Whatever you are making or whatever service you are providing, chances are good some other business organization is already performing this service and doing it efficiently, and would love additional business ... a strategic alliance that makes sense for all involved.

Consider no more employees in production, no more expensive warehouses, and no other overhead burdens. In essence, you become a sales organization supported by the Internet, website sales, and marketing efforts, all low cost and working 24/7.

Your territory becomes the world.

You can even off-load sales to other organizations, call centers, brokers, representatives, telemarketers, and so on, all willing to work on sales success and share the proceeds. It's possible that you are the only person involved in your own organization, with everyone else a strategic partner. Sounds a little utopian, but it's possible.

Just ridding yourself of manufacturing would result in an immense savings in overhead and time burden. Why not manufacture offshore in India or China? There are brokers and reps willing to assist you in making these connections. A fulfillment arrangement will allow drop shipping directly to your end user.

Since you will know all your costs, you simply mark up your product adequately to absorb the costs and add your profit.

You have to either buy low and sell high or buy high and sell higher.

Both are possible, not for every product or service, but for many. It used to be a strategy reserved for large manufacturers purchasing shipping container loads; these manufacturers would experience huge economies of scale based on the low costs of labor and materials in other countries.

Now small business owners can piggyback on this opportunity because there are brokers handling the transactions and providing savings for them, as well. Now small business can compete effectively. Because few small businesses are embracing this opportunity, those that do will experience competitive advantages.

> **Consider becoming a virtual company by creating a business plan that relies on outside sources handling the entire chain of business or at least significant parts of it.**

Telemarketing can be off-loaded to companies in India willing to charge in direct proportion to revenue earned. How can you lose? Printing can be handled this way, as well as many other aspects of your business. Think about the possibilities. Consider becoming a virtual company by creating a business plan that relies on outside sources handling the entire chain of business or at least significant parts of it.

Your immediate response will probably be, this is an interesting idea but it will not work for me or my product. Think again; there is little that cannot be accomplished through strategic alliances offshore or onshore, creating a true virtual business without any bricks or mortar.

This does not have to be an all-or-nothing decision. You can go virtual on parts of your business.

## Notes

1. David Goldman. Worst Year for Jobs Since '45, January 9, 2009, http://money.cnn.com/2009/01/09/news/economy/jobs _december/index.htm (accessed March 2009).
2. Tom Peters, *Crazy Times Call for Crazy Organizations* (Vintage, New York, 1994), p. 6.

# Chapter 2

# Look at Your Options

## Escape When You Can't Recover

It is clear as of this writing that we are not in a recession. Let us get that clear. A recession implies the situation is temporary and will soon be over, and we will return to where we were. Dream on. It ain't happening.

What is happening is a sea-change in our economy. Many changes that are occurring will have a long-term impact. We may lose our auto industry—or better said, it will exist, but it will look different than it does today. The same with the financial, housing, and building industries, and on it goes. This will be a five- to 10-year cycle, maybe even longer, not ending with where we were, but evolving into a new reality. Understand that the same jobs will not be available on the rebound, and many older, experienced workers will not regain their previous or even comparable positions—ever. The ongoing prognosis for business survival is poor, with millions of businesses likely to fold in the next few years and with those that do survive having to downsize. In fact, 1.5 million businesses closed in 2009 and 2010, and more will close in 2011; many will file for bankruptcy, and many will simply shut the doors and be done.

Another aspect of this extreme change is that entire industries will be altered beyond recognition. The office furniture market, including new and used furniture, is in deep trouble. New office openings are rare at the moment, and closings are too numerous to mention. Clearly, there will be warehouses filled with office equipment and furniture, and it will take a decade to absorb this inventory.

The general furniture industry is experiencing severe pain as well, as the purchase of new furniture is frequently associated with acquiring a new home, and that activity has come to a standstill. Layoffs as well as cuts in bonuses and pay additionally drive the demand for this discretionary purchase to be postponed for a while, maybe indefinitely.

Car dealers are hemorrhaging, as no one wants to buy cars. People who do cannot get credit. Many are losing their jobs or fear they may, so they will make do with their current auto for another year or so.

And so it continues. Some industries simply slow down, such as the restaurant industry; others dry up completely. It's one thing to adapt to a slowdown; it's another to try and adapt to a drought. Endure the slowdown and redesign your business equation.

If you are in a drought industry, you must plan your departure with broad-based exit workouts, preventing further harm to come to you personally. It is crucial to exit safely, or reemergence becomes extremely difficult. Plan your exit, especially the cash requirements, and make certain you can bridge the gap.

> **If you are in a drought industry, you must plan your departure with broad-based exit workouts, preventing further harm to come to you personally.**

We are living through a huge transition. Those that recognize it will make the correct decision: be it adapt, cut and run, or self-liquidate. Think clearly, plan and implement effectively.

## You're Unemployable—Make Your Business Work

An entrepreneur, typically the small business owner, is unemployable in the traditional workplace. Therefore, you'd better make your business work: Pay its bills, pay you, and retain some earnings.

I can explain this reality.

You are all unemployable, not because you are unskilled—you are in fact very skilled—but because it is unlikely you will find a satisfactory job opportunity based on your financial requirements, experience, skills, and expertise. Consider the risk factors any prospective employer would have to weigh: Few would pay what you need or would trust that you would be loyal and in for the long term. Add to that the questions of whether you will take orders and not disrupt their organization. The net result is that you are unemployable.

They are probably correct in harboring those doubts, as an entrepreneur cannot work for someone else for long. An entrepreneur is a different type of person and does not have the personality required to be a successful regular employee. You are a dreamer, a planner, and a strategist. You lead and do not follow. This is not a good employee profile.

Unfortunately, millions of small businesses will fail over the next few years. Those businesses that survive will do so because the owner made the necessary changes to successfully navigate this economic meltdown. You need to succeed if you want to continue your independence.

It's your choice: Make the changes necessary, including:

- Doing preemptive debt workouts
- Downsizing deeply and then rebuilding slowly
- Adjusting your marketing, sales, and production programs and utilizing the Internet
- Reducing your inventory
- Collecting your receivables more effectively
- Implementing greater employee productivity through an incentive-based reward system
- Developing a flat management organization
- Installing and reviewing a key indicator system and financial statements weekly
- Training and cross-training within
- Creating career paths
- Reinventing your business model to reflect what works and what does not
- And using any other systems that allow a manager to make the best decisions possible to maintain profitability

Implement all this, and most important, implement a preemptive debt workout while you still have something left to save.

If you do this before you have drained all your resources, are under siege by the bank, and are reacting to disaster as opposed to leading through adjustment, you will survive and possibly prosper. You will not need to attempt to "get a job." You are unemployable. Trust me, I know.

Even if you are under siege, confronting total loss, there may be time to preserve the core business, shake off all the debt, and reorganize ... or make a safe transition to another business model.

## What You Can Do If Your Business Fails

OK, the economic meltdown is forcing you out of business. We all know that many small businesses will not survive a severe downturn. Many failed business owners will be out of work and looking for a new way to earn an income. The old ways are, for many, all but gone and will not be returning.

But you still have valuable skills, as well as contacts, knowledge, experience, and perspective that you can convert to a business opportunity. You can leverage your years of entrepreneurial experience into a new way of earning.

Let me describe some scenarios:

1.  Be a broker for the product line you were involved with. Certainly you know the players; and based on your experience and knowledge and established relationships with major customers, you would be a great broker and possibly very successful. There are low barriers to entry, one of which is that it will not require a lot of start-up capital. It is a great fit.

2.  Be a sales manager for a competitor that survived, with a commitment to bring in certain favorite special accounts you have excellent relationships with. Sell your relationships. It's time for you to cash in, and it could be lucrative working for your major competitor.

3.  Reduce your product line down to one or two items, the best sellers; remove all excess employees; subcontract as much as possible; and run a small but lucrative specialty shop. Use the Internet for sales and market like crazy, making a living off a few items with low overhead. Expand your territory to be the world, as that's what the Internet will bring you. Reinvent yourself and your business model.

4.  Write a book, a manual, a how-to, and become a consultant for the industry. Market yourself through the industry trade organization and convert your knowledge to a marketable commodity for start-ups. Offer specific problem-solving expertise that will make you a natural for others to turn to for help. Be a consultant—you have done it all.

5.  Get a job with your industry trade organization. Start by writing an

article for the organization's magazine and offering to speak at the annual convention or trade show. Work your way into the organization, or perhaps an industry business will be attracted to you as you increase your contacts because of your new visibility.

## Why You Need Advisors

Every business owner needs a board of directors. First, we do better when encouraged by others to leap further, stretch more, achieve more, be more creative. We see this in so many places: home team advantage with the crowds screaming encouragement, moms and dads at Little League baseball games. We all can accomplish more with support than we can by ourselves; yet most small business owners do it all themselves with no one to cheer them on, support their efforts, or push them harder.

Coaches know (and everyone has, at one time or another, experienced) the benefits of encouragement. Yet where it counts the most, in our business life, we all seem to prefer to do it ourselves, fighting our battles alone, winning or losing with our own drive and effort. It makes little sense for so many reasons; still we seem to prefer to be there isolated.

With a board of directors, a coach, a mentor, or a consultant, not only do you have a cheering section, a driving force greater than yourself, but you also have checks and balances, as well as an unemotional point of view. It's important to have someone to try your ideas out on, to make certain your thinking is clear, to test your theories, and to have someone challenge your logic.

> It's important to have someone to try your ideas out on, to make certain your thinking is clear, to test your theories, and to have someone challenge your logic.

There is always some aspect you won't foresee or consider that someone else may think important and challenge you on. This prevents mistakes, oversights, miscalculations. It provides performance, success, mistake insurance. A board helps you reach your goals, to achieve greater success than you can on your own. Not only is this important for your overall success; but you will consider new ideas you otherwise may not have had.

I recommend you ask someone to be on your board who is willing to be totally candid, someone who is willing to challenge your thinking and your performance, wanting to make you better, unwilling to compromise.

You may consider paying someone to be an outside director, paying a consultant to watch over you, or using your lawyer or accountant to review your work; but an active, concerned, aware board of directors is the best way to achieve this goal. You should meet periodically but often, certainly no less than quarterly, or perhaps monthly and possibly weekly. You should review all aspects of your business including finance, operations, and sales and marketing, providing a complete review of all financial reports and key indicators.

The best situation, however, is having a board of directors of interested participants, be they investors, lenders, friends, or family. There should be an odd number on the board, and majority should prevail unless you decide that unanimity rules. The board cannot be a rubber stamp for the owner.

Even if the owner is the majority or even the 100 percent owner, he or she must allow the board to determine the actions, providing checks and balances at the highest level.

The big corporations do this, so why not learn from the best and follow suit? We all need the help, support, and guidance such a system provides. Your business is important enough. Get help, get support, create a board of directors, empower them, and listen to them.

## Have Your Business Inspected

Are you familiar with the old saying "You can see a flea on another's nose, but not an elephant on your own"?

We all believe our own stories. We all see ourselves through our own filters. We may be able to advise others on what to do and how to do it, but when it comes to evaluating what we do individually, we typically flunk the test. That's because we believe our own effort is the best—we cannot see the elephant on our noses.

If we had a board of directors to watch and check our actions, programs, and systems and operations, and if we produced daily, weekly, monthly, quarterly, and annual financial reports, along with tracking key indicators, and if we had a flat organization, we might be able to say with confidence, "I am doing it right!"

But most of us are doing it alone; we do not have a board of directors. And we lack the appropriate reporting mechanisms and systems installed and operations to help us guide our businesses effectively and successfully. If there are no checks and balances and no flow of critical information, how can we tell if we are operating profitably, effectively, and successfully? We cannot. Admit it. We believe our own evaluation and analysis, but this is usually a mistake, because we also usually believe our own stories—and our own stories are fraught with our own biases.

> We believe our own evaluation and analysis, but this is usually a mistake, because we also usually believe our own stories—and our own stories are fraught with our own biases.

So what are we to do?

Simple, call on the services of a certified public accountant, a CPA. We all probably know a CPA trained in business systems and financial reporting. Maybe it's the CPA who does your annual taxes, maybe not. However, there are competent CPAs in every market. They are trained and possess the experience and expertise to evaluate your business systems to determine if you are operating truly effectively, efficiently, and profitably.

Take the test! Hire your CPA or hire one you may not know yet. This exercise will in all likelihood cost you less than a few thousand dollars and may be the best money you have spent in a long time.

Ask the CPA to come into your business and inspect your systems, reporting mechanisms, and procedures and then make recommendations. Let the CPA loose to talk to your managers and review and evaluate your business operation.

You will be amazed at what the CPA's report will tell you and the recommendations he or she makes. Without judgment, follow those recommendations. Do not reevaluate the CPA; do not argue with the findings; do not say glibly, "I do not need these systems and recommendations. I know what's going on without these reports." Listen to and follow your CPA's advice and maybe you, too, will have a profitable and successful business operation.

Inspect yourself through the eyes of an expert.

Do this quarterly, and you will be assured that you are on the right path. Do not do this, and you will probably wander off the trail.

## Follow Your Gut

I read an article many years ago that has stuck in my mind. It was about a Harvard study on how the best business leaders make decisions. It described how they would collect data, test hypotheses, do research, ask others' opinions, and do the numbers. But in the end, after doing their best research and evaluation, they all said they would lean back in their chairs and trust their gut instinct.

> **In the end, after doing their best research and evaluation, they all said they would lean back in their chairs and trust their gut instinct.**

Wow, I thought, as important as outside opinions, research, and evaluation are, in the end the best decision makers of the time, the leaders of successful corporations, trusted their gut instinct to make the most important decisions.

I was both amazed and excited, as I have had a lifetime of making intuitive, gut decisions. I get that feeling in me when I know I am onto something good. It is difficult to explain; my wife calls it the "ping of truth." It is a sensation, an energy, a feeling. When it happens, I know it. When it is not happening, I feel its absence.

At one time, I had been eyeing with great interest a building that had been for sale for a while. I called the broker, who informed me it was under contract. I asked him to call me if the deal fell apart. It did, and he called me back. The deal was exceptional; the property appeared right for my intended use. I should have been very excited, but I wasn't. I did not have that gut feeling of excitement, my "onward through the fog I go" feeling. There was no ping of truth, no inner belief that it was the right decision despite every logical analysis screaming, "Buy, buy, buy!"

So I stepped away and did not act on the opportunity. Will I be remorseful when someone else buys it? No! Do I have any reason not to buy it? No, not one! I simply do not have that gut feeling telling me to do it, so I will not.

I am following my intuition rather than deciding by empirical evidence, numbers, and any other analyses. All other evaluations scream buy it, except the absence of the one I deem most important—my intuitive, unexplainable feeling of yes.

I believe this is the soul of entrepreneurial decision making: instinct, gut, intuition. I believe the Harvard study had it right. The executive leaders used empirical evidence to evaluate and analyze and then rested on their intuitive feelings to make the final decision. If empirical evidence says no, there may not be a reason to go further; if the empirical evidence says yes, then check the gut and decide based on intuition.

If you're good at this skill, irrespective of empirical evidence, research, or numbers, do whatever your gut says despite what the more traditional evaluation process says.

If this is foreign ground, you can learn to do this. Start with small decisions and try and feel the right decision. Experience success. Get familiar with the feeling so you can identify when it happens again. It may be a skill you have but have ignored because you did not understand its power. Trust your gut . . . it knows.

# Chapter 3

# From Innovator to Manager

Many small businesses start growing, and managers with little or no training apply what they learn from having been managed. Those who've never been managed will follow their gut doing what they think is needed to get the job done. For entrepreneurs, who have only worked for themselves and grown their businesses hands-on, changing styles can be a difficult transition that many never make. Some have a natural skill at leadership; others fall into the trap of overmanaging, or micromanaging.

How an owner and those who work for him or her manage also has a lot to do with the organization's management structure. Following are the strategies I have found that create the most successful environment for a thriving, growing, successful business.

## Management by Doing or by Leading

There are two styles of managers. The first is the doer. The doer does it all, controls it all, and everyone under the manager is an assistant. The manager makes all the key decisions, and the workers simply implement. No one can make a decision without the manager, and the manager steps in to complete tasks and correct and adjust the process when needed and even if not needed.

Obviously, this is not an effective managerial style. Here are some other characteristics of ineffective managers. They:

- Deflect criticism for failure to perform adequately by blaming the staff.
- Undermine the authority of workers or staff by countermanding decisions, compromising their ability to lead, and damaging the loyalty of their people and the teams they are trying to create.
- Are ego driven and must be in the spotlight, at all times taking credit for success.

This style of management does not inspire long-term relationships, support employee career paths, or foster peer development.

The second is the manager who leads, not by doing the job, but by teaching, directing, training, and, yes, leading employees. This kind of manager is there to assist if and when necessary but not to do. Here are some of the characteristics of managers who lead. These managers:

- Accept responsibility for screw-ups and failures.
- Gain full cooperation and commitment from the people they are responsible for by allocating responsibility to them and trusting them.
- Pass off the limelight for success to the individuals and teams who performed the tasks well.
- Lead by example, by showing, teaching, and training the people how to be better.
- Encourage employees to make decisions and take risks, and then support them when they make mistakes or fail, knowing their support encourages growth and builds confidence, as well as trust between the manager and the workforce.
- Inspect frequently to be assured of success, but allocate responsibility and authority completely. A true leader is invisible.

These are the leaders for whom the employees will walk the extra mile, will stay late and come in early, will produce better products with fewer rejects, and will become team players working together for a common goal because there is reason to succeed.

Give to your employees, and they will return your leadership many-fold. Manage by doing, and you sacrifice being a leader and become a babysitter. A leader develops the employees to become their own decision makers and risk takers. By making decisions and taking risk, they will succeed frequently, which is good. They will also fail occasionally, and that, too, is acceptable because without allowing them to be decision makers and risk takers, all you can do is babysit.

In short, try managing without doing; pretend you cannot do but can only lead, teach, train, and support. See what happens. Aside from your employees being shocked at first and then becoming much happier and more productive and successful, they will build a better team, and you will have to manage less and less as they get stronger and better.

## Do You Have a Pyramid or a Flat Organization?

There are many styles of management, and depending on how big your business is, what its organizational format is, and whether or not you have departments and department managers, all may help determine how you manage your business. However, the real issue is the personal preference of the owner about how to run the company.

There are two basic formats. One is the pyramid organization, where the head of the company, typically the owner, makes all the decisions and the managers simply implement the company's mandates.

Alternatively, there is the flat organization, where the managers make the operational decisions, with the management team and owner only reviewing results or discussing issues and problems. Managers resolve daily operation issues, with reviews on a timely basis such as in a weekly managers' meeting. Of course, the owner can always determine to review critical issues as required, but the company is run by the managers in this flat format.

### Style Differences

There is a huge difference in these styles. The pyramid organization concentrates all power and decision making typically in the owner's hands. The owner micromanages every aspect of the business with a constant flow of managers asking him or her for immediate short-term consideration and response to whatever is happening at the moment. There are typically few systems installed, as the owner makes decisions on an issue-by-issue basis. This is more often called putting out brush fires and babysitting, as these are the main functions such a style promotes. It means endless hours of work and total self-absorption on the part of the owner.

On the other hand, the flat organization allows, encourages, and even requires the managers to make all the operational decisions without going to the owner or company head for the answers to every micro issue. A flat organization requires that managers be held responsible for success and also be held accountable for their achievements or failures.

> A flat organization requires that managers be held responsible for success and also be held accountable for their achievements or failures.

**Flat Organizations Empower Managers.** As you can see, the choice of management style must emanate from the ultimate boss, the owner. Owners who are committed to controlling it all—who impose a pyramid format—are establishing their and their business's limitation. As there are only so many decisions an owner can make in a day, this style eventually stifles the effectiveness of the organization.

The second style, the flat format, requires the owner to trust the managers, who are expected to rely on key indicators to track, monitor, and control their actions while the owner makes policy decisions. The managers manage the daily operations and attend meetings to share and discuss information.

**Flat Organizations Empower Employees.** To develop the style further, if the decision is to manage a flat organization, why not empower the employees to also contribute to management decision making? This way, you involve the entire team in the responsibility and accountability for success. Holding periodic department meetings, managers can frankly and honestly discuss the workings of the operation and ways to improve it.

This approach works best when the employees are rewarded for success on an incentive basis. It puts everyone in the same boat, all pulling together trying to achieve the same goals; everyone is held accountable and is rewarded for success.

I believe the flatter the organization is—where the employees and managers are held responsible for success, are accountable for reaching goals, and are rewarded for achieving stated benchmarks—the more effective, efficient, and profitable the business will be.

### Emulating Flat Organizations

To become a flat organization, you must start from the top. If the owner selects a strong management team and lets the team members manage, if the managers can create quality teamwork in each department, and if the departments can work together to create a larger team effort, success will be assured.

The owner's job changes from crisis and brush-fire management to training, planning, and reviewing—what it should be. This is the way many successful companies are being run today. While neither style is wrong, it appears that flat organizations are the current trend. Major business successes such as Toyota and Whole Foods are truly flat organizations, and these businesses are growing rapidly and profitably. Perhaps they should be emulated.

## Why Flat Is Best

Let's dig deeper and see why a flat organization appears to be more effective and, therefore, preferable.

In a flat organization, managers make direct operational decisions with limited overview other than being held accountable for successful performance. Wow, it already sounds good! Can you imagine holding your managers accountable for the performance of their section, group, or division?

This requires a significant discussion with your managers to agree upon the goals and objectives, but the managers are responsible for achieving them. Each division or group acts as if its manager was the CEO of that group. The manager's answer is the final word, and he or she does not have to retreat to the mother ship for ratification, affirmation, or permission. The manager is empowered to truly manage for success.

It further requires a CEO who will expect that managers will make errors in judgment and will support them when this happens. This is critical since every decision will not be correct or the best. As long as enough of the decisions are appropriate, then the CEO should cultivate decision making by supporting managers. The best professional baseball players hit one out of three or four at bats, and that's success. Basketball players, likewise, shooting over 50 percent, are all-stars, and no one beats them for missing a shot. These athletes are encouraged to swing or shoot again and again, because in the end that's how they win.

Managers should be encouraged to occasionally take risks, a leap of faith, a daring experiment, and maybe they will hit a home run, bringing additional profits into the company. Low-percentage shots are missed more often, but players are encouraged to take them because great players make enough of them to justify the risk of missing. Your managers should be encouraged to experiment. They should be supported in their efforts and encouraged to try again if they fail, even if they fail more often than they succeed, as long as they reach their objectives and projections.

Ask your managers to draft their own department business plan and supporting budget, and then give them the authority to implement it. You will have the basis of a very successful flat organization, with far less management and babysitting for you. Your managers are now the CEO in their group or division responsible for success, and they will work as hard as they can to deliver—it's their plan, their budget, their operation.

> **Ask your managers to draft their own department business plan and supporting budget, and then give them the authority to implement it.**

How about rewarding them and their workers with incentives for successful implementation of their plan? Let's really get them involved, committed, and invested in your success.

By the way, you and your managers will waste a lot less time in meetings together than if you were in a pyramid organization, where the CEO micromanages every decision and affirms all managers' activities. That's not necessary anymore. Give them the ball, and let them run with it. Let them create the plays. Of course, be involved in an orderly fashion with scheduled weekly meetings to discuss actions and projections and review performance, but let them control their game plan and implement it directly. No assistant managers and assistants to the assistants required. That's flat.

Bill Belichek, manager of the New England Patriots football team, sets the tone, direction, and goals with a game plan, but his offensive and defensive coordinators determine the plays and formations during the game. That's flat. Belichek does not make every decision, nor does he even review the plays during the game. His men are free to manage and do their job ... and win.

This act turns the manager's job from a boss's messenger boy and babysitter to a productive manager. He or she is no longer just transferring the boss's wishes and managing for limited success, preferring not to make errors rather than to score since it's not his game. His job focus changes from damage control to victory, and that is what we truly want.

Why not even leave hiring decisions to your managers? It's their team; allow them to pick their own players.

This begs the question, what does the CEO do if he or she is no longer responsible for the operation and is running a flat organization with the managers controlling and operating the game?

Plan, train, and review: That is the CEO's real job.

- **Plan.** Chart the future course and goals. Plan for capital investments, growth, and development.
- **Train.** Make certain your managers are constantly learning new skills and acquiring additional capabilities. Provide training opportunities and make them mandatory.
- **Review.** Always monitor the results and the key indicators so you have a pulse on your progress and success. If faltering, you're there as soon as possible to help make corrections. You're supporting your managers' efforts, not doing their job for them. Inspect your managers' work, often and deeply.

It is important to free your managers to act independently and not merely reflect your wishes, style, or approach, and it is as important for the CEO to encourage and support contrary styles and approaches to problem solving as you flatten your organization and empower your managers.

This style of management design can eliminate levels or specific jobs of middle management—these are managers who report upward and downward but do little productive work and less managing.

That's a flat organization. Can anyone do it? It requires a CEO who can resist being a control freak and who can let go in exchange for the benefits of greater success with less work effort and greater success. Let your managers do their job. Why pay them a lot to watch over the employees when they should really be managing them.

Jack Welch, the most successful CEO in modern history, spent his career flattening General Electric, one of the most successful organizations ever. He spent years converting a huge pyramid to a flat organization, division by division, and he claims flat is the only way to go.

## Management Lessons from President Obama

Many criticize President Obama for doing too much, starting too many programs, biting off more than he can chew, so to speak.

Not so, I say. While I am not endorsing his programs, I take note of his ability to manage a diverse, complicated, lengthy list of agenda items. He is the perfect example of implementing an effective flat management approach, and we see its benefits. He is accomplishing much in a short time. Whether we agree with his programs is another issue.

He states the goals he wishes to achieve and then he empowers his cabinet to do what it takes to reach his objectives, figure out the strategy to get there, and implement the strategy effectively. Of course, Obama inspects their process, reviews their findings, affirms their strategies, and checks on achievement.

He further accepts final responsibility for the results, whether they are good or bad, and respects the managers whose efforts the programs represent by giving them credit.

The man is an excellent flat manager and is demonstrating how more can be done when he removes himself from making every decision and trusts his managers to do their jobs. That is why he has cabinet-level appointees handling major areas of his agenda and authorizes them to create programs to reach his goals. Without flat management, he would accomplish far less, buried by the enormity of the tasks.

Take a page out of his book, manage a flat organization, get more done, take responsibility for the failures, and applaud the managers, giving them credit for their successes. Inspect, review, and project, but let your managers carry the heavy weight. That's flat management. If Obama can do it, you can, too.

> Take a page out of Obama's book, manage a flat organization, get more done, take responsibility for the failures, and applaud the managers, giving them credit for their successes.

## Inspecting Your Managers for a Flat Organization

The challenge in managing a flat organization is for both the owner and the managers to learn how to communicate—how to transfer the pertinent information effectively and honestly without fear or risk, ego involvement, and interfering emotional junk. Here are the two basic communication requirements:

1. The managers must understand that the owner requires informa-

tion in order to effectively manage the growth and direction of the company as well as to generally understand what's happening.

2. The owner must foster an environment that supports the managers in taking reasonable calculated risks when making decisions and not being penalized for failure or mistakes, but being encouraged to try again. This opens up the full throttle for self-direction, self-responsibility, and growth, while removing daily operational responsibility from the owner.

Given these two requirements, the owner's need for information and the managers' need for support of reasonable risk, the managers must accept being inspected and transfer all pertinent information to the owner, and the owner must learn how to inspect the managers to gain insight, but not interrogate. There must be a frank discussion about the reporting process so both the owner and the managers learn and understand the requirement for inspection and the difference between inspection and interrogation.

*Inspection* is the close examination of what is working and what is not. This is not intended to be a judgmental evaluation of a manager's performance; it cannot be an attack on character or capability. It is a real-time report to extract vital information so management and ownership decisions can be effectively made regarding what is occurring and what can be done to further the business goals and objectives.

There are two issues that most often interfere:

1. The owners tend to make it personal and emotional.
2. The managers feel as though they are being interrogated as opposed to inspected.

Unless done effectively, failure will result in a return to a pyramid-style organization, with all decisions being made by the owner. The other possibility is losing your managers. The difficult, yet crucial, understanding between the owner and the managers must be that inspection is all about the communication. Any opinion from managers to owners must be transmitted without emotional baggage and the interference of personal, judgmental attitudes.

The managers have become the owner's eyes and ears and are closer to the line of action. The owner must refrain from making judgments regarding the managers' performance by entrusting them to do their jobs. The result will be a quality, flat organizational experience, enhancing the likely success of the business and the people running it.

Manager inspections are not social events or personal discussions, but are designed to achieve specific business goals. That requires communication training to achieve the full potential for success.

This is an important and necessary system for all business organizations, flat or pyramid. If you have a pyramid organization, inspection of your managers is not as vital because the owner's involvement is closer to the scene of action.

Even so, the ability to regularly inspect is always helpful, and you should train your managers to be inspected.

If owners and managers can learn how to perform this function, both will be happier and more successful, as it will help the underlying business entity also reach its greatest potential.

## Flat Management Practices

The idea behind using flat management practices is to create a team approach to management and as flat a hierarchy as possible. If you have department heads, say sales, marketing, operations, and finance, while you have written and determined the overall plan, each manager should be deeply involved in his or her own division planning. Since each manager knows intimately what works and what does not, this is an appropriate opportunity to ask your managers for their ideas and plans. What would they do given the opportunity to chart this year's course?

> **The idea behind using flat management practices is to create a team approach to management and as flat a hierarchy as possible.**

I would start with a meeting to explore the parameters, being careful not to poison their thinking with your ideas. It is appropriate to establish the guidelines, which should be well known anyway. Let the managers determine the program, the strategies, and the plans required to produce the desired results; see what creative thinking you inspire.

Better yet, have them determine their budget based on their plan. What do they need to get to where they want to go? This is called zero-based budgeting. Rather than starting with last year's budget and adding on a bit here and there, so they can spend more, ask them to determine a budget starting from zero. Require them to create the best possible plan and cost it out.

The results will be terrific as certainly you will see strategies that you otherwise would have overlooked. The people in your organization dedicated to the various parts of your business may see those parts more clearly than you.

Also, consider the effect on the individual managers, as they are now willing to defend their thinking, plan, and budget. They will have invested themselves into the program and will do what it takes to have it work as projected.

In a follow-up meeting with all your department managers, you play the role of mediator and integrate all the plans into one coherent, integrated overall plan, one with separate budgets. This will work better than doing it all yourself and then asking your managers to implement it. This approach has their input and budgets, as well as the benefit of all managers reviewing one another's work and making it fit together.

That's a plan that has power and precision. Launch that baby! It's bound to work better than your own plan done without the input of your key managers. As well, consider the enormous job satisfaction, pleasure, and enrichment experienced by your managers when you show them the respect of including them in planning the rollout for the new year. They will stop at nothing to make certain it succeeds. Watch their self-esteem, confidence, and pride build. You will have successfully begun to create a real team effort.

 # Hiring Right

To build a business, you have to hire people. Getting the right people and the right number of people into the right jobs can be a challenge. It takes time and resources to hire people and more to train them, so it's important to get it right from the start.

## When to Hire, When to Fire

Don't hire until you see the whites of their eyes.

This statement exemplifies the exact attitude you must have when considering hiring additional employees. It comes from the famous instruction uttered at the Battle of Bunker Hill. The Revolutionaries, who were greatly outnumbered, had little ammunition, no training, and few experienced leaders, but they looked into the eyes of the enemy without fear. The actual quotation was, of course, "Don't *fire* until you see the whites of their eyes," exclaimed to make certain every bullet counted and none were wasted.

We can take a lesson from this situation and save ourselves a lot of money while making certain we install the attitudes necessary for effective management.

**Hiring When You See the Whites of Their Eyes.** The tendencies are to hire sooner than necessary or wait too long and allow overtime, which is expensive.

Managers and business owners tend to ramp up before they absolutely need to, and thus they incur excess overhead and build in low productivity as a benchmark.

My advice is never to hire until you are forced to, until you are unable to process the workload in a reasonable time. Then, when it seems as though everyone will burst from overwork . . . hire.

Along the way, find ways to increase productivity, so the same number of employees put out more work. That's efficiency, that's building profit, and that's controlling overhead while maintaining or increasing production. That is a better plan.

Focus on increasing productivity rather than simply hiring either in anticipation of need or even after the need is clearly evident. Wait until you see the whites of the enemies' eyes—late delivery, backed-up orders, paperwork not being processed in time, a bottleneck somewhere. Finally, after extracting the most productivity you can out of the existing situation and current work team, then and only then, when it feels like you are unable to absorb one more order . . . start looking for additional help.

Only when you have exhausted yourself and your people with training and incentives, creating greater productivity and bringing it to its maximum potential, then hire.

Excess payroll and the resulting payroll taxes and employee benefits, coupled with accepting lower productivity from the existing employees, is a major cause of lost profitability. Overhead that is too high can cause an early demise. Lean and mean coupled with high productivity is the best path to go and needs to be a fanatical commitment to succeed.

**When to Reduce Your Workforce.** Too much payroll—too many employees—is the cause of many business failures. When revenues are declining, reduce the payroll as soon as the trend is identified. Yes, you may want to overlook small declines or momentary reductions in demand, but over time adequate enough to identify a trend, cut the payroll. Keep all your employees working to their maximum potential while maintaining the highest productivity.

Reduce the employee base as soon as you identify the downward productivity trend, and do not increase it until the existing group is producing at the highest efficiency. It's tricky balancing the employee base with productivity and always working toward maximizing the outflow with the least number of employees. Every manager is reluctant to fire, because the effect it can have on the individuals and their families; but, remember, if you do not control costs, increase productivity, and hold the payroll down as low as possible, you may be shutting down altogether in a few months, costing all their jobs.

Hiring too soon and holding on to employees too long are the two most costly management judgment errors. Wait until you see the whites of their eyes before you hire, and fire as soon as you see the trend.

> **Hiring too soon and holding on to employees too long are the two most costly management judgment errors.**

We are in a downturn that is going to last a long while. Downsize deeper than you believe is necessary, allow the remaining employees to work harder to make up the difference, cut deeper than you believe you need to, and watch the team rebuild itself with increased productivity and do a better job. Reward the smaller employee team with greater rewards based on productivity, and everyone wins.

## Job Descriptions

Creating job descriptions is something that should be done before the business opens and hires its first employee, but seldom is. Too often the step is skipped over as obvious, boring, or trivial, but I suggest it is a basic building block and cannot be ignored. How can you address any of the following issues without job descriptions:

- First, in designing your employee teams, if you fail to put together a detailed job description as a starting point, how is a potential employee to determine exactly what the job requirements are? Or do you expect the interviewer to create the job description during the interview? Are the specific duties of the position clear? Are the goals and objectives discussed in the interview clearly recorded so they can be referred to in the future?

- Even if the interview process went well, and everyone believed the potential employee is in tune with the hiring manager, what if the hiring manager incorrectly assessed the person or the job requirements; there are no guidelines. What about the lower-level jobs hired by managers; shouldn't there be guidelines to follow in describing the job requirements? How do you determine if an applicant is suitable for the job if there is no job description?

- Are job titles so descriptive that they adequately outline what the jobs require? Are the width and the breadth of a job to be left up to the prospective employee to determine and create? And even if they are, who determines if they are in line with the vision of the owner? How are differing visions kept in balance? How do we make certain we will never hear these words: "Oh, I thought ..." or "I didn't know you wanted me to do that." By then, it's too late, as management has already determined failure and the employee had not a clue about the specific expectations. How could he or she?
- Is the line of reporting clear in a title?
- Are you assuming that your employee handbook covers most of the issues and details of each job in your company?
- Can job success be evaluated effectively if we have neither benchmarks nor clearly stated areas of responsibility, goals, and objectives to measure success against?

Here is an exercise that is fun, informative, revealing, and helpful in the hiring process. Why not write your own job descriptions and carefully evaluate them to make certain they coincide with the vision and requirements of the business. Then, after a careful interview of an applicant you think highly of, why not ask the person to write a description of the job based on the interview; you will learn an enormous amount from this exercise. You will:

- Learn more about the applicant, the applicant's vision for the job, and the business
- Make certain there is a fit between the applicant and the business
- Assess the applicant's writing and evaluation skills

In the end, exchanging job descriptions, with each reading the other's, makes for wonderful discussions and clearer communication.

It is an excellent opportunity to make adjustments to your own job description, as it is highly likely the applicant will add insight, thoughts, ideas, and direction for improving the vision. It's also possible that an applicant will reveal a fatal flaw during this process, which is better to happen before you hire.

When your first employee review occurs, wouldn't it be helpful to be able to pull out both job descriptions, the employee's and your own, and compare them to the job performance assessment. This can be a huge help in directing improvement or rewarding excellence.

A job description is critical. It tells everyone what the job requirements are, and if satisfactorily accomplished, the employee can be recognized for a job done well.

If you are not already using job descriptions, I strongly recommend a commitment to creating them for every job in your business. The next time you hire, you will be pleased and will better understand the value of this tool. Even introducing a newly drafted job description after an employee has been long on the job can be valuable in bringing goals and objectives in closer alignment with the current situation.

The message is this: Every business requires written job descriptions. Make certain you have them and that you review them from time to time as jobs evolve and the business matures. You will find they are valuable references.

> Every business requires written job descriptions. Make certain you have them and that you review them from time to time as jobs evolve and the business matures.

## The Worst-Employee Problem

I recently had an opportunity to see the incredible dynamics of "the one bad apple can ruin the entire bunch" theory at work, and it's an eye-opening process.

The bad apple worked for a towing company that offers 24/7 service in a metropolitan market. He was using the trucks, equipment, and work time to repossess cars for another business while collecting paychecks from both the original employer and the second employer, the repo company. The result, of course, was that the tow truck driver was not able to do his primary job very well and had to lie and con everyone in the shop. That was the scene.

For a month while this was going on, the company seemed as though it was going through hell. Nothing was working well. Employees (all men) were undependable; they were showing up late or not coming in at all. They were underperforming or performing erratically. They argued and bickered among themselves. They were behaving poorly with customers, did not complete their paperwork appropriately, and made their manager look bad.

We could not figure out why everything was nuts for the entire month. The business's numbers were off, of course, and the manager blamed it on the summer slowdown.

The owner and manager sensed something was very wrong, and while not being able to immediately put a finger on the issue, knew there was a problem they needed to ferret out. Ultimately, they confronted the man and fired him on the spot.

Then just as everything had fallen apart so quickly, everything smoothed out without a word being said. The men absorbed the bad apple's production requirements without replacing him; the arguing and bickering disappeared, and their attitude became improved. They all began showing up on time, taking care of the equipment, cooperating, and working effectively with motivation and determination, the way they had been trained.

The entire business appeared to breathe a huge sigh of relief as the employees came together, working efficiently as a team, and revenues increased dramatically. Once again, the business was productive and profitable and ran smoothly.

From members of the office staff to the cleanup guy, everyone stepped up a notch, and the business resumed producing at a high level with less stress and greater results. It appeared as though everyone wanted to come to work and enjoy the entire experience. In essence, it became a great place to work and earn.

Watching the men begin to smile, joke around a bit, and enjoy their work again was the most amazing and dramatic transformation I have witnessed in a long, long time. It was as if someone had cast a spell over the company the previous month, and everything that could possibly go wrong did, with everyone having a bad attitude at the same time.

Never before have I seen such a blatant example of one bad apple spoiling the bunch. The disease had spread throughout the company, and without even knowing why, everyone was dysfunctional and acting poorly. The moment the bad apple was rooted out, the employees responded and miraculously became the model group any manager would love to work with. I am certain many companies have bad apples, but because of many barriers, they are reluctant to confront and remove them, and so they allow the entire "bunch" to go bad, along with the business itself.

Examine your own business, and if appropriate, immediately get rid of the bad apples.

## Work-at-Home Employees

I know. We all have this vision of our work-at-home employees sitting around in their pajamas watching soaps, talking on the phone to their friends, and maybe doing an hour or so of work. Few small business owners feel secure in this relationship, believing they will not get value for the effort. Thus, most will not even consider this as an alternative.

Change your thinking . . . it's not so. It works.

Large corporations are way ahead of small business owners, as they have been experimenting for years with this alternative work program, and here is what they have found:

1. They first offered this program to experienced, reliable employees in small doses to see what would happen. Once deemed successful, they awarded the option to successful deserving employees as a benefit, a little at a time. They started with one day a week and slowly expanded to two, three, four, and then five.

2. The results have been stunning. Productivity was measured and compared, and the findings showed that productivity went up with work-at-home employees. The studies indicate a significant increase in productivity for the worker. In short, these workers got more done than when they were in the office.

3. Important to the success of the program was determining exactly how productivity would be measured; and once determined, the stay-at-home worker knew exactly what was expected and could assess his or her success independently. Giving the employees the guidelines needed to increase productivity, they exceeded more than previously attained in the traditional work environment. Performance improved mostly because the work-at-home employee appreciated this benefit and wanted to keep it.

4. Finally, to keep the office culture going and to maintain the social network, which is also important, the work-at-home employee would

come to the office one morning a week to attend face-to-face meetings and to stay in touch with workmates who were still in the office.

I believe this model will work in the small business environment, as well. There are fewer reasons than ever, with the advent of computers, fax machines, e-mail, and cell phones, for all the employees to sit in the same office. Everything required can be accomplished without being able to touch the person you're doing business with. In fact, with video conferencing and conference calls, this work-at-home organization is practical, valuable, and satisfying to all involved, and the employer gets more productivity in the bargain.

> **There are fewer reasons than ever, with the advent of computers, fax machines, e-mail, and cell phones, for all the employees to sit in the same office.**

To try it, start slowly and follow this basic model: Select an excellent employee and start with one day at home, followed by more as the practice develops and works to everyone's satisfaction. Then expand the program. Make certain you design a measuring process to determine productivity; it's crucial for successful implementation.

## Independent Contractor versus Employee

Using contractors is a high-stakes strategy. Independent contractors or their company gets paid the gross amount owed them. It is a total business expense to the contractor without payroll tax deductions. Employees who work directly for a company rather than independently for themselves have federal and state taxes deducted and paid for by both their employer and themselves as an employee.

That's a big bet. Approximately 7 to 8 percent of the payroll tax is paid by the employer and the same amount by the employee. Many creative business owners contrive every possible way to satisfy the requirement for hiring independent contractors rather than hiring direct full- or part-time employees.

There is an IRS form that can be submitted in which the service predetermines if an individual is an employee or independent contractor, although the forms lean toward determining all are employees (other than licensed and regulated professionals and bona fide business enterprises).

The general test is the degree of control the employer has over both the process and the conclusion delivered by the proposed employee. The more control over the would-be independent contractor, the less likelihood that independent contractor status will be established and the more likely the person will be deemed an employee.

Hiring contractors is an opportunity for employers to avoid paying not only payroll taxes but worker's compensation insurance and other benefits that come with employee status, including health insurance, vacation, holidays, and overtime. Using contractors instead of permanent employees is, therefore, an important strategy to implement carefully and knowledgeably after considering the facts.

Contractor status is frequently contested and more frequently lost by the employer when independent contractor status is claimed but eventually denied. Here are some of the controlling questions used in determining if a worker is an employee or an independent contractor:

1. Who controls when and where work is accomplished?
2. Who determines how the job is done and what materials are used?
3. Who hires and controls the subcontractors and service providers?
4. Who determines how the process is accomplished?
5. Who designs the tools used?
6. Who determines what the results should be?
7. Whose equipment is used? Who cares for and pays for replacements?
8. How is the payment for services assessed?
9. Does the worker have other clients?
10. Is a professional skill or a professional business organization involved? Is there a written contract?
11. Is there any risk of investment or chance for loss involved on the part of the worker?
12. Does the worker have his or her own letterhead and billing system?

As you can well imagine, every prudent businessperson would prefer to have his or her employees categorized as independent contractors.

The IRS has the opposite in mind, and so the battle lines are drawn. Control is the issue, and it is the burden of the employer and employee to determine that control vests with the worker. Only then can the employee be considered for independent contractor status.

So be prepared to argue divested control and see what happens; the more effort put into the response, the better the result will be.

In the end, the truth will usually be reflected in the outcome; an employee who controls his or her working environment will be awarded independent contractor status, although it is definitely an uphill battle.

## Big Mistake: Making Your Best Salesperson the Manager

Making your best salesperson your next sales manager is frequently done, and seldom is it a good move. Most effective salespeople do not possess the necessary skills to successfully manage a sales department. The two jobs require significantly different personality characteristics as well a different skills. The best salespeople are fiercely competitive and get adrenalin rushes from the excitement of stalking their prey and then killing their prospect with a great close.

> **Making your best salesperson your next sales manager is frequently done, and seldom is it a good move.**

Most great salespeople are unable to do anything well other than close a sale. They typically do not do their paperwork well—too boring. They are usually unable to train others, as they have no idea how they do it ... they just do it. They often come in late and then leave when they are exhausted, as selling requires an enormous amount of energy.

Great salespeople typically are paid more than sales managers because salespeople create revenue and managers do not. Managers must be able to deal with upper management as well as their sales group, which requires diplomacy and other skills salespeople do not always have.

Another frequent and potentially bigger mistake is to make a great salesperson split his or her time, devoting half to sales and half to management. That's an impossible challenge, as great salespeople cannot split their time that way and do a good job at selling and also managing effectively. Sales managers must manage full time to get the best results out of their group.

Frequently, salespeople's personal issues and problems become the issues and problems of the sales group, and the manager must handle the issues. Salespeople do a poor job in this area, as it requires compassion, understanding, patience, and managerial skills, which salespeople typically are short on. In fact, great salespeople do not have this capability at all as they hunt and kill and compete to the last breath, showing little compassion or caring for weaker salespeople.

What normally happens is that the great salesperson becomes a mediocre or, worse, a terrible manager and ends up being fired or leaving for a better sales opportunity. Now the company has neither its star salesperson nor a sales manager. The moral of the story: Think deeply before you try to convert a great salesperson to a sales manager!

 # Employee Management Musts

## Smile, Your Employees Are Watching!

**M**anaging your business successfully requires effective leadership skills. This we all know. Such skills require us to focus our efforts on training, allocating responsibility, inspecting constantly, taking responsibility for failure, and giving credit to those who deserve it.

Frequently, however, managers forget that our employees are always watching us and listening to what we say and, just as important, what we do not say. They take their behavioral cues from our words and actions, and we must always be aware of and use this reality to our advantage.

Good managers understand that their employees will react to and adopt the manager's demeanor. When things are difficult, no matter what the problems are—goals not being reached, customer problems, cash flow shortfall, employee issues, and so on—the manager must always keep the faith outwardly, demonstrating the "no-problem" attitude that breeds confidence and success.

Frequently, when times are tough, if the boss demonstrates fear, depression, failure, desperation, or a negative belief in his or her potential success, the employees will begin looking for other jobs. When you show a lack of confidence, lack of optimism, and overconcern with an issue, then this attitude will rock the world of your employee base. If the boss is worried, they'll think, "We'd better be looking for another job, soon."

In fact, the wrong attitude can create a worse problem, destroy company morale, and make it difficult to rally the troops and gather their support as you navigate whatever difficult issues you are encountering. Your employees will no longer be supported by your vision, as it has become clouded.

The manager must always keep a straight face, handling issues that are barriers to success and leading the employees through the storm with confidence and assertiveness. No matter how you feel inside, no matter how distressed you may be, no matter how serious the issue may seem, as the manager you must show fearlessness. If you demonstrate a positive attitude no matter what the situation, your employees will feel comfortable, in good hands, and they will be willing to follow you through the maelstrom.

The quickest way to lose control of your workforce, and therefore be unable to overcome adversity, is to demonstrate your inner fear. Watch your people scurry for cover, feeling abandoned, without trustworthy leadership, and having to take care of themselves, whatever that may mean. A manager showing weakness also generates a "who-cares" attitude, and it becomes more difficult to gain traction when your employees give up. Worse yet, this attitude can continue long after the issue at hand has been dealt with. It can poison the entire workforce.

> **The quickest way to lose control of your workforce, and therefore be unable to overcome adversity, is to demonstrate your inner fear.**

It is possible that the issues you are confronting are impossible to overcome in the short run or are extremely damaging. Irrespective of the degree of difficulty, and even if the employees realize the extreme nature of the problem, if the manager demonstrates fearlessness and optimism, the employee base will feel comforted and protected. Even if the employees don't know the facts or the obstacles seem impossible to overcome, they will respond favorably and will follow if they believe the boss. Even if the manager personally questions his or her own ability to overcome the adversity, they are comforted with the knowledge that the manager believes we are OK, so we must be OK and do not have to worry. A positive disposition and a belief in future success will inspire employees to strive alongside the leader and achieve greatness despite adversity.

Review your level of optimism and pick it up if necessary; there is no room for whining at the management level. Your employees will follow you to hell and back if you demonstrate a no-problem attitude.

## 11 Ways Your Personal Attitude Affects Performance

You have heard it many times before because it is true: Attitude, good or bad, starts at the top and spreads throughout the organization.

This is an important fact to understand, as it frequently determines the success or failure of a business organization. Here are just some of the factors that can affect a business's attitude:

1. Bosses who show up late and leave early present a bad example to the staff. Bosses who come in early and leave late set an example that is productive and respected; they foster better work ethics and commitment.

2. Bosses who treat the employees with consideration, who demonstrate care and concern by getting to know about their employees' personal lives and families will get the same respect in return, and their actions will promote the same good behavior among employees and with customers. Employees will enjoy their work more, they will perform more effectively, and the customers in turn will be happier.

3. Bosses who take cash from the till in plain sight of the workers are inviting the employees to steal. It becomes common knowledge that the boss steals and there are no cash controls so anyone could steal.

4. Bosses who have no inventory controls, who allow staff workers to take reams of paper for their home office, are acknowledging that stealing from the company is acceptable.

5. Bosses who pay no heed to quality control will foster poor-quality workmanship. Cutting corners becomes the standard.

6. Bosses who have high standards and implement an exacting and professional-level quality control program will instill pride in the work effort and quality in the product. This will also be demonstrated in the pride the workers have in working for such a company.

7. Bosses who bend over backward to honor their customers, who do anything to please them, demonstrate their ethics to their employees. Thus, employees will act similarly toward the customers, doing the same, going the extra mile, doing the unexpected and the unrequired.

8. Bosses who condone bad behavior from employees, who support bad behavior by treating it as an acceptable way to act, create an environment for good employees to start acting poorly.

9. Bosses who do not fire employees for breaching important company standards and instead condone the employees' bad behavior make breaking rules acceptable.

10. Bosses who speak poorly of their difficult customers will develop this attitude throughout the organization. Eventually the customers will feel this attitude and return the same toward the business, or not do business at all.

11. Bosses who allow specific employees to behave badly without chastising them or somehow demonstrating what is expected and required, will allow these employees to spoil the attitude of the others they come in contact with.

It seems so obvious; yet when I recently spent a week at a resort and found everyone absolutely surly, uncooperative in every possible way, unwilling to please the customers, and definitely not going the extra step to accommodate anyone, I was amazed. I investigated this aura of bad attitude and determined, after talking with the manager, that he treated his employees poorly. Likewise, his disdain for his customers was also obvious. No wonder this attitude was prevalent. It spread throughout the entire workforce, because attitude starts at the top, whether it be good, bad, or ugly.

The lesson? As an owner, your business reflects you, your personality, character, attitude, and standards. You are the definitive leader, the owner, the trendsetter. Make what you want of it, but be aware that your default mode is what you bring to the business every day. Respect your employees and customers, and respect will be returned to you threefold. Treat your business, employees, and customers with contempt, and that is what you will get back. Reflect anger and frustration, and that too will be reflected in your company. You are the leader, and where you go, the entire company will follow.

Your business is the mirror image of what you bring to it. Check yourself out; you may be the source for required change if your company is underperforming.

## Managers Manage Systems; Systems Manage Employees

We say many things about systems. The line I like the best is "Managers manage systems; systems manage employees." Systems are a guideline telling you how to do the parts of your job. If your business plan is on point and you follow all your systems, you will succeed.

Not having financial reports because the bookkeeper did not follow the system to create them is fatal. You will find out you're broke after the fact. Without a comprehensive sales and marketing system, procedures aren't followed. Not having guidelines for operations prevents orderly production and destroys productivity. These are the barriers that prevent us from reaching our goals. Systems are the tools to overcome these barriers.

If you analyze each procedure, draft exactly how you want it done step-by-step, and provide tracking forms and information storage tools, you build a book of systems. The more systems you create, the better. Why? Business is not about reinventing the wheel each time. It is not about improvising, doing it differently every day. It is about doing it consistently every time, the right way. It is about training the employee how you want it done every time.

If the systems are written, rather than word of mouth, then you have the basis of a training manual. If someone is out or a new person hired, you can make certain the job is done correctly because you have a system to follow. People get comfortable. They skip steps, fail to keep records of important information, and you only find out when something goes wrong.

Companies, especially new businesses, frequently add systems as they develop. So documenting systems as they are added is an ongoing process. This is not about stifling creativity or innovation. Systems support innovation and creativity in the proper place at the proper time. Adjustments to the system can be made based on experience and trial and error, as long as you have a foundation to grow on.

Systems allow managers to manage by tracking the systems. You have common benchmarks, reports, and procedures so you can tell what your employees are doing and if they are doing it correctly. A system delivers the reports you need when you need them. Your salespeople will call your customers on time with the minimum contact interval dictated by the system.

Ask your employees to draft the systems they follow. You will learn an enormous amount about how your business is being run, and most likely, it will not be as you want. A business without systems is a free-for-all, a gang of people going in different directions doing what they think they should be doing.

Having systems increases productivity and makes employees happier as they know what is expected and how to do their job. Systems manage people; managers manage systems. Finally, you will gain control over your business and stop babysitting employees.

> **Having systems increases productivity and makes employees happier as they know what is expected and how to do their job.**

## Systems for Managing Everything Imaginable

Systems assure continuity, prevent errors, provide training, prevent power grabs, reduce wasted time, and overcome absentee issues. Thus, systems increase profitability and reduce costs. Create systems for everything. It's what the big businesses do. You should do it too, because it works.

Taking telephone messages, for example, as simple as it seems, is important to running a successful business. Documenting an incoming call requires a system. The message should have the full name of the caller, the company the caller represents, the person's callback information, the message, the best time to reply, the degree of urgency, the name of the employee who took the message, the date, and the time. Why? Because these are critical details and calls need to be handled professionally, consistently and accurately, no matter who the caller, the intended recipient, or the message taker. With effective training, no one will miss a beat ... or a message.

This system, as with every system, must be described in writing and inserted into a systems book that can be duplicated and sent to every office that takes incoming calls.

Other examples of appropriate systems include:

- Fax system and reports … in/out
- Petty cash system and expense reports
- Shipping/receiving, returns, rejects, do-overs
- Appointment scheduling
- Raises, promotions, hiring, firing, purchasing
- Managers' budget projections, quarterly department plans, advertising programs
- Work processes, service processes, guaranty procedures
- Credit, collections, payables

Describe each system in detail so it can be repeated easily—so the process runs smoothly, consistently, and accurately no matter who is operating it. A written system that is disseminated and followed throughout the business supports a higher-quality operation.

## Be a Good Manager … What's Stopping You?

I see it all the time. Employees determine when a product gets completed, set their own schedule, choose how they act and dress, with the managers and owner running around complaining about it but afraid to do anything about it. In the end, the inmates are running the asylum.

There are three reasons why managers and owners allow such bad behavior:

1. They are afraid to lose employees by disciplining for breaching the rules.
2. Managers and owners are more concerned about how their employees feel about and regard them than managing by the rules.
3. They are more concerned about missing a deadline or getting the order out than disciplining the employees for breaking the rules.

> When we bend the rules to try and make everyone happy, the result is inconsistency, instability, and organizational disaster.

This management behavior encourages employees to take further advantage of their situation; it demonstrates that the rules are not important, and it is OK for employees to self-govern. When we bend the rules to try and make everyone happy, the result is inconsistency, instability, and organizational disaster.

So in the end we have no rules and no respect for a management that has demonstrated it will not enforce its own requirements, and the employees are free to do as they please when they please.

Management often will reach a breaking point and then usually overreact by firing someone for a small infraction, while really expressing general dissatisfaction over a long list of breaches. The managers think, "We will show them we mean business here. We will set an example that we do not tolerate this type of behavior."

They do tolerate it, inconsistently. So here is the deal. Carefully consider the rules you require to ensure the operation runs smoothly, for example, attendance; production standards; lines of communication; productivity; interaction among employees, customers, and management; and so on.

Once determined, you must require compliance equally by all involved. Breaches are handled consistently for all and immediately by the direct supervisor. As a result, employees will do what they should, when they should, and with respect.

If you have an ongoing training program, which you should, then you will never be afraid to lose an employee. If you do not, begin one immediately, and cross-train, as well, so any position can be handled by multiple people. Restore order and decorum in your workplace. Managers will return to managing, rather than letting the inmates be in charge.

## Incentives, Training, Reviews ... a Career Path

One seldom-recognized, yet valuable, goal of management is developing a career path for each employee in your business. By making it a goal to develop a career path plan for each employee and executing it successfully, your business will succeed beyond expectations.

There are the three components of a career path plan:

1. An incentive-based reward system
2. Manager and employee training
3. Productivity reviews

Taken seriously and implemented effectively, career path form the foundation for operational success in your business. If you develop your employees' skills and capabilities and give them a vision of where they can go in your business, along with what they have to do to get there, they will have a plan and a course of action for their own development.

This will yield many positive results for the business, as well as the individual.

**Incentive-Based Rewards.** An incentive-based reward system that includes the rules and regulations for how you expect your employees to act and work is the starting point. This tool maximizes productivity, improves and defines the appropriate attitude, and supports self-direction and commitment to success.

It is with this tool that our workers become engaged as if they were part owners—and in a way they are: Because they are rewarded for success, their goals become success for the job, the company, and of course, themselves. Watch the changes occur as your employees come to work early and leave late, support one another and work together well, and increase their productivity. They become long-term employees, and everyone earns more than expected, including the business.

**Manager and Employee Training.** Then we train our people in many ways: to do their job more effectively, to increase their skill level, to manage more effectively, to do any number of things better. Training adds to their career path in your business, creates a long-term commitment, and increases the effectiveness of your employees, as well as their productivity and your revenue.

**Performance Review.** Conducting performance reviews cements the employee and employer together as we advance the employee to new heights with a unique plan of personal development and business success.

When effectively implemented, you will see a business become a culture, a community, with everyone caring, growing, and achieving. We create standards for all to work with.

## Why Managing Salespeople Is a Must

Salespeople are a special breed of people. They have a difficult and important job to do. They must be managed to achieve maximum success, or they will cost you a fortune and deliver far less than they are capable of.

For most salespeople, their job is all about successfully absorbing massive amounts of rejection and still feeling successful and positive about themselves, their company, and the product or service they are selling. It requires a manager to harness their positive energy and keep them productive, or most salespeople will fall into one or more of the following 15 traps:

1. Failing to prospect for new business, spending most of their time on safe ground talking to established customers.
2. Spending most of their time on the biggest accounts, feigning the importance of those accounts to the company. Safe ground again.
3. Selling only the best items you have and not the entire spectrum of products. It's safer to sell the winners than promote all the items you sell.
4. Selling the items that are out of stock, not the items that are still in inventory.
5. Always asking your company for something you do not have, explaining that this is what the customer wants, rather than successfully selling what you have.
6. Letting the customers cherry-pick the bargains, discounts, and specials without purchasing anything meaningful. Even helping them do this by pointing out the best deals.
7. Selling bad-credit-risk customers, or existing customers who are a few invoices in arrears, trying to protect their relationship to preserve their commissions.
8. Making side deals to get a sale, extending terms, guaranteeing performance, guaranteeing the sale.
9. Violating stated company policy to create a below-standard sale, for example, selling below minimum levels, mixing and matching different colors, sizes, varieties, and so forth.
10. Cutting price without authority. Making any promise, even one impossible to keep, to make the sale.
11. Wasting time, such as by not filling out required paperwork.
12. Complaining about the company, the boss, the product line.
13. Coming in late, leaving early, saying, "No sense in making calls Monday morning or Friday afternoon."
14. Saying anything to avoid rejection, yet appearing busy and committed.
15. Claiming entire months are not good times to sell: December is bad because of the Christmas season; during the summer, claiming "Everyone is on vacation," and so there are no sales opportunities. And on it goes.

You need a sales manager who can control the salesperson, get the most out of him or her, and prevent wasted time and money. A good sales manager is like a good team manager in professional sports; they both play a primary role in overall success. A good sales manager will get lots more out of an average sales force than a great sales force will get without a good manager.

Track, monitor, and control ... train, plan, and review ... this is what a sales manager must do, this and a lot of babysitting; it's the nature of the beast.

## Sharing Your Business Financials with Employees

Many business owners keep their financial performance information close to their chest. They believe that gross revenues, profitability, and other financial information are secrets not to be shared with anyone, especially not employees.

I am not certain why, and I cannot fathom the issues or the problems with sharing this information. I can only see benefits if done in a meaningful way and for specific reasons.

> **I cannot fathom the issues or the problems with sharing financial information. I can only see benefits if done in a meaningful way and for specific reasons.**

For example, if we want to increase sales revenue, don't we have to know where we are to figure out what we have to do to beat the high-water mark?

If we are measuring costs and expenses and attempting to control these factors, don't we have to share these numbers to measure success?

In production or sales, don't we have to have historical production numbers to know how we are performing?

Some say that these examples are OK. Because they are isolated aspects of the business, they do not show the entire story. No employee will know how we are performing overall with only a sliver of information.

Apparently, it's the whole picture that business owners do not want to or are afraid to reveal to their employees. The fear is that the employees will become upset and unhappy if they know how much profit the organization is making or how much money the owner takes home.

In the end, most employees know all there is to know, including the owner's take-home pay, because it is nearly impossible to keep information secret in a small business. But what is the real issue here?

Publicly traded companies disclose everything for the entire world to see, analyze, and judge.

> **In the end, most employees know all there is to know, including the owner's take-home pay, because it is nearly impossible to keep information secret in a small business.**

Government agencies and employees, which are a huge percentage of the marketplace, reveal all and make public every financial aspect of running the government.

It's only small business owners who believe it is not in their best interests to reveal this confidential information.

Somehow, small business owners believe that such information, if revealed, is detrimental to their well-being. If you asked small business owners why this is so, I doubt they would be able to answer, as I am not certain there is an answer that makes sense, other than it's none of anyone's business. After all, it is a private business.

Some believe that such information in the hands of their competitors will be detrimental to their competitive position. Again I hear the words but fail to see the reasons. How can such knowledge hurt the business in the marketplace?

On the other hand, I believe that if a company is well run and making profits, the employees should be taken care of appropriately and all will be proud and satisfied with the group's accomplishments. They will feel secure and follow the leader, who obviously must know what he or she is doing to be as successful as the numbers say.

It's a report card, and if the business does well, it's a higher grade. Aside from a sense of accomplishment and pride, the overall profitability is a benchmark of success that the employees are entitled to know since they contribute to it. This sort of knowledge is beneficial, as it includes them in the well-being of the entire community. Even though the individual employees may not personally benefit any more than receiving their paycheck, they are still proud to be part of a successful organization.

On the other hand, it is possible that the owner has created various benchmarks for incentive-based rewards, and not only are the individual department numbers relevant, but the final score is the ultimate benchmark. The gross revenue and profitability numbers may be an excellent measuring stick for some aspect of the performance of some key managers. Thus, it is an important number to share. A quality employee who played an important role in this success ought to be appropriately rewarded. Thus, sharing this information is a benefit.

In the end, however, I believe all the negativity of revealing personal revenue numbers of closely held small businesses is overblown and does nothing other than to create mistrust between the owner and his or her team. Conversely, sharing these numbers demonstrates trust and respect.

I say share your information with pride and include your employees in a demonstration of trust, respect, and appreciation, as they contributed meaningfully and ought to know how it all worked out. After all, isn't that the overall goal, to develop the most gross revenue you can at the highest profitability?

> I say share your information with pride and include your employees in a demonstration of trust, respect, and appreciation, as they contributed meaningfully and ought to know how it all worked out.

## Scheduling Vacations

Giving employees their well-deserved time off is always a challenge, especially if you are running a lean organization and are not overstaffed. Each person should be playing an important role, and so the organization will feel the loss of an employee every time one goes on vacation. This could cause major interruptions in the workflow for many weeks during the year. It becomes a built-in excuse for lower productivity if someone key to a function is absent for a week. It's an allowable excuse not to be able to deliver on time.

You also have the annoying scheduling competition to control. You must decide who can take what week off and in what order of priority, juggling to prevent interrupting the work process while recognizing seniority or whatever measuring stick you use to allocate priority among workers.

The cost of vacations is far more than the payroll; it's the lost productivity that's devastating, with bad habits and lower standards developing, which can carry over when you're back in full force. How can this bundle of horrors be controlled?

There is a plan that has worked very well, and I highly recommend it. But before I present it, I want to mention one more relevant observation. Low productivity occurs naturally at different times of the year and results in inefficient operations. At these times, requiring employees to come to work is probably not worth the expense and possibly could be damaging to your development.

For example, the Friday after Thanksgiving is a silly day to work. Depending on what days Christmas and New Year's fall, the days before and after are typically another waste. In fact, the entire week before and the week after Christmas are two weeks during which little happens, unless you are a retail store or a restaurant. Productivity is universally at a near standstill, and yet we maintain a full-force effort.

The July Fourth weekend is another holiday that employees stretch out. Based on the natural low productivity around this day, attempting to implement any productive plan during this week should be reconsidered. The entire business world takes time off.

So I say, let's solve two problems with one strategy, as follows:

- Acknowledge there are two or three holiday periods that will yield low productivity.
- Acknowledge that staggered vacation scheduling is destructive to the productivity of the business.
- Close all operations during these three or four weeks and give everyone extended holiday time; this solves the vacation scheduling issues and the low productivity around holidays. Everyone will be on vacation at the same time during these low-productivity times, and both the business and the employee base will benefit and are much happier for it.

This plan is a net gain anyway you evaluate it.

While this may appear to be generous, and it may be, it is my belief that you gain far more at a lower cost, well worth the implementation. You can adjust this plan to meet your personal needs; it's merely one way to resolve this common issue. There may be a need or a benefit to always staff the office with a skeleton crew performing limited, basic activities.

This is a wonderful time to implement special projects, be it overhauling equipment, cleaning, building, repairing, whatever. You can allocate a few people to execute special projects during the period.

So shut the door and send all the employees home during some combination of the following times: the July Fourth week and the two weeks from before Christmas through New Year's Day.

Everyone is scheduled at once, and the business is either totally shut or partially closed, so there are no additional interfering vacation interruptions to contend with during the year.

Everyone gets the best time slots and possibly more vacation than normal because of your acknowledgment that there are naturally slow unproductive times. You will spread great goodwill and bolster long-term employment, as well as save the company much wasted productivity.

 # Training with Purpose

## Develop from Within

Let's face facts. Most jobs can be taught to anyone with a solid work ethic, a willingness to learn, and good general skills. So if a position is vacated in your business, why not draw from within, train, and create a very loyal and devoted employee, someone who can be trusted to go the extra mile for you, as you are doing for him or her?

I have seen someone inexperienced develop into a superstar when trained from within. Everyone benefits. The company, the person, and the rest of the employee base are better off. Other employees watch and think well of the boss, the company, and their own possible opportunity for advancement from within.

I am a firm believer in training. You can train anyone to do anything if the individual possesses the right attitude and skills. So we are looking for a responsible, competent, and clear-thinking person who has a good work ethic. Find that person, make him or her an employee, and then find a place to fit the person in, as business is built around people, not vice versa.

If you have an employee already demonstrating these qualities, develop the person into a better job position—better for the company, better for everyone. Make it a rule: Hire from within ... expand from within ... train and develop the expertise required to staff your jobs appropriately. Create office managers out of staff, create a production manager out of production workers, create salespeople out of production workers, and on it goes. It's called a career path and will keep employees interested for a long while as they climb the ladder of success within your organization.

Developing from within adds to the bottom, and gives everyone an opportunity to work their way to the top. It will cost less than hiring from outside, take less time, and create a reward system that cannot be beaten. When you hire from outside and use inside employees to train, you create problems.

## Cross-Training

It matters little how large or small your business may be. I see it occur all the time, and it goes like this: "Paul is out today, so we cannot_____." You fill in the blank. Another rendition of this theme, "Phil is on vacation this week. We cannot get to this until he returns next week."

Or "Betty had to leave for the day ... afternoon ... early ... we will get to it tomorrow."

In small business, we tend to design our businesses so individuals perform specific jobs. Thus, if that individual is unavailable for any reason, that job cannot be fulfilled and production stops, be it manufacturing, service, or internal office paper flow. If Nancy is out, bills do not get sent that day, or we cannot look that up. In other words, unless we have full attendance, the operation cannot run smoothly. It bottlenecks somewhere.

Think about this absurdity. If you have 10 people working for you, and each person has one week of vacation and five days of excused absence for whatever reason, this amounts to five months of not having full employment when things will not flow smoothly or some task cannot get done, completed, or even started. It waits for the person to return so the business can do its job as designed. That's nearly half a year of inefficiency, lower productivity, and the unfortunate likelihood of making someone unhappy when the job cannot proceed.

Is this a way to run a business smoothly and effectively? Of course not, but this is how it's done. Productivity and customer service seem to be forgotten concepts when it comes to keeping a small business running smoothly. It seems that business owners accept this issue as part of the business dilemma.

Few owners consider cross-training. Everyone seems to be a specialist doing one thing. So here it is: If every job or task is learned by at least one additional person, when the primary person is out, the secondary person cross-trained to perform the task can leap in and save the day. And so work continues, and productivity remains high despite the absence of a key player. Smoother production, greater productivity, and happier customers mean a better bottom line.

Every job in the business flow should have a trained backup so that any job can be completed under any circumstance. A manager can make the decision when to call in the substitute and how to best allocate the human resources, but the key is by investing in cross-training, the manager can decide about how to allocate the talent; at least there is a choice.

> **Every job in the business flow should have a trained backup so that any job can be completed under any circumstance.**

This also applies to the occasional situation where a person must be fired. If someone else is cross-trained to do the job, there is more freedom for the manager to fire when necessary without fear of interrupting the workflow.

If an incentive-based reward system has been installed, this bit of management prerogative will go a long way in maintaining high productivity and reaching the organization's goals.

It takes time and effort but is worth the investment. Cross-train your employees so every critical task has a backup capable of doing another job when needed.

## Use Training to Eliminate Do-Overs

It's the hidden killer of profit, the destroyer of client and employee goodwill, the client eliminator. It leads to the destruction of positive cash flow and profitability. I can think of few things worse than having to go back to fix an error, a poor installation, a mistake, or whatever you call it. Do-overs are something that must be controlled as much as possible. Using the punch-list concept is an excuse for allowing shortcuts and performing below standards. Do-overs happen when you have no one trained in the leadership role required to develop and maintain on-site control. Certainly at least one member of the crew could be learning that role.

> **Do-overs happen when you have no one trained in the leadership role required to develop and maintain greater on-site control.**

Frequently, mistakes appear to be the result of a poorly managed team. Crews are sent to clients' houses to install, repair, or build something, and because of unclear communication, poor work habits, poor on-site management, a mistaken assumption, low standards, or not caring, they do not perform the job acceptably, meeting neither the client's nor to the business owner's standards. And it must be redone.

I figure that if all the downtime and hours spent discussing the situation were tracked, a redo takes as much as one-and-a-half to two times the time and cost required to do the job correctly the first time.

That's a huge loss, and depending on the complexity and value of the materials and labor, the cost of a fix could be disabling. Worse yet, this may not be a singular experience. It may be a trend. If it happens frequently, the cost should be the cause for concern.

First, it reveals a number of flaws; for example, possibly the instructions were not in place or were poorly communicated.

Second, it may be a failure of providing effective on-site management, quality control, supervision, and accountability, which indicate poor management systems or no systems.

It may point to another issue, that there are no training programs, no mentoring programs, no teamwork, no way to support the quality of work desired.

It probably also means there is no incentive reward system and no attention to quality as a requirement of the job; at the very least, it appears there are no consequences for inferior work, just lost profits.

I have seen businesses fail because of this problem. Many business owners I talk with tell me it's too expensive to add the management they need to supervise effectively and provide the quality control required. I say, "Whatever the cost, it's cheaper than failure."

Here are just some ways to curb the costs of do-overs:

- Install a tracking system with accountability and rewards for success.

- Add incentive-based pay for successful work.
- Add overview and quality control.
- Train effectively; have a program to help the younger workers improve with the help of a dedicated mentor.
- Create a culture where errors, repairs, and redos are unacceptable.
- Create working teams.
- Create career paths.

Major errors need never happen again if you create a company culture in which employees take pride in their work. If you train employees and have quality control systems in place and if you track, monitor, and control the work effort, you will reap the benefits. It can be done if you raise your standards and provide the systems to support them.

## Forging Leadership Skills in Times of Crisis

Like molding steel into a shape you want over a hot flame, leadership skills can also be forged over the hot flame of a crisis.

There are many other ways to develop leadership skills, undoubtedly, and probably a whole lot better and safer. However, crisis situations do occur all the time, and when they do, someone has to step up, take control, and lead the pack through the storm ... and that's a leader.

A leader must inspire confidence, so when necessary, the employees will follow what the leader says. A leader must be able to delegate responsibility to others, choosing the right person for the job. A leader must see the bigger picture and yet also understand that reaching a goal requires lots of small acts done by many people.

There is nothing like a crisis to see who has it and who doesn't or who comes through it alive, smarter, and more skilled. Whatever the crisis and resulting problems may be, it takes a leader to rise to the occasion and do the job.

Rudy Giuliani, mayor of New York City during the 9/11 crisis, demonstrated that he had the real stuff. He was an excellent leader already, and while this was a crisis demanding enormous capability, he demonstrated he had skill sufficient to lead the city through this crisis successfully with the least loss and the greatest amount of protection possible.

Not all crises are as horrific as 9/11. That was so enormous, it was a good thing we had an experienced leader at the helm, and we witnessed what skilled leaders can do when needed—they step up.

So what should we as business owners take out of these situations? Fortunately, our small business environment provides ample opportunity for us to allow our managers and executives in training to learn and practice their leadership skills during smaller crises.

Crisis situations happen all the time. Machinery breaks down, raw materials are not delivered on time, a large account goes to a competitor; storms interfere with delivery, and power outages occur. There are cases where absenteeism or untrained employees can be the source of a major problem.

All such occurrences are typically handled by the CEO, who takes charge and cautiously makes all the necessary decisions to safely navigate out of a challenging situation.

Turning adversity and disaster into success—that's the challenge, and that's what we must train our future leaders to do. We train them by allowing them to manage small emergencies and learn how to turn disaster into success.

> Turning adversity and disaster into success—that's the challenge, and that's what we must train our future leaders to do.

Unfortunately, the knee-jerk reaction of many owners and CEOs is to take over and steer the course, as much is at stake. The right answer is to let the manager handle the emergency and to learn how to make decisions quickly and effectively, how to lead people, how to see the bigger picture, and determine the best path and implement a plan to get there.

That's leadership training under fire, and it works well, forging strength and effectiveness.

Remember that management is not about doing it yourself. It is about training others to do it; and if all are working together toward a common goal . . . the goal will be achieved.

Stand next to your manager, provide counsel during the crisis, and let the manager talk things through. This is good training if you let the manager make the decisions and implement the plan, even if it fails to achieve the desired results. The experience is worth more than the amount lost.

So take advantage of the next crisis and accept the risk; let your manager handle it and learn on the job. It's the best training possible and the only way to learn this skill. This action also demonstrates that the owner or CEO trusts the manager with the responsibility of averting disaster and controlling losses. The commitment requires great trust. It shows respect. Much can be gained out of a crisis, including developing your next leader.

# Chapter 7

# Meaningful Evaluations

## Performance Reviews

Performance reviews are frequently considered worse than going to a dentist, for the employee as well as the manager. It doesn't have to be. Instead, it can be an exhilarating, positive experience for all involved, a celebration of success and positive development, a helping hand to find the path to success. It can most always be a beneficial experience for the employee, the employer, and the business if you do it the right way.

For it to be successful, the employees must evaluate their own performance, as well as have an opportunity to discuss their desires, their objectives, and needs for training, education, licensing, and whatever other support they may need to develop and succeed. The employer must use this opportunity to develop a plan for greater success. The performance review should become a total career path discussion, reviewing, planning, and evaluating the past, the present, and the future.

Change the review from a typically expected one-sided evaluation—from the employer to the employee—to a joint-effort planning and evaluation session, with positive and productive conclusions.

This change makes a huge difference with incredible results. You can convert what has always been a stressful, unpleasant, and usually unproductive experience to a productive and wildly positive one that affects the ongoing performance and development of the individual and the business.

The performance review becomes a joint venture between the employer and the employee. With a goal to support personal development and growth, this kind of review strategy promotes excellence, happiness, longevity, productivity, and loyalty.

The important aspect is self-evaluation by the employee, with the employer building his or her assessment into a career path for development. The outcome is a specific plan developed by the two of you that maximizes the employee's opportunities within the organization.

> **The important aspect is self-evaluation by the employee, with the employer building his or her assessment into a career path for development.**

Conduct performance reviews every six months. Take the time to develop and customize your own questionnaire for each person you evaluate. Keep notes on what was agreed on, as you will want to review the assessment and plan at the next review session. When combined with an incentive-based reward system, your employees and your business will flourish.

## Self-Assessment to Start

While it is important and valuable for employees to get feedback from their manager on current performance, as well as expectations for the future, I believe in letting employees review themselves first.

Here is an example of a short questionnaire that I distribute to my employees to guide their self-assessment.

1. What areas of your job performance did you do your best? Worst?
2. What additional training do you feel you need to perform more effectively?
3. What do you think about how you have been managed?
4. How do you rate your ability and performance in handling your clients effectively?
5. Overall, did you do your best? If not, why? How can you do better?
6. Do you have complaints about any aspect of the business and how you were treated?

7. What would you change in the business if you had the opportunity?
8. Do you believe you are adequately paid? Do you have adequate benefits?

We discuss the answers during our review, after which you review the performance of the employee from your perspective.

If there is a manager involved, you may have the manager conduct the review, or both you and the manager might do the review together, or you may do it without the manager. It all depends on your situation.

It is interesting to see the differences between my review and the employee's own self-evaluation. It reveals much about the character of the person.

## Mastering Productivity

Productivity is the measurement of how much product or service your employees create over a given time. Since you must have projected some level of productivity in order to determine selling price and, therefore, profitability, you must monitor these benchmarks during the production process. Why presume you are as productive as required? Here's an example.

Assume that it requires 2 employees 2 hours each to produce an item that sells for $100 and earns the company $50 gross profit. The employees earn $10 per hour. Thus, labor costs $40 of that $100 receipt. What would happen if it took the employees 4 hours each? The labor cost would double: $80. The business would make only $10, not the intended $50, each time it sold an item. That's productivity or the lack of it. If the employees make the item in 1 hour, they increase the profit measurably by an additional $20 for a profit of $70. That's greater productivity and lots more profit.

Unfortunately, productivity is not a concept many business owners relate well to, nor do they use it to control their production process. They tend to allow their employees to work at their own pace, believing they are working as fast as they can, and the rate of production is, therefore, reasonable.

Productivity is typically unmeasured, and in America it has been allowed to hover around 30 percent. That means, in our example above, the employees would work for 6 hours to produce the item, and the business would lose money every day.

Worse yet is the typical solution. To build production to meet consumer demand, the company hires more people and loses more money, as opposed to increasing efficiency and productivity. To add insult to injury, if the business owner truly wants to get more items out the door, he or she allows overtime, a reward for low productivity, which creates greater losses while the employees make more money.

This is typical American small business management. In most businesses I review, the production workers have no idea what is expected of them. They are unaware of the time the business owner has determined should be spent building the item, so the employee has no reference for delivering adequate productivity. I even see businesses where productivity is measured but not told to the workers, so it does no one any good. It is clear many business owners have not done productivity analyses and have no expectation about how much time must be spent to produce the product or service profitably. Thus, they rely on the standards the employees determine are appropriate.

> In most businesses I review, the production workers have no idea what is expected of them.

Further, if workers know what production time is expected and if they are given an incentive, they will do their best not only to achieve this standard but to beat it ... greater productivity.

The more advanced business owner ties compensation for the workers to their productivity and rewards them for greater productivity, and, yes, fires them for low productivity or, better, trains them to work more efficiently.

Develop a key indicator system to track, monitor, and control productivity. Measuring productivity allows management to make the changes required to maintain profitability. Never allow overtime. If everyone works fast and effectively maintains quality as well as speed, then the business makes money, as do the employees, who are now paid for production, not for time spent.

## How Firing Benefits Employer and Employee

Firing ineffective, underproducing, problem employees is usually a difficult situation for the employer, and, presumably, no one likes to do this. However, it is a blessing for all: the employer, the employee to be terminated, and the remaining employees. It will be easier to do if we understand the principle that everyone benefits.

Here is why. If the working relationship is not good for the employer, it cannot be good for the employee. As with most relationships, the employer–employee relationship is a two-way street, and so the relationship cannot be good for one side and unacceptable for the other. It is either good for both or unacceptable for both … that's what I have observed.

> As with most relationships, the employer–employee relationship is a two-way street, and so the relationship cannot be good for one side and unacceptable for the other.

Unfortunately, not every employee may understand, and so the job of the firing employer is to explain this concept as the basis of the firing … freeing both the employee and employer to find a better relationship.

Everyone wants to be appreciated, respected, and successful. Nearly everyone wants to be productive. If an employee does not achieve success—and in fact is experiencing the exact opposite: negative feedback, complaints, low job satisfaction, feelings of low self-esteem, self-doubt, and perhaps discomfort with the job—release from this situation is good for all.

Explaining this principle to an employee whom I am about to fire will typically arouse agreement and relief. "If it isn't working for the employer, it must not be working for the employee," I explain, "so it's best for us both to part ways. It's a positive decision."

Met with agreement that this firing is best for all involved—so the employee can find a job better suited to his or her skills and, likewise, the employer can also find a better-fitting relationship, the exit strategy becomes a win-win discussion.

An unhappy employer firing an unhappy employee is a blessing in disguise for both. It's an act of benevolence, and when presented in this manner, most employees say thank you and appreciate the opportunity for candid communications and positive action.

It does not have to be as negative or destructive as most believe it is. It's now about what's best for both.

# Chapter 8

# Get On Board with Social Media

## Social Media for the Business Arena

We have all heard about the power of the Internet as a business tool, and so we all have websites. Many are enjoying the benefits of blogs and video attached to our sites. The next Internet wave of business tools is social media: Twitter, Facebook, LinkedIn, YouTube, and blogs. These tools are more subtle, as they resist direct marketing efforts, but when used effectively, can have a huge impact on the marketplace. Yet many businesses have been slow to adopt social media marketing strategies.

MarketingSherpa compiled a chart based on a December 2008 survey showing the effectiveness of social media's uses. There are some interesting statistics in its report.

Most striking is how the effectiveness of social media far outweighs ineffectiveness. Over 90 percent of companies interviewed believe social media is most effective in building brand reputation and awareness as opposed to direct marketing strategies.

"You might expect the revenue-producing goals of direct marketing to rank higher than branding during a recession," says MarketingSherpa. "The conversational and relationship-building nature of social media, however, is more synonymous with PR, which is more likely to help accomplish branding goals."[1]

Still, the direct marketing potential is nothing to shake a stick at. MarketingSherpa's data illustrate wonderfully that there are a variety of ways your business can benefit from social media. Irrespective of your specific goals, social media tools such as Facebook, YouTube, Twitter, and LinkedIn apparently reach the market very effectively and influence your customers' actions and opinions.

If you are unsure of what this is all about, ask your teenage son or daughter to explain it ... you'll soon get the picture of how powerful and far reaching these tools can be.

## Social Networking Is the New Wave

So, yes, folks, it's time to tweet on Twitter! Make friends on Facebook, and star in your own video or podcast on YouTube. You might be saying, "Why should I be thinking about this? What are the benefits? What happens if I don't do 'it,' whatever 'it' is?"

Your opinion about social media and your belief in its potential value are irrelevant. If you are not using it, then you need further enlightenment along with an introduction, so you, too, will "get it," as did I. It's simple; pay attention, follow directions, implement effectively, and reap the benefits.

The point of being involved in social networking is action, growth, and development. It is about how we as a society, the world, are changing our ways of communicating. Social networking tools, vehicles, and contexts are what we need for this new way. By exchanging real thoughts and views and getting personal, the message comes along for the ride; it is not the main act. This approach is refreshing and relevant. You will be surprised how many people are awakening to this new reality. Be a leader. Millions upon millions of people are tweeting, making friends on Facebook, watching video clips, and reading blogs, far more than anyone imagined.

The revolution has happened; let's usher in the changes. To market effectively, we must utilize effective business modes, tools, and vehicles for delivering our messages.

Social networking is the next wave. Be early; stay ahead of your competition. Grow and prosper in the face of a declining marketplace; take a share from your competitors. Social networking is how to communicate effectively to the world today.

As I theorized when I wrote my first blog post on Wordpress, it would change the way I marketed and communicated. It did. My entire marketing program is based on sharing valuable information and creating relationships through social networking, which sometimes result in a sale.

Now is the time to get on board and take your business marketing to the next level. Create a broader, deeper, more dynamic, and powerful social network, and then do something with it.

> My entire marketing program is based on sharing valuable information and creating relationships through social networking, which sometimes result in a sale.

## The Power of Social Networking

If you are still questioning the viability of social networking, look at the following statistics:

- The Facebook nation has the third largest population in the world after China and India.
- Twitter is experiencing upward of 2 billion tweets per hour.
- YouTube had 100 million visits in January 2009, and the frequency is way up since then.

If these statistics do not convince you to reconsider the viability of social networking, consider that Pepsi-Cola decided not to advertise on the Superbowl and instead invested $20 million into social networking media . . . are you paying attention?

These numbers tell it as it is. To ignore social networking is to do so at your peril. The future is here, today, and you must get on this train or be left behind. If not yet, your competition will figure this out sooner or later; and when it does, you will be playing catch-up and losing. The opportunity for you to create more revenue, develop additional sales and marketing tools, and reap the benefits is important to your long-term survival and success.

Yes, we are experiencing the deepest downturn in our modern economy, and many are suffering from declining revenues. Downsizing and rebuilding is the mandate. Utilizing the Internet for marketing purposes is a necessity. It is cost efficient and potent. Forget newspaper ads and other traditional media tools. It is like what is happening to the telephone booth and the landline, taken over by the cell phone technology. Join the revolution before it passes you by.

## Facebook, the Next E-Commerce Wave

If you have kids, you understand the power of their Facebook insertions. You can see the importance that this social networking application has in your children's lives. It is the face of America. The first to know the value of and become immersed in Facebook were the demographically young, under 30. Typically, small business owners are older and thus are missing this tidal wave of connections and communication.

The important point is that these social media networking tools are a marketing opportunity of immense power if used properly and consistently. They allow us to reach a huge market in a personal and meaningful way. This is not about pandering your products or services or hard selling. It is not advertising. It is all about talking with and becoming part of this social media revolution. The business applications of social networking have enormous potential.

> The important point is that these social media networking tools are also a marketing opportunity of immense power if used properly and consistently.

Blogs are a huge part of this as well, allowing a dialogue with your readers that is transparent, unmonitored, uncensored, relevant, contemporary, interesting, valuable, and powerful. And free! Yes, free. Can you imagine what it would cost to talk to hundreds of thousands or even millions of people? Yet social networking is free!

It requires integrity, sincerity, candor, focus, and relevance. Delivered effectively, you can reach millions of people and subtly create a relationship with your market, which eventually will result in revenue.

It's a new way of thinking and a new way of marketing, and it requires a new mind-set. It forces you to understand what things interest the marketplace you are seeking to communicate with. It forces you to be relevant. It moves advertising and marketing to a whole new atmosphere, an atmosphere typically foreign to business. It's a place where people can exchange ideas and information and explore thoughts, beliefs, and feelings. It forces us to become transparent and real.

Ask your kids about it. My 24-year-old daughter called me the other day and insisted I investigate Facebook and become a part of this social media revolution. She said, "Everyone is in it."

Businesses are using Facebook and other social networking vehicles to communicate with this vast marketplace. I am listening to her, as I am out of touch. I am exploring Facebook. It is uncomfortable for me because it is different and new, but it is the direction the communication train is going and I want to be on it. The numbers are staggering. We cannot ignore this revolution. Get relevant. Get on board.

## How Social Networking Works for Small Business

Social networking is a new concept—Facebook, YouTube, and IM (instant messaging). The big question I have is, how does this help business? I have learned quite clearly how blogs work; I write posts for my blog every day. Thousands of visitors read my blog. It's the free dissemination of valuable information and appreciated by many who read it. I know, because they tell me this in their comments. What does it do for me?

Sometimes a blog post creates business opportunities; most times the reward is the gratification of offering help to someone ... without my expectation of a return. How does that help my business? I believe it helps me become a resource and a recognized part of community with members all over the country and around the world. People return and learn from my posts and become part of my unique community. They develop a relationship with me, one of trust, and when needed may become clients.

I speak with a half a dozen people each day whom I invite to consult with me on my blog posts about their business debt issues with no obligation. To most I give advice; some retain my services. That some hire my services is welcome and the obvious benefit that works for me and my clients, but the true value is in the dissemination of valuable information. The ones I *give* advice to are the more interesting as that is the true meaning and value of social networking: sharing valuable information, solving problems, and doing it without expectation of a return. The blog interaction creates a social network that supports my business mission. I enjoy it thoroughly and benefit from it. Yes, it is tough to figure out, but go with it; the benefits will become clearer as you develop your own community.

Verizon has discovered the same worthwhile results in a different application with a social network twist. The company is experimenting with the 1 percent of its users (customers) who are experts in setting up networks, HDTVs, and all the other applications it offers. These services are typically handled through India customer service support. In this experiment, the other customers' issues are handled by volunteers, online experts who want to help others needing technical assistance.

By nature, people want to help one another; they crave community. It may be hard to believe in this day of greed, but it remains true. People who are good at something, say hooking up in-house telecommunication systems, which is very confusing to most and mastered by a few, are willing to spend time assisting others in overcoming their technical barriers. Verizon reports that some volunteer experts are putting in upward of 20 hours per week, doing an incredible job helping customers hook up their electronics.

> Verizon reports that some volunteer experts are putting in upward of 20 hours per week, doing an incredible job helping customers hook up their electronics.

Instead of talking to India and getting a low level of uncaring technical support, people can talk to online volunteers for the purpose of helping others overcome their issues. It costs Verizon nothing, and the results are stunning. The people who constitute the 1 percent are willing to help the other 99 percent because they get the point of social networking. They participate because they care and enjoy the rush of helping others in need, free of the expectation of a return. That's a new business model. That's radical.

It requires a leap of faith to implement social networking. Perhaps you can try a blog first; maybe Facebook second; then advance to a video on YouTube, and then Twitter. By then you will be a regular participant in Web 2.0, the new world of social networking. Welcome to the future—it has arrived.

## Note

1. Chris Crum, The Business Goals Where Social Media Is Most Effective, www.webpronews.com/topnews/2009/02/17/the-business-goals-where-social-media-is-most-effective, February 17, 2009.

 **Marketing Without Money**

## Effective Low-Cost Marketing for Local Markets

As we carefully measure the degree of damage, or in more precise terms, reduced revenue and increased costs we are experiencing from the decline of our economy, advertising spending tends to be one of the first cuts owners make. Yet this may be a great time to expand marketing to take a share of the market away from your competitors.

I witnessed a contractor who climbed from a new-entry start-up in the local building market with no clients to the market leader in a few short years. The owner participated in the local political arena, first volunteering for various positions and slowly building political strength. In time he was appointed and volunteered for higher-visibility positions, and eventually he was elected to public office.

Along the way, his involvement attracted business automatically. Without a mention of his work or his desire to build business, he simply attracted business by his selfless volunteering for local political positions. It took a year or two to catch on, but after that, he was able to build business, and it has not stopped since.

A second rendition of this public service idea was developed by another business owner I know, who built a successful regional business on the backs of children. He offered to sponsor any sports team anywhere within his region, which spanned a number of towns in a county or two. He provided the printed T-shirts. Over the years his sponsorships amounted to many dozens of teams and a $60,000 per year budget in every imaginable sport. He created such goodwill and such local brand recognition that it was all the advertising his company needed. He literally built his business on the T-shirts the kids wore. The parents were grateful, and the community knew the company name. His business is now the leader in the local market area.

A third approach offers sports teams, Boy Scouts, classes, clubs, and so forth the opportunity to sell the services of the business and then split revenues for sales brought in. With the right product, it is a great idea that is inexpensive, creates goodwill, and brings in local business.

We must continue to market, advertise, and build our share of the market, even in a declining economy.

## So Many Wasted Advertising Dollars

Advertising and marketing are crucial programs that too frequently result in wasted dollars and disappointing returns. What seems to be the problem?

Successful advertising requires an investment. Small, infrequent ads have limited power and usually limited success in competing against powerful, frequently run large-space ads. So why waste important dollars on ineffective, traditional space advertising?

Here are a few suggestions that may result in a better response for fewer dollars:

- **Referrals.** Ask your customers for referrals. This is an often-overlooked form of networking. Past and current customers are a likely source of additional business or valuable referrals.
- **Press releases.** Will Rogers said it best, "It must be true. I read it in the newspaper." It's free, and it works. Write a press release and send it to the press in the market you are serving.
- **Your website.** It is crucial, as it is expanding your use of Internet technology, which is available for low-cost promotions such as blogging or videocasting. Powerful, not necessarily expensive, and it works 24 hours per day everywhere.
- **Handouts, fliers, newsletters.** All are low cost and have potentially high impact.

- **Postcards.** Use them to make a statement; use humor. Here is a tip: You must plan to send at least three to a potential customer. By the third one, your message will be noticed and recalled.
- **Tradeshows.** Attend as an exhibitor, but you must be more than an exhibitor. You must use trade shows as a springboard and support your presence with all the above programs before, during, and after. Have a well-thought-out display and interactive program. Walk the show and talk to the other exhibitors in the same industry, and you may be able to sell to them or create positive strategic relationships. Everyone important in your industry is there.

Finally, and perhaps most important: Define your message. If you are telling your audience what it already knows and expects, then you are wasting your money. If you are telling potential customers why they should do business with you, what separates you from your competitors, you will achieve success. For example, is it important for a moving company to promise safe drivers? I would imagine that's expected. What do you do that is special or that differentiates you from your competitors?

> **If you are telling potential customers why they should do business with you, what separates you from your competitors, you will achieve success.**

It is all about creating a relationship with your prospects by stating what you do uniquely and what a consumer would want to learn about. What is your guarantee, for example? Or how can customers communicate with you? What do you know that they do not know about your service? Talk meaningfully to your prospective customers and teach them something with your ad. Once you create the relationship, the sale will come. Remember to sell yourself, your company, and your service … in that order.

Financial stress is not an adequate excuse for not marketing; it is a necessary function for any successful business. There are many avenues to pursue. Find the right ones for you and use them. The only bad advertising program is no program at all.

## The Forgotten Benefits of Public Relations

For small businesses especially, which are almost always searching for additional capital to invest in their growth and development, advertising programs tend to go first when cash is scarce. That's unfortunate but understandable. Advertising is a necessary support for the sales and revenue projections but quickly dispensed with when cash gets tight. Advertising support tends to dwindle in the face of inventory requirements or payroll. Frequently, inadequate dollars are assigned to support marketing from the beginning, as the demand for cash for so many other good reasons is typically overwhelming.

So consider including public relations in your program. It's free, it's powerful, and it works well if executed appropriately, either in support of a major marketing effort or standing on its own. Here is how it works.

Write a press release about some interesting aspect of your business or service. Use a soft sell, as the story carries your name with it, and that's the goal; that's what counts. It cannot be about price, nor can it sound like an advertisement. It cannot be completely self-serving. There must be a human interest aspect to the story. If it is printed, it will support your brand's name or company's name recognition.

A press release works best with local and special-interest newspapers or magazines. They tend to have low budgets and few writers, and they appreciate and use quality space fillers, news, or human interest stories, especially when the stories have community ties or a relevant special interest.

There are also many coupon books and other high-distribution advertising pieces that print news releases about local businesses, especially if supplied and well written. You can get significant, quality coverage at no cost.

A similar approach, but possibly even more self-directed, can be accomplished by sending a release to local, regional, and national trade magazines that focus on your product or services. This approach, of course, should carry more of a wholesale message, business to business, while the public press release should carry a consumer message.

Sometimes purchasing a small ad will help grease the way for a press release to be printed, but a press release still must be reasonably well written. Don't be discouraged if your first two, three, or four releases are rejected; eventually your fourth or fifth one will be printed. It will be worth the effort and wait, as the results can sometimes be stunning.

Public relations—in this case press releases—should be part of a larger marketing plan because it works well, even if the cash has run out. Add your press release to your website for your Internet visitors to read. (If you do not have a website, get one as soon as possible.) E-mail a newsletter, with your press release in it, to your mailing list. Purchase e-mail services that will blast your press release to your prospective customers. Try to drive them to the website and compel them to inquire about your product or services.

## Great Logo Graphics Reasonably Priced

Image is important. Marketing begins with your name and logo. Your logo says much about you and your business. Graphic artists can be very expensive, and you never know what you are going to get. So hiring a good logo designer can be tricky. Unfortunately, as happens most often, you get what you pay for. If you go for low-priced graphics, chances are you will get inadequate results.

Frequently, small businesses opt for no graphics, but instead use a computer-generated, type-only display of their company name for a business logo. Using a standard type font to communicate your brand name is not inspiring and communicates no message other than you did not bother or could not afford it.

There is a way to create a logo with outstanding graphics without breaking the bank. Recently *The Wall Street Journal* reported on four national logo design companies it tested that work through the Internet and telephone, providing quick turnaround services and delivering high-quality results. At the time of the report, the prices for developing a custom logo ranged from $99 to $1,499.

Here are the companies the *Journal* looked at:

- The LogoCompany.net
- LogoDesignCreation.com
- LogoDesignGuru.com
- LogoLoft.com

All four were given the same company name and asked to submit four concepts. The resulting logos were all professionally done and worthy of consideration. All appeared high cost and provided a variety of quality choices to match personal taste.

While not free, they are affordable, with quick turnaround and great results. Using one of these recommendations is an excellent way to go.

There is no excuse for not having a quality image and an excellent logo.

Here is another great idea: Promote a competition, promising a prize for developing your next logo, ad, or anything graphic you may need. Put it out to the community at large, and let all the aspiring graphic designers compete for the prize and provide you with hundreds of suggestions. The results can then be a press release with more bang for your business.

## A Dozen Fast Ways to Become a Recognized Expert

Frequently, it helps to be recognized as an expert in your field, a specialist with trustworthy credentials, to establish your credibility. How does one become an expert? The traditional path: Spend a lifetime in the industry and earn relevant educational certifications and degrees. The traditional method takes a long time and is impractical for the new entrepreneur who wants to enter the business arena as a player.

There are alternative paths to reach the goal of being recognized as an expert. Here are 12 ideas:

1. Learn about what's important in your industry today and become current. Every commercial niche has one or more trade magazines. Obtain a few back copies, three at least, and read them cover to cover, noting the editorials, as that's what's currently on the minds of the industry leaders. You should understand and adopt the opinion of the lead editorial from the lead magazine in that genre. The editors and writers know what is best for their industry. You should be adept on the subject and have an opinion or two of your own, of course, as you are an industry expert.

2. Note the advertisements, as they will tell you what's new and important to the industry as well as what the leading businesses are talking about and selling. Of course, read the letters, the articles, and everything else, as it broadens your awareness.

3. Write an article and submit it for publication in one of the industry magazines, which is not as hard as it seems. Once done, you are a published writer in the industry. If you have trouble getting an article published, write a letter to the editor or respond to one; that's easier, and it will start the process going. People will see your name and read your material.

4. Create a website and a blog. Begin to communicate with your mar-

ket, discussing the issues and creating an open forum with you as an expert. Highlight your involvement, as well as your diverse commitment to the industry. You can further establish your credentials and publish your materials, including press releases, articles, and so forth.

5. Create your own podcasts (video or audio) based on your blog entries. Post the video on YouTube. You can post your audio to iTunes. Some people find it easiest to start with Audio Acrobat (www.audioacrobat.com); you can phone from anywhere to record your podcast, and Acrobat feeds it to podcast hosting sites such as iTunes.

6. Just about everyone lives near a university, college, state school, technical school, or some other bastion of higher learning. Offer a professor or department head the opportunity to have you speak at a forum run by the professor or department head on a subject relevant to you and the educator's interest group—at no charge, of course.

7. Offer a local club, association, or service organization programming chair the opportunity to have you speak on a relevant subject both at no charge.

8. Run your own seminar—building your credentials.

9. Become a corporate speaker. If your subject matter has commercial application, you may be able to get a local leading business to let you speak after hours, during lunch, or at a business meeting. Being a public speaker at leading businesses and corporations adds to your credentials.

10. Send out press releases to the local press. Repeat your credentials and promote your speaking, or writing, or seminar, or whatever you have to promote that you believe is of interest to and important for the general public to know about.

11. Join a national trade organization for your industry and offer to write a monthly column on interesting aspects of the industry for the organization's newsletter or magazine. Of course, mention your name and business at the end to insert yourself subtly and tastefully. Be sure your article at least includes a byline with your web address. Now that you're writing a monthly column for the industry trade magazine, you must be a respected expert.

12. If you can afford it, give a seminar, have a booth, or get on the board or any committee for the organization's national trade show. All these options give you enormous credibility and visibility. Speak at the trade show; sponsor an event; be a presence.

You have begun to cement your reputation into a solid foundation of respectability. Now you can add to your credentials the facts that you are a nationally recognized and published author, a lecturer at universities and colleges, and a nationally renowned expert on _____. In the end, marketing you as the expert leads to more business.

## Eight Rules for Using Specialty Items

We see specialty advertising items everywhere: pencils, pens, T-shirts, refrigerator magnets, plastic rain hats. The list is endless. There must be something to it; the ad specialty industry does multibillions of dollars of business annually. There are a few tricks and tips that can help you make your investment worthwhile. Specialty items can effectively support an advertising and marketing program.

1. The medium is part of the message and carries your message and image.
2. To have any impact at all, and therefore, not waste your money and effort, the item must be memorable for some reason: originality, humor, quality, design, or type of item. People are inundated with tons of ad specialty items every year, so your choice must stand out.
3. The item must suit the working or living habits of your potential clients, so that it is often used and appreciated and serves as a reminder when the time is right. It might be your logo and slogan printed on coffee cups, water bottles, or stickums for office workers. The go-to coffee cup for the right client is useful because it is used daily, and it will be there when the reminder counts.
4. Buy something of quality and give out the item everyone really wants, the good one. Do not distribute junk and believe the return on your investment will pay off in quality clients. Junk carries the message of junk. The item must be even better than expected. It must not only work, but provide some valuable or frequent service or pleasure, something that clients will want and use. It's worth a few more nickels or dimes or even dollars to make the right impression. T-shirts can be great reminders, but golf shirts may be better,

more likely to be worn by your client and not his or her son.

5. You want something that will last and be a constant reminder to the recipient that you exist when your service or product is required. The hope is that the prospect uses it frequently and it stays around for days, months, or even through the year.

6. Calendars can work if they are tasteful and not too self-serving. Even pencils can work, but the item must be distinctive, well done, and memorable, as well as usable.

7. Keep in mind who at your client's business makes the buying decision, as it is frequently not the owner but an empowered staff person. That's your customer. Give the well-thought-out item to him or her and repeat as necessary.

8. For a high-value client, purchase a top-of-the-line specialty item costing over $200, which instantly becomes a favorite item for the recipient and a constant reminder of the giver ... you and your business!

Maybe you will need to have a few gift levels, differing in value and purpose: one or two to remind potential clients of your presence, one for existing clients to say thank you, and one for special potential clients that you want to impress.

One of my clients tells me American flag refrigerator magnets are his best promotional item. Another says the Red Sox schedule, while another uses printed Post-it® notes. Hats, T-shirts, and coffee cups can be great items as well, but the design and message will determine the long-term effect. If they love it, they will use it, and the goodwill occurs. If the design and function aren't adequate, then it will deliver nothing.

A planned and effectively executed ad specialty item can work wonders for you. But if done without appropriate thought and planning, it's a waste of money. Select carefully, design well, and have a quality distribution plan. If it's a winner, you will achieve your goals.

## Attend State and Regional Trade Shows

You're probably aware of and may even attend the national trade shows in your industry or profession. Frequently, we make the significant investment required to attend these shows and display as an exhibitor, hoping to connect with distributors, chains, and significant stores; create broker relationships; and so on. It is an opportunity to create a national presence and impression. Usually the results are disappointing, however, as it is difficult to be noticed and taken seriously if you are an unknown trying to break into the national scene.

The major national players usually only exhibit at the national shows, as they are way too big and important to show up at state or regional shows. As well, most business owners wanting to make a national impact seldom, if ever, consider the state and regional trade shows. The savvy few understand the potential. For the others it's a missed opportunity.

The state and regional shows are really owned by the state and regional players. Often only a handful of exhibitors display; and while most major players in the state or region do appear, it's primarily a social event. Typically, significant communication occurs between the exhibitors and their attending clients all year long, and so the local or regional show acts more as a social gathering than a place to do business.

Although few ever see it this way, these regional and local shows present a gigantic opportunity to make inroads and create an impact on the exact market you want to penetrate. Even at the local level, a trade show puts hundreds or thousands of potential customers in your reach, instead of your having to drive, fly, or spend an entire day to see two people.

> **Although few ever see it this way, regional and local shows present a gigantic opportunity to make significant inroads and create an impact on the exact market you want to penetrate.**

Let's assume you are a smaller manufacturer, distributor, or importer and want to do business nationally. If you make the huge investment to travel to a national event, bring a few salespeople, and exhibit, you need to pray you attract enough business to break even because the large players, the national stars, monopolize and dominate.

It is extremely difficult to have a turn in the limelight in a national show if you are not a nationally known and well-established company. But at a local or regional show it is quite a different situation altogether, and what an opportunity it is.

Attending a state or regional show outside your state or region makes you unusual. National players, even small ones from outside the region or state, rarely turn out for the shows. They are too small. Thus, you can play a high-impact role as you may be one of the only exhibitors from outside the region that cares enough to show up.

All of a sudden you're in the limelight, or better said, you are the limelight, and you have everybody's attention as the only new exhibitor at the show. Everyone will be at least a little interested to see what you are showing. You will experience this advantage just because you showed up.

Better yet, you will be able to speak with any distributor, chain, or store in the state or region, as you will be the place to go. Why not sponsor the lunch, be the keynote speaker, or do whatever is offered to stand out further. Make it clear you are there out of deep respect for the state or regional association and market area.

If you have a broker, he or she will use your booth as a hangout. And your broker will drag every important and interesting contact into your booth to meet, greet, and get to know you. Business will be done; maybe not on sight, but the introductions will result in business.

If you want to pick up a broker for the state or region, the brokers will all be there and will flock to you like flies, hovering, bringing business, and wanting to represent you. You are the new action.

One final point: State and regional shows are typically inexpensive and only last for one day. So it's low cost and a huge-impact opportunity. It's being the big fish in the small pond. What would happen if you did the California, New York, Southeast, and New England shows? They would probably result in a huge and successful marketing strategy generating far more business than any other tradeshow strategy you could devise, especially for the cost.

In addition, you can socialize, create relationships, and hang out with the state and regional big dogs. The large players in the state or region will know you, do business with you, and open doors for you, as you have gone where few others bother to go ... to the local and regional shows.

## How to Successfully Work a Trade Show

While a regional trade show provides a great opportunity to reach your market in a high-impact, personal way that is both cost- and time-efficient, it requires serious preparation and a game plan.

Depending upon the type of show and the type of product or service you are marketing, frequently the objective at a trade show is to create personal relationships and fight for the order after the show. So even though it can be difficult, restrain yourself. Rather than sell first, make friends. Talk business later after you've developed the relationships.

Some shows are very local, designed for businesses marketing to individuals, homeowners, parents, kids, men, women, athletes, and everything in between. Some are wholesale distributor or chain shows. Frequently, they are divided up by the commerce the show represents so that everyone there is a potential customer and is interested in your product or service.

I have a client who makes a half year's business volume at one of the regional agricultural shows selling a professional service. Knowing that out of every hundred people that walk by, five will be interested in talking, he takes their names and creates appointments for follow-ups after the show that result in dozens of paying customers.

OK, so how does it work? What should you do? Prepare and begin long in advance. Here are some of the things you need to do:

- The booth itself must be designed and built to be easy to transport, set up, and break down.
- Have your information and samples, price sheets, catalog sheets, and business cards all in adequate quantity to be given out to thousands of people and last the length of the show.
- Decide what your strategy is for engaging prospects. Are you going to be the three-table booth with fliers on the table and that's your presentation? Are you creating some point of interest so the show walkers will gravitate to you and want to engage? Will you have samples? Maybe you will create a specialty advertising item to give away. Think about which approach will work best to introduce your product or service.
- Why not begin calling key distributors, store owners, or whoever you feel will be a quality customer and arrange meetings weeks in advance. Announce your intent to be there and ask to meet and get to know potential clients so there can be future business discussions. Suggest meeting at your booth and then going out for drinks after the show, or get contact information where the person is staying at the show so you can make plans for dinner or something. Get the point?
- Why not have dozens of contacts and calls with a variety of potentially important relationships? Invite some to come by the booth to

review your product line. Others you may want to meet off the floor and invite the spouses to go sightseeing while you and your customers do business.

There may be a show newspaper. If so, advertise in it and ask the paper to do an article about your business. The publication will report about the interesting exhibitors. Advertising should get you a mention in the review sections. You need to create a buzz.

I have attended dozens of trade shows and have displayed in dozens, observing those who win and those who lose. Here is reality: The buyers who go to the show intend to see the people they already buy from or sell to. They leave little room and time for the unknowns, those they are not doing business with. So what do you do to break through this barrier?

Hook 'em into the booth and talk fast. Attract them by personal drawing power using an intriguing question, a clever line that promises a benefit, or an irresistible offer. A show special might be giving an extra discount if an order is written at the show. Even though we all know that the customer can have that price any time by asking, it's a good deal opener.

Pull them in using a spectacle … a model, a superhero, an athlete, a star, a contest, whatever you can imagine that will attract attention, slowing passersby and giving you an opportunity to sell or at least to talk to them.

Will it work? Some tactics will work better than others, and that's a whole lot better than none. Some people will become customers now, some later, some next year, but the opportunity is magnified and concentrated at a show. Meet and make friends. Get to know as many people as possible. Also, next year's show is around the corner, and next year will yield returns as now you are a regular. People will know what to expect from you and will be delighted to have you entertain them.

Take business cards from everyone, because after the show you're going to send them a mailing to continue developing the relationship, inviting them to sign up for your newsletter, subscribe to your blog, and furthering the sales talk. You may even call them personally or have your sales staff follow up.

You have seconds to attract passersby into your booth and then maybe a minute or two to talk to them and involve them in meaningful discussion. Over and over just do it, having no idea whom you are talking to, big or small buyer. You will get some of both, but you must pitch to as many people as you can. That's the only way to make a show work for you. If you stand in your booth and wait for people to come in because they are attracted to your presentation, you will get little out of your investment.

While you're at the show, you have a captive audience with the other exhibitors. Early, before the doors are open, walk the show and talk to as many exhibitors as you can. There will be natural relationships and potential customers. Talk to the other vendors, but be respectful as they are there to sell, also.

> **If you stand in your booth and wait for people to come in because they are attracted to your presentation, you will get little out of your investment.**

Work 24 hours per day. This is your opportunity. Make early appointments and late appointments; take different people out to dinner each night. Do not entertain your staff. Ask them to make a similar commitment and take similar action with potential customers, hooking them in, meeting them, talking to them, and going out with some.

Take your salespeople to the show. It's a selling event and having your sales staff there is an excellent strategy. Give them credit for and commissions on sales made at the show; incentives always work.

The best advice I can give is to talk to as many people as you can. Be aggressive, as anyone may become a customer, and you never know who it will be. It is all up to you: your excitement and your sales skills, your product or service, its positioning, unique qualities, pricing.

For the right business, exhibiting at local and regional trade shows can be one of the most productive, cost-effective marketing strategies. With the proper attitude, a plan, and an understanding of how to work a show, you will generate sufficient leads for enough new business to make the experience worth the investment.

## Business Is Out There ... Go Get It!

Yes, we are in a deep recession. There is massive employment reduction, home foreclosures are rampant, and revenues are down in most every business sector. Yet we must recognize this is not universal. Even those in trouble are still spending some money. The question is, what are you doing to attract business?

I see too many businesses eliminating, cutting back, or wasting money on their nonproductive marketing campaigns. Some are using the same tactics and material they have for years and are experiencing zero or limited return.

There is business out there, but you must go out and get it, aggressively, actively, focused, with determination, and with a recognition that you need new tools, new approaches, new methods to pierce the barriers preventing customers from shopping in your business.

The business landscape has changed dramatically; your marketing techniques must also change. You must be different, interesting, attractive, and current. You must reflect the changing attitudes in the market. The market demands quality and a good deal. People will spend if you deliver the right message. Small stores can now compete effectively with large stores, competitive differences are huge, service is more important than ever, choice and variety rule ... but in the end it is a combination of many factors that bring your clients to you to spend.

Talk to your clients about why they should shop with you. Tell them your competitive advantage. Be aggressive but have a message. Tell a new story. Be different; use humor; be outrageous; use sex appeal if it applies. Telling the same old story is a waste of time and money.

There are customers, and you must outdo your competition with a newly thought-out campaign to get more of what is available. Waiting for the customer to show up and buy will not work. Use marketing that creates relationships and then sell. No matter what your business may be, it's a war, and you must fight aggressively to win customers.

 # Generating and Closing Sales

## Relationship Building, the Heart of the Sale

We spend a lot of time worrying, plotting, and developing a sales strategy. We spend a great deal of energy determining price and discount procedures, such as who pays for shipping and what terms we should provide. We focus on describing the merits of our product or service and specifying why the customer should buy it.

We consider our advertising and marketing schemes, allocating huge amounts of money, time, and effort to devising the best possible marketing plan we can imagine and pay for. Print, radio, trade, consumer advertising, we experiment with it, all hoping to find the one avenue that does the job best of all.

Sometimes we hire brokers, sales representatives, or dedicated sales employees. We display at trade shows, we send direct mailings, hand out fliers, use telemarketing, create expensive and powerful websites. We create expensive brochures and design powerful presentations. We service our top accounts, which we know represent 80 percent of our revenue. We spend a lot of time waiting for the big order to come over the fax machine.

All these exercises and efforts are appropriate and result in some degree of success. These are all tools of the trade, but not the real issue.

Understanding the sale is what is so critical before we pick the media or the venue or the tools we believe will do the job the best.

## Creating Relationships

So what is the bottom line, the heart of the sale, the heart of the sales strategy? This question is infrequently asked and seldom answered correctly. Is it price? Is it value? Is it specifications, terms, options, quality? All are important but not the heart of the sale.

The real heartbeat of selling is creating the relationship between the business and the potential customer. Once you make that connection, the sale follows. It's that simple, or difficult, as it is not always easy to create relationships, but this should be the goal: create the relationship and the sale will follow.

People prefer to do business with those they know and trust. This is the heart of the buying decision. Do they believe the sales message? While the choice of communication tools is important, what you say with them and how you use them are more important. You should spend more time creating the message that supports the relationship rather than selling the product.

> **People prefer to do business with those they know and trust. This is the heart of the buying decision.**

Of course, product or service information is also important, but who you are and why we should do business with you and not your competition is equally important—creating a relationship. What differentiates you is a key question, not the choice of colors available or delivery times. Create a dynamic relationship, and the sales follow, automatically.

So check your yellow page and print ads, your website, and your direct mailing pieces. Ask if they support and create a relationship. Or do they merely try to sell your goods or services? It is an important distinction. It is the difference between a campaign that fails to connect and one that successfully competes for your share of the market.

Remember, everything, everything you do and present to the potential customer, is part of your sales presentation. So create the relationship, and you will win more than your fair share.

## What Are You Selling?

I recently learned something valuable from a friend of mine. He proposed a solution to an age-old question in a way I have not heard before, "What does a salesperson sell?"

The typical answer is service or himself (or herself) or the company or the product, but these were not the answer my friend proposed. He leaned back after we all gave up and said, "Trust."

A successful salesperson sells trust. If the salesperson is successful at creating a trusting relationship, the customer will buy the product or service the salesperson represents. Trust is the cement that holds the client to the salesperson: trust that what the salesperson says about his product or service is true and that he delivers what he promises.

If problems occur, he will stand behind his commitment. A good salesperson understands that his word is worth far more than any one sale. Once you've established a bond of trust, it must be cherished and nurtured. When trust is nurtured, the next sale will always be waiting and competition will never succeed in penetrating this relationship.

## Sell What They Need, Not What You Think They Want

The marketplace is changing. Unemployment is soaring, and millions cannot afford to spend anything other than for necessities.

We do, however, make daily spending decisions, all of us. There are many who are doing well. There are many with disposable income, but they are making decisions differently than they did in the past. Now they question the need for every purchase. Even if they have more than enough money and income to warrant the purchase, they are asking the questions. People are changing their habits and spending less, more carefully, with a specific purpose, and with clear intent. Along the way they are demanding a good price.

For the first time in years, more people are saving money, while others are facing the loss of their homes and jobs. All of which results in less discretionary spending.

Consumers must believe they are getting a good deal, or the wallet will not come out. Quality is crucial, so products will last. Precision shopping: consumers will buy exactly what is required, so less is better. That's the new purchasing equation. Figure out how this trend applies to your product line or service for your market. The revenue will follow.

My tree service client, for example, is cutting dangerous limbs that overhang wires, roofs, and walkways. He fertilizes valuable trees to protect the owner's investment. He added cordwood to his revenue projections, because demand always goes up in tough times, and he has even invested in machinery to support it. All services are reasonably priced. People are contracting for essential services.

My glass installer client is installing solar panels following the large stimulus package investment in the market. He focuses on what the market needs. Glass installers for solar panels are in demand, more so than for replacement windows, and there is no demand for new construction.

Traditional print media companies are failing to sell the advertising to support their business model, and the smart ones are offering computerized, customized, individualized printing, a new trend made for the times. Companies are innovating or falling by the wayside as social networking invades the media world by providing what the marketplace is demanding, not what the magazine marketers think the consumer wants—what they used to want.

We are watching the near collapse of the American auto manufacturing industry because the automakers refused to make and sell what the marketplace needs, thinking they knew better.

The business world is changing, and the consumer is changing. Frivolousness and excess are out; minimalism is in. Figure out how to deliver this new wave and get in front of your competition. Such radical change provides great rewards for the opportunistic entrepreneur.

## The Power of Personal Presentation

How often do we recite these excuses rather than meeting with someone:

- It takes too much time to do it, and I am too busy.
- It is too expensive.
- It is too long a trip.
- What, fly?
- It is not worth it.
- It is just as good over the phone, by fax, or by e-mail.

Excuses, excuses, excuses. In this age of cell phones, e-mail, and fax machines, and with our very important and busy schedules, we frequently forget one of the basic principles of doing business successfully ... do it in person. Create and support the relationship.

Personal presentation is more powerful and successful than any other form of communication, and yet we leave the office as seldom as possible and resort to the more convenient forms of communication.

We have forgotten that while the technology age has made communication easier, nothing will replace the power, effectiveness, and success of a face-to-face conversation, lunch together, a round of golf, or other personal setting.

Years ago, I had a business relationship with a distributor who represented my line of manufactured goods. The man owed me a sizable amount of money and agreed to pay me $20,000 per week for a number of months. Every Wednesday, I would call to make certain the check "was in the mail," and almost every time he told me that he couldn't do it this week, sorry. I told him I would jump on a plane and be there in a few hours; he was in Detroit, and I was in Massachusetts.

He would always say, "Don't bother. There is nothing I can do for you this week." I went anyway, and each week I came home with a check for $20,000. This went on almost every week until the bill was paid. Why did it work? Personal power, my very presence—just going was adequate. I never had to hard collect. Frequently, we would go out for drinks. Sometimes I would stay over and visit with him, but I always left with a check. From then on, I never forgot the power of personal face time.

Closing a deal, discussing details, creating relationships, selling, collecting, solving problems, planning—whatever the mission is, if it is important, then it is best served with a personal presentation.

Recently, I flew to Florida for a one-hour meeting that expanded into lunch and another few hours of getting to know one another. I was inspecting a small business to determine if I wanted to do business with these people. It was possible that they would become a provider of a specific service I deemed very important.

They are a credit rehabilitation company, credit repair, it is sometimes called. Since so many of my clients require such service, I felt it necessary to meet, interview, inspect, and get to know the staff, the managers, and, yes, the owner, as well as discuss details of working together.

Much was accomplished as we got to know each other over lunch and discussed a wide variety of experiences, opinions, personal matters, history, business strategies, including the specifics of our deal and business relationship. It was wonderful, and we accomplished more than we all intended.

The owner was impressed that I cared enough to come down for a personal discussion, taking a day out of my busy schedule. My willingness to invest in our meeting indicated the importance of our possible business relationship. Now we have a personal relationship, which will soon grow, both in the business we do together and in the understanding we have of each other. This relationship and the trust that has begun to develop never could have been accomplished over the phone.

Lunch was crucial as we relaxed and got to know each other. Afterward, communicating with his staff, showing them respect, and letting them get to know us were added benefits. I believe anything important is worth my effort to do personally as it works better, and most frequently results in the desired conclusion. It helps convert strictly business relationships to personal relationships.

> **I believe anything important is worth my effort to do personally as it works far better and most frequently results in the desired conclusion.**

Yet in today's hurry-up world we seem to ignore this truth. We are too busy, it's too expensive, and everything else is so much more important. I think otherwise.

## Increase the Perceived Value

While frequently attempted, lowering the price to increase sales seldom works as planned. In fact, it could lower sales. It certainly lowers profits. It's not always the price that counts the most.

The true underlying principle for closing sales is to deliver value to the customer. It has been demonstrated time and again that price alone is not always the determining factor in a customer's decision process. Service, quality, guarantee, and perceived value are more important than price every time. These factors combined can cause a buying customer to purchase something more expensive because of the perceived value and what the whole package offers.

So offering a training program, in-house repair, or whatever the added benefits may be, will support a customer's decision to purchase a more expensive deal over a less expensive solution available elsewhere but sold with less perceived value. Increasing the perceived value is frequently accomplished by add-ons to the basic product or service, be they unrelated gifts, additional accessory packages, upgrades at no additional charge, extended guarantee—anything to increase perceived value.

In other situations, such as wholesale-sales business to business, it may be the preparation of the sales presentation. It can demonstrate increased intrinsic value by identifying cost savings while operating this product or service, which may result in extra longevity, future savings, or greater earning potential of the service or product; all add value to the customer's perception of the product or service, inspiring the wholesaler to purchase.

Thus, the retail return or gross profit percentage when reselling the product to the business purchaser may be more important than the purchase price.

The conclusion is that for any sales presentation or marketing program to be as successful as possible in this down economy or any economy, the presentation or program must include a serious effort to demonstrate and elevate the perception of value, and if successfully done, will result in more product or service sold. To increase sales revenue and profitability, don't lower the price; increase the perceived value.

## Find a Market Niche

A client's business offers powder coating on metal, also called heat-baked painting. There are many who perform the same skills and deliver the same product, and so competition is fierce. It is difficult to elevate oneself above the crowd in an environment where everyone is the same, and all that remains is price competition. Not good.

Searching for a competitive advantage, we discovered two passions the two owners of the business enjoy and determined that this could be the added opportunity we were looking for.

- One partner owns a parrot and is involved in marketing parrot products on the Internet. We decided to powder-coat a parrot cage and offer custom colors to discerning homeowners who want their cage to match their bird, room, or whatever. No competition, high value, very profitable, and a huge potential market. A great market niche. She created a proprietary idea to support the services she offers with added value, added revenue, and greater profit in an uncluttered market.

- The other partner rides a motorcycle, and so we expanded into custom-powder-coating bike parts. Others do this as well, but the price point is excellent. Because the cost of shipping is high, the service is geographically sensitive. We can grab our fair share of business by focusing on the local and regional market, which created a significant market opportunity.

I have another client who owns an electrical service company. He has developed a specialty in pools. He has a steady stream of valuable business for wiring pool installations. A towing company client specializes in big trucks and has huge equipment capable of handling any size truck, and as a result he gets most of the truck business in his area, large and small.

Specializing is not always possible in every business situation; however, there are many creative ways to distinguish your business from the rest of the market and then reap the benefits: higher profits and a niche that remains less competitive than your core business may be.

Overnight delivery, short orders, custom work, unusual market segments are all ways to create your niche. Then the rest of your typical service or product line goes along for the ride and carries the basic overhead burden while the profit is in your specialty or niche item.

> **Overnight delivery, short orders, custom work, unusual market segments are all ways to create your niche.**

I have a tree service client who says he is an expert with large trees, which he is; yet customers with regular-size trees figure he must be the best as he does large trees, and so they hire him for all sizes.

A pizza chain puts out a terrific product, truly superior; yet the company's signature item is a specially designed box that has built-in feet and cooling holes preventing soggy bottoms. The customers love it, ask for it, and come back because of the great product and the great box.

A pipeline company performs much of the work of constructing its pipeline systems over the winter in its own large building, and then it installs the pipe systems in the spring and summer. Doing it this way saves money and time, a brilliant move that keeps the customers coming back. The company has become a preferred supplier to a number of businesses and makes more per job because of its preinstallation winter work. Could others do this? Of course, but they don't, and so the pipeline company enjoys a huge advantage.

A landscaper has a distributor relationship for a source of high-quality pavers for making driveways, and so not only does he get an inside price for his own jobs, but he is the main source for this item. Others who bid against him frequently purchase the pavers from him for a job he was outbid on, so he makes money on the job anyway. A competitive advantage.

The standard business, the core effort, must carry the day, but the specialized niche provides a competitive advantage, a better profit position, and more revenue. It has the power to carry the core business into many areas it might not ordinarily get to. It may mean the difference between success and failure.

Find your niche and then exploit it, not to the exclusion of your core business but in support of it.

## Ask for Referrals

It's not an unfounded criticism. Business owners, frequently men, have problems asking for help. I am not certain if this is a male thing (like not asking for directions, which is also asking for help) or a unique characteristic of business owners, whether male or female. But I know one thing for certain: Business owners do not ask for help until an issue becomes a huge problem and so beyond the business owner's ability to handle, that they finally break down and, ask for … help! They mutter as quietly as possible as if such a request is an admission of weakness.

This behavior is the sidekick of doing it alone, another bad habit of business owners, whether it is our fear of rejection, our unwillingness to appear weak, or our ego that prevents us from asking for help. The conclusion is that we do not do it, yet we should.

We are probably more concerned with what others think than achieving the objective. We must be adequately self-sufficient so that the goal of getting additional work referrals is more important than what the person you are asking may think. Besides, the likelihood is that the person will think none the worse and perhaps better of you.

So the request for referrals for new business falls into the trap of not ever asking for help, and what a self-defeating trap that is. Think about it: You have a satisfied customer for whom you provided acceptable goods or services, you were paid, and everyone left the experience happy and better for it. Why not ask that person for a referral or two? Happy customers will be delighted as they had a uniquely positive experience and have therefore developed a trust relationship. And with that trust and because your clients appreciate the relationship, they will be delighted to make a referral and help advance your cause. Also the customers would be delighted to share the benefits of your services with friends whom they know would also benefit from the goods or services you provide.

Yet we seldom ask our satisfied customers for such referrals, and thus the chain stops.

I suggest this because industries that make a living on referrals and that enjoy significant success because of this are proof enough that this works. Real estate agents, insurance brokers, and car salespeople are always asking for referrals. Why? Because it works.

> **Real estate agents, insurance brokers, and car salespeople are always asking for referrals. Why? Because it works.**

Referrals produce more new business at the lowest possible cost. Over time they create an ever-expanding client base as each customer gives referrals that result in more business and more referrals. The geometric progression results in an ever-expanding new business chain feeding off your original successful delivery of quality goods and services.

Yet we seldom access this potential well of wealth and success because we fail to utter the most valuable words: "Can you give me a few referrals?"

Most customers will gladly offer a helping hand when asked. I believe people want to help, but I also know they must be asked. Of course, asking for help from others expands to a myriad of opportunities to advance your own business program. For the moment, let's concentrate on a meaningful request for help that benefits all involved and furthers your mission.

Ask for referrals, have a specific system that all employees follow, and focus on developing referrals as a primary marketing effort. It will bring you much business in return.

## The Tipping Point Through Referrals

The *tipping point*, a term coined by others, represents an important concept in the context of a business life cycle. It is the point in a business's life when repeat business and referrals create adequate cash flow, revenue, and profits to propel the business forward on its own merit. This key indicator is important for many reasons.

For example, it may mean you need not invest dollars heavily in traditional advertising, as you have created the ultimate guerrilla marketing plan: word-of-mouth marketing and referrals. This is the most valuable form of promotion and cannot be purchased; it must be earned.

Once you have accomplished this benchmark, you need to cultivate it, honor it, support it, and preserve it, as it, too, can erode to your competition if you are not constantly working your referral system.

In fact, establishing a referral-based business growth plan, while sometimes a happy accident, can and should become part of a purposeful marketing program, using every aspect of direct communication and indirect communication. It requires a plan of attack and should be a first priority.

Of course, the ultimate referral is one made directly to a friend or neighbor that results in additional business as opposed to a referral given to you by an existing client, which you then must pursue. Both are valuable; but if you are doing a good job delivering your product or service so your clients feel good about the relationship and pass the word along, you have hit the mother lode, and success is knocking at your door. But you must cultivate and nurture this response to achieve it.

Referrals do not happen by accident. While it is crucial to have a great product or service, you must promote repeat business, word-of-mouth recommendations, and referrals as seriously as you promote your product or service in traditional advertising.

Newsletters, Web 2.0, social networking, video, blogging, Facebook, insider special deals, surveys, rewards for referrals and recommendations, and on the list goes. As important as all these are, delivering unprecedented service accounts for a huge amount of successful word-of-mouth marketing, all adding to your reaching the tipping point.

It costs less than creating new customers to reach your sales and financial goals. It deflects competition successfully and promotes long-term success. Make this objective one of your goals.

## Testimonials Sell

Testimonials may be one of the most important and powerful tools available in closing a sale. Testimonials are the positive recommendations provided by customers who have satisfactorily concluded a working relationship with the seller of a service or product. In their testimonials, the customers describe their experience and how they feel about the experience. This is what people want to hear. People love to hear a success story.

> **Testimonials are the positive recommendations provided by customers who have satisfactorily concluded a working relationship with the seller of a service or product.**

So help your new prospective clients make their decision by sharing the stories from your satisfied clients. Let your satisfied clients tell their story in a testimonial format. This is an expanded reference because a testimonial is the customer's story, not only a recommendation. Phrases such as "wonderful experience," "would recommend to anyone,"and "excellent service" are all good, but we can do better. We can tell the story so the new prospective customer lives the experience and envisions his or her own successful story. That's your objective.

Here are the seven steps to accomplish this:

1. Ask an existing satisfied and happy client if he or she would be willing to participate in a testimonial. Explain that privacy will be protected. Remember, this is not a referral, but a written or spoken testimonial; the customer does not have to be involved in ongoing discussions with potential clients. The customer's job is merely to tell a story with a happy ending. Assure the client it will be easy, that you will do all the work, even writing the story down, as most people are willing to tell but not write the story.

2. Include a picture. This is easy to do today with a digital camera. Capture a picture of the client telling the story. If possible, include the product or service in the photo; not critical, but it adds a nice touch. If your business provides swimming pool services, take the picture around a pool. It adds credibility and sets the scene in the customer's mind to envision a successful completion. You are already halfway home to a sale, as the prospect begins to see the vision.

3. Here is the key to success. Have someone in your organization who has an established relationship with the customer giving the testimonial to briefly interview him or her. Use the interview to remind the person of all the positive points of the experience and the relationship, all the points you want to expand upon, such as quality, timeliness, friendliness, ease of doing business, excellent price, and value, whatever is important. Then help the customer tell the story.

4. Then *your* employee writes the testimonial right on the spot, shows the story to the customer, and asks, "Is this OK?" Ninety-nine out of a hundred times, with minor insignificant adjustments, the customer says, "Yes, it's perfect." You have the testimonial you want.

5. People are afraid to write, do not necessarily have the skills, and may not understand what you want, so make it easy and do it for them. Never ask clients to write anything themselves.

6. Have the client sign the testimonial, using only his or her first name, so it has more authenticity.

7. Put this on your website, in your presentation book, and enjoy the benefits of a signed, illustrated story written by your employee with the support of your client—a testimonial you can use.

This creates trust and confidence easily and effectively.

## Free Samples ... Be Innovative

We see free samples offered in many places. Supermarkets do it frequently, and it works. Vendors offer tastes in anticipation of customers liking what they sample, buying the product, and creating a new customer. Think about it. How much does it cost to send a free sample to a potential customer, buyer, CEO, or other key decision influencer? Not much, and there's a huge potential return.

Store owners should explore creating a cost-sharing relationship with their vendors. You can also do it yourself. Customers love to shop where they experience free samples. It draws them to the store, and sales increase not just for the free sample products but for store's entire line. I heard a friend tell his wife, "We should go to Costco. They have tons of free samples." The wife said, "OK, let's go shop there." Those free samples draw traffic.

This concept can apply to services and to wholesale distributors and will work in any level of sales organizations. It makes sense to let the product or service speak for itself. Let the consumers test something they would not ordinarily try. How valuable is a new customer? Sampling is not that expensive and pinpoints the potential consumer in a buying atmosphere. It increases product awareness and sales. It is a marketing program with immediate direct revenue impact. Especially in this tough consumer market where purchases are debated . . . samples will win the day.

Depending on the type of product you sell, offering free goods to the sales staff of your distribution system is another way to promote your products. Recently, I went shopping to buy winter hiking boots and was not certain what to buy. The salesperson told me he personally used a particular brand and loved it. When I questioned him further, he informed me that the company gave the boots to the salespeople for free, but he loves the product and freely recommends it. It made the sale— another great use of free sampling.

## Sometimes the Best Choice Is One

Many years ago, I went to a highly regarded graphic designer to have a corporate logo designed for a business I was starting. We talked about my ideas, and I concluded by explaining to her that I was not a designer so I wanted her to use her skills and design something for me that fit the business purpose and looked good. I was hiring her not just to execute the project but to design the concept.

She did not get it. When she finished, she showed me 20 variations. Frankly, all of them were good. I was totally confused and at a loss as I could not determine which was best. They all looked good. So I told her, "I'll take them home and think about it."

I then hired another designer and gave the same instructions. She showed me one design. It was terrific, perfect, and we used it. I was happy; she had given me what I asked for.

This exercise taught me an important lesson, which I carry with me to this day. I call it the "choice of one."

In short, when asked to provide a response of any kind, resist the temptation to provide unlimited options. Options are a way of saying in many instances that you are not sure of the best answer. Choices may be appropriate in specific situations, but over all people want, respect, and appreciate the right answer when asked. Giving choices shifts the responsibility for the right decision back to the person who asked.

If you are an expert or a source, or represent authority, or are selling something, give the answer, the opinion, the conclusion, whatever is requested. Be the expert you are perceived to be.

> Choices may be appropriate in specific situations, but overall people want, respect, and appreciate the right answer when asked.

Even at a restaurant with a full menu describing a dozen choices, I frequently ask the waitress what's best. I just as frequently go along with the recommendation.

Yesterday, when working with a client who was providing a proposed program for his client, he expressed annoyance that the people he was dealing with were not getting back to him. I asked him how many options he provided. He said, "Three."

I remarked, "That's two too many."

He looked at me quizzically, and I said, "They are now bogged down in deciding which one they like best. This will take awhile and may prevent a final decision altogether. The choices create uncertainty and do not support a secure and comfortable, easy-to-make decision. You lose the momentum and focus and waste a lot of time on the wrong issue."

"Give them one program." I suggested. They can reject it or make adjustments and suggestions, and then you can redo it and close the deal. It's the 'choice of one.'"

I have applied this concept repeatedly throughout my business career, always limiting the choice to my best effort and then worked back if necessary, making adjustments to satisfy the client's needs.

Many mistakenly believe that by providing numerous options that you are enhancing the likelihood for success, when in reality you are diminishing the potential for success.

Try the "choice of one." It works.

## How to Beat a Competitor's Competitive Advantage

I was talking to a very wise and successful friend who had returned from a European sales support trip for his company, an IT business with some proprietary software. He operated in a highly competitive environment, competing with a few much larger companies that are well supported in Europe. They successfully outsell his company with excellent products perceived as better in many ways. His approach is exceptional and clearly successful. Here is how he tackles this sales dilemma.

He understands his competitors' strengths and weaknesses, as well as he knows his own products.

He acknowledges that his competitors have successful products and that they do well in accomplishing stated goals, and then he freely states his opinion regarding the strengths of his competitors to his clients. He acknowledges that his competitors do a better job in some important situations. As he explains it, his honesty and accuracy create credibility because he is saying what the prospective client thinks anyway. It doesn't make sense, therefore, to bash the competition. That only takes away from his ability to sell.

After acknowledging his competitors' advantages, he frequently outsells them by further understanding what his program does better than his competitors'. He wins when the advantages of his product are what the client needs to solve a particular problem. He outsells his competitors by selling what his program does better while recognizing and acknowledging his competitors' strengths and weaknesses. While it makes sense, I rarely see the strategy implemented.

So many salespeople simply believe in their products or services and, right or wrong, sell blindly with the belief that their product is the best and everything else is inferior, whether true or not. Successful salespeople are more sophisticated than that, and customers are more knowledgeable. Selling without knowing your competition will not work. Selling intelligently is a requirement. Understanding your competitions' strengths and weaknesses is a fundamental requirement for success in today's market, and acknowledging what they do well and, yes, what your product does better is the key to successfully selling against your competition.

> **Understanding your competitions' strengths and weaknesses is a fundamental requirement for success in today's market**

Reconsider your approach and see if this strategy can benefit you.

## No Means Yes ... Just Not Now

In business, I believe "no" means "yes," but just not now. That's the attitude a salesperson must maintain to be successful. Of course, this assumes you're talking to a bona fide potential customer who does, should, or could use your product or service. As long as the potential client is talking to you, "no" is an acceptable answer, not to be considered a rejection, a postponement.

The danger is when the talk stops, and there is no further opportunity to penetrate and close. When your potential client is not taking your calls, you may have a real no.

Yet in spite of the no implied by avoiding your phone calls, I still say, "It's only a harder postponement." It will require a strategic reconsideration of how to approach that client next, not a sign for a retreat or abandonment.

If you are talking to enough potential clients, some will close immediately, some soon but not today, some later, and some a lot later. Your sales and marketing plans must include working the line, knowing you have clients in development—tomorrow's sales, next month's sales, next year's sales. All may be saying no but are really saying, "Not now, but let's keep talking. I am getting closer to a yes."

There is the low-hanging fruit, those prospects whom you merely have to ask once or twice to receive a yes. This will not happen all the time. Many excellent, bona fide potential clients need a longer time to consider and accept. So how many noes must you receive before you get a yes?

> **Why give up on anyone, if qualified, especially if the person is not throwing you out the door or hanging up on you?**

Frankly, my answer is unlimited noes, as many as it takes; never give up. It may not require a weekly call or even a monthly call, but I would have a sales and marketing program that manages my communication requirements. For every person I speak with who says no, a carefully considered return call, letter, e-mail, newsletter, postcard, whatever you can imagine, will be scheduled and implemented, designed to keep the prospect in play and working toward an eventual yes.

Why give up on anyone, if qualified, especially if the person is not throwing you out the door or hanging up on you? If you are convinced you have a product or service that the potential customer could and should use, the answer no is a postponed yes.

So how many times does it take? The consensus on this issue suggests that on the average it requires eight rejections before an acceptance or a yes is received. That's a lot of rejection, but how sweet the acceptance is when it finally arrives.

Perhaps the strategy requires you to figure out how to deliver at least eight approaches, so you can get the 8 rejections (or 10 or 12) before the yes occurs.

I would, therefore, never consider another postcard, e-mail, call, visit, or other contact a waste of time until you have provided at least a dozen passes and received a significant number of rejections. You must ask for the sale, and either get a rejection, which simply means more work is required, or a yes and a sale is made.

Deliver at least a dozen communications to get through the noes. Keep score, and if you stay in the game and play all nine innings, making 8 to 12 sales pitches, you'll receive a dozen noes but eventually the yes.

Maybe the sale requires creating a relationship, demonstrating professional tenacity, service, commitment, empathy, or follow-through. Maybe it's a no to you and not your product or service, and thus you need the time to convince the potential client that you are worthy of his or her business.

If sales are all about creating a relationship, it cannot be done in one or two communications. It takes many, and maybe they should not all be sales calls but should be relationship-building calls without a word said about product or services. Maybe your conversation is about the industry, or whatever subject you think the potential client would be interested in.

Remember, the mantra is "No means yes, just not now." You require at least eight rejections before you will receive an acceptance, so get on with the job. You have a ways to go, and giving up before you have made at least eight passes is leaving potential sales on the table, wasting the time already spent because you failed to keep the ball in play long enough to win.

Think about it. Every salesperson has experienced success after a significant string of noes. Make the "no-means-yes" philosophy part of your sales and marketing plan. Since companies make such a large investment originating and presenting to a new prospect, it seems pennywise and pound foolish to give up on the third or fourth effort. How much more does the additional contact cost? Not much.

## Increasing Your Call Volume to Increase Sales

There are great salespeople. Anyone who has worked in a sales force knows what I am talking about, the standout, the one who has the gift and closes sales almost at will. We have all seen this person in action, and it's a natural skill, a God-given gift.

Not necessarily so. An average salesperson can increases sales dramatically by using the secret of sales success.

It's all in the number of calls made. Double your sales calls, and sales volume will go up manyfold. It's that simple. This may seem obvious, but in my experience it's a well-kept secret. And when I say double the number of calls, I mean just that.

The more calls, the more sales. Believe me, it sounds obvious, but so few do it, allowing the sales force to be as inefficient as humanly possible. Track how many new calls are made per day, and then come back and tell me it is impossible to improve the call sheet.

Here is one reason. Sales calls have a built-in potential percentage of success. However, let's say, for example, a salesperson must make 100 calls to get 10 appointments that will yield 2 successful sales. That can be interpreted to mean a 2 percent success ratio. But if the salesperson made only 50 calls, does that necessarily mean 5 appointments and 1 close? No, as it is entirely possible that the 50 calls would yield zero appointments and zero sales. Why? Because the minimum threshold of calls for sales to occur was not reached, the percentage of success does not work. Arithmetically, you need the volume for the ratio to work.

If you made 10 calls per day and failed for weeks to produce anything, you might draw a wrong conclusion that the entire program is built on a bad premise. Conversely, the person who made 100 calls daily and received 10 appointments and made 2 closes would conclude it's a runaway success. The same program produces a different call level, so an incomplete effort may result in an incorrect conclusion.

If your belief is you're reaching the right market with the right product or service and at the right price, but you are not getting the results you expect, then making more calls may be exactly what is required to cross the threshold to reach the results you want.

So it's not just that more calls make more sales, although that is true under most circumstances; it's also that you may not be triggering the threshold level and no daily or weekly effort will be successful until you do.

How do you know what the threshold may be? You don't, and so double the effort and see what happens. You will find out when the results roll in. Initial failure may not be an indicator of the potential results.

Do this, and for no additional investment, you will see sales increase dramatically. It's possible the super salesperson is making enough calls to trigger a better response than the average salesperson who calls less frequently.

## Going Up Against Major Competitors

We all understand that we cannot compete with the big box stores or major service competitors on price. Their buying power gives them a competitive advantage. So stop trying to compete on price; it's a losing battle.

Take advantage of the competitive edge small retail stores and local service providers have that the big box stores and major service businesses cannot compete with you on: customer service, and more specifically, customer relations.

Most small business owners or their store managers or salespeople know who their best customers are. If you're doing your job, you know who all your best customers are, by first name for many. You also know a little about their lifestyles, families, and habits, at least for your best customers. Since your best customers already have a relationship with the store and the staff and have already acknowledged that they appreciate your product mix, the objective is to get as much of their spending dollars as possible.

Focus on marketing to your existing client base, spending even more special attention on your best customers. How about a sale just for customers, a private sale for the best, maybe off-hours, maybe catered, maybe fun, interesting, personal, and all about the relationship, not the price. It will attract your best customers, and then let your sales staff go to work on them and capture their spending budget for your store, without giving it away.

This is not the time to compete for new customers—they will be attracted to the big box stores as they have not developed a relationship with you or your store, and so they have no incentive to shop there. Clearly, general advertising will bring some new customers in, but in view of the likely reduced spending because of the economic downturn, the high investment in ad dollars may be best saved, replacing it with a smaller marketing budget directed at your most likely successes: your existing customers. Induce existing customers to bring a friend along.

This strategy is more effective, costs less, and yet yields more. There's no point in advertising massive discounts to all comers, because in the end you are giving away the additional profit to your existing customers who would have shopped with you anyway. You cannot make it up with new business volume while trying to compete with the big boxes. Be smarter. Focus on existing clients, have private sales that are moderate, and keep your customers spending with personalized service.

You will gross less but profit more, and that's a good thing. Be smart. A lot is at stake. Change your approach—the times have changed. This strategy can apply to service businesses as well.

> **Focus on existing clients, have private sales that are moderate, and keep your customers spending with personalized service.**

A great two-for-one suit sale at very large men's clothing store got me to take my son there to improve his wardrobe at a reasonable price. Was I ever disappointed! Despite the wonderful ad, it was a come-on deal. Just a few suits were included in the two-for-one sale, and everything else was regular price. I was annoyed, as the suits they were offering were unacceptable, and I felt it was a bait-and-switch deal. They have lost a potential customer.

Furthermore, as a small retailer, you can beat the big box stores by specializing and expanding your niche, being the best with the most, including the obscure.

## Selling to the Major Chains and Distributors

Attempting to do business with the major distributors, chains, and similar businesses is frequently fatal, is most always painful and costly, and seldom provides the intended additional profits anticipated.

In short, before selling to the major distributors or direct to the major chains in most retail or wholesale markets, be aware of the following issues:

- Promising to pay in net 45 days is an illusion; net 60 to 90 days, or whenever, becomes the expected. Can you imagine the audacity—

you financing their growth with net 60- to 90-day terms? Amazing!
Try supporting the increased overhead, cost of goods, and so on,
while waiting for the big check to arrive.

- Everything is a guaranteed sale whether you agree to it or not. When
  they feel justified, they will simply deduct the remaining inventory
  from the past due invoice and send back what didn't sell. They also
  deduct a handling fee, shipping, and other add-ons, with the
  remaining payable still being postponed for payment.

- Did I mention the bone-crushing discount they will demand, as they
  must enjoy their enormous markups at your cost?

- Samples are required for the various buyers, all the stores. Sometimes, if it's a distributor, you are expected to supply a significant load
  of free merchandise, say three to five pallets, to disperse as samples
  to buyers. Not a bad idea but costly. They sell it anyway, but there is
  no benefit to you; they end up with increased revenue and you with
  increased costs.

- The distributors and chains will both want additional opening-order
  incentives, such as one free with three or whatever they can beat out
  of you to sweeten the pot for them on the first order and decrease
  your profit further.

- They also require contributions for printing your catalogs and
  including your product, and the more you are willing to pay, the
  larger your display will be. But you pay for it ... translating, once
  again, into less margin for you, more for the distributor and chain.

- The dreaded slotting fees, which began in the food industry, are
  spreading across every industry. Why not? It's a grab for all the
  remaining profit that may have been allowed you. More realistically,
  you are now investing only in your customer's profit. You are now
  losing money, and the customer is getting it all.

- "But this is how it works," says the broker (an additional 5 percent).
  This is what you have to do to sell into this chain or distributor; and
  once you do, the others will follow, and we will make better deals.

- It gets worse, should you miss a delivery date. Then they either
  threaten cancellation or fine you, further increasing your investment
  in this transaction.

- Then there is the automatic deduction for waste and spoilage irrespective of whether or not there was any. Now don't forget you are

building inventory with expensive payroll and cost of goods. You must absorb this additional investment for approximately 90 to 120 days from the time you begin to build inventory to the moment you get your invoice paid. Since there may not be any profit coming, you may simply get a credit notice telling you how much you owe them!

Wow, can you imagine doing business under such conditions? So what should we do when contemplating doing business with the big dogs?

Unfortunately, the predator habits of chains and distributors must be evaluated and changed to meet your needs. If they can't be changed, refuse to do business; it's your terms or no deal.

Do not fall into any traps that promise you future business that will be profitable despite the lack of profit on this order. It's ridiculous; either do business profitably and safely or say no. Better you should do more work with smaller businesses than take the extreme risk and smaller return from larger, less profitable big business stores.

Another common theme, one that I have witnessed too many times, occurs in the construction trade. The small subcontractor reaches for the moon and bids and wins a large job, and then the general contractor fails to pay the sub until the sub eventually goes broke and never has to be paid at all. This usually happens near the end of the job, so most of the work has been completed; the sub hangs on doing everything possible to remain alive, waiting for the check, which never comes.

What also happens is when the sub finally refuses to continue without payment, the general contractor hires a replacement to complete the job. Then the contractor charges the sub payable for the replacement work, and there goes all the cash owed. Go fight it, and the contractor claims you failed to show up, so there was no choice; or the contractor complains about issues like inadequate work or untimely completion— anything to not pay. Meanwhile, the subcontractor has paid huge payrolls, purchased materials, and rented many large, expensive machines for the job, investing in the contract and waiting for the check, eventually failing to pay his 941 taxes or running out of cash.

I have seen this too many times to count. Stay smaller, grow profitable, and enjoy life. Big suppliers should handle large jobs; small businesses should stay in their own arena. You can reach your gross revenue and profitability goals in the market you are best suited for. Growth and development are fine, but accepting a large contract requires huge stamina and lots of cash and lawyers in the construction business. It may be profitable if you have the cash.

> Stay smaller, grow profitable, and enjoy life.

## The Problem with Using Brokers

I am certain there are some good brokers. I have heard many legendary stories about some major brokers that do a phenomenal job, selling Coke, or M&M's, maybe Budweiser, or other well-supported, nationally advertised consumer lines.

I have also heard stories of excellent brokers representing dry goods lines, sporting goods, and clothing as well, so I am sure they exist somewhere. I have never found one, nor have I done business with one who ever delivered the orders to me or my clients that added up to more than a hill of beans.

I have worked with broker organizations—the national brokerage firms—over a few dozen times, maybe more. If you count each broker relationship I have tried to squeeze an order out of, hundreds.

I will tell you one universal truth in my experience: Brokers do not work well for pioneering a new product or a product without national advertising and without support such as huge discounts, guaranteed sales, catalogs, sell sheets, specials, push money, and free goods—all given in addition to the commission to the broker presumably required to stimulate the successful introduction of your item and to help your broker to do the job . . . hmmm.

Maybe we are getting a clue here about what is wrong. A broker can do a fair job of taking orders. If your product is a runaway winner with huge brand acceptance and supported by a major ad program and all the other goodies mentioned, then yes, a national broker firm may be just the thing for you. But the likelihood is you are not in that position.

If you are a small regional manufacturer or importer, are attempting to develop a more significant national distribution, and are currently using a broker network, I will make a bet that you are unsatisfied with the results. Why?

Brokers are not designed to place new items in the marketplace. There is way too much risk. They are order takers, not pioneers. The retail buyer has no desire to take risk, so brokers sell only with the winners ... taking orders. It does not pay for them to experiment, as there is far less money in it for them and far too much risk since some will fail; in addition, their loyalty is to their buyers, not to the manufacturers.

Brokers tend to represent a number of lines and can only expect so much commitment from one buyer at a chain.

Brokers push whatever the buyer wants or is asking for and dare not take their precious time and limited influence to push something new, such as free goods, discounts, and other killer requirements meant to weed out anyone other than the large, successful items that everyone wants.

Thus, while your item may be innovative and unique, if there is not an existing demand, brokers are not the way to go.

If you cannot afford all the whistle and bells, free goods, long terms, sell sheets, huge opening discounts, extra push money for the brokers, an opening deal that will destroy any hopes of profit, ad money, guaranteed sale, and so forth, do not waste a moment of your time on a broker. It will not be a successful relationship.

If you are going to brokers who specialize in either your industry or product line and you hope to capture your share of market on their successful coattails, it is unlikely, as the brokers are more afraid of failure than the buyers, who are protected by a guaranteed-sale deal.

If you do use brokers and are lucky enough to capture one with great contacts and a successful sales background, one who is willing to pioneer your item, I have only one suggestion.

Ask your broker to arrange for a two-day field trip with you and the buyers (the broker's clients). Tell the broker to make appointments with his best accounts. You will come bearing gifts of a better deal and will help him make the sales, as only an owner can do. This works, as the dynamic is set up.

The buyer understands she must behave appropriately, as the buyer typically has a relationship with the broker and she understands the dynamics of a manufacturer coming out with the broker to meet and sell the buyers.

She usually feels obliged to cooperate in such a setting and should give an order, as the broker will look bad if he does not create a sale for the manufacturer. Thus, the buyer is inclined to buy. You will do all the selling because the broker does not really sell, and thus the job gets done, with everyone smiling except the manufacturer, who had to give away the ship to get the sale.

But at least a sale was made, and now maybe the broker can use his influence by telling the next buyer that the last chain he visited bought quite a bit. That's about as good as it gets!

In short, the broker picked you up at the airport, took you to your hotel room, ate lunch with you on your tab as you explained the strategy and he explained whom he has lined up for you to see, and he then takes you to each buyer he could in the two days you're there.

After that trip, you will not see additional sales, as the broker is waiting to see what happens. If the product sells, he may sell into another chain. If the product does not fly off the shelves, he will not promote it to another buyer no matter what. So now you know that a broker's highest value is in making you appointments and driving you around, and for that he gets 5 percent.

Oh yes, he will want a commission for all existing customer sales within his territory. That's to be expected. He will tell you that he will do a better job and will get much more out of them than you will. It demonstrates commitment and helps override the expenses of creating new sales which are huge, he will tell you.

Have I ever had a good broker relationship? Sadly, no. Has anyone? Maybe, probably, yes for the well-established and well-supported product line. Is it all worth the effort and cost? I do not believe it is.

It's a great concept but seldom works in pioneering situations. My answer is, "Do it yourself." It will take longer, but the results will be more effective and profitable under your control.

# Chapter 11

# Run a More Profitable Business

## Consider Charging the Highest Price

Given the downturn of the economy and the massive unemployment, it seems everyone competes by reducing prices, giving back profit to the customer, be it wholesale or consumer. Therefore, the competition focuses on just that: discounts, sales, special deals, always lowering prices. This does not mean you have to start out or even end up at a rock-bottom price to compete. There is also the top of the feeding chain, where customers are still excited about discounts and special deals, but are satisfied with higher pricing because they demand the best and want the extra service.

Expensive cars, clothes, jewelry, homes, every product line has a high end. Every service has the best providers, be it lawyers, accountants, or architects. They have earned it through their own success or because they provide the best service and are much in demand.

There is a significant marketplace that wants the top end and is willing to pay for it. While still desiring a discount or a good price, these customers understand that top-end work gets top-end pricing. While the top end of the market may be smaller than the bottom with fewer potential customers, there is typically competition, but not as much. The competition is less, and the profit is greater.

Perhaps the best business strategy may be to find and fill niche markets that are not yet overexploited at the top end. For example, there are high-end lawn-care firms, cutting the same grass with the same tools as the low-end providers, but somehow they are getting more for their effort. Why? Typically they give more or better services or products by doing something that represents higher value added. Maybe they offer a guarantee or follow-up services, which creates the perception and the reality that they are best the industry has to offer.

In the end, to be successful at the top end of the price chart, to build a reputation and a successful business, a business has to deliver top-end service and top-end results. It is not just about pricing high; it's about pricing high and delivering high, satisfying expectations. You can achieve this many ways, depending upon the nature of your service or business, but customers who are willing to pay the highest price expect and deserve the best product or service.

> Your customers will still want a discount or a special deal on occasion … but the higher profits are worth it. Perceived value, that is the concept.

A highly profitable niche, that's where I want my business operating. Make certain you're delivering the best possible product or service, and you can succeed. Your customers will still want a discount or a special deal on occasion … but the higher profits are worth it. Perceived value, that is the concept.

## Service, Service, Service … and More Service

It is absolutely the way to beat price competition, the big box stores.

It is absolutely the best way to beat local small business competition.

It is the way to boost profits, as great service allows for slightly higher pricing. The best service may allow for significantly higher pricing, especially in certain industries and product lines where service is more important than the product.

Not everyone is more interested or swayed by great service. Those who will buy based on price alone and look for whatever they can get free will switch loyalty for a dime. These are not the type of customers or clients you want to do business with or build your business on.

You must identify the customer profile you want to do business with and then create a service program that keeps them coming back year after year. That's how to succeed in this down economy. That's how to avoid discounting and create word-of-mouth promotion and long-term loyalty and growth. It is all about creating relationships by serving your clients' needs.

There are many ways to accomplish this. For example, you might offer free extended guarantees … really how much does it cost to replace or repair a few widgets each month or week, in exchange for a long-term profitable relationship?

Here are just some of the services you can use to attract customers and encourage their loyalty:

1. Free installation
2. Liberal "no-ask" return policy
3. Value-added design consulting services
4. Free assembly
5. Seminars, courses, how-to advice on your product or service
6. Telephone support
7. Refill reminders
8. Upgrade service
9. Low- or no-interest financing
10. Free delivery; then pick-up and removal of the old product
11. Coffee or other amenities while waiting
12. Home consultations
13. Gift services
14. Try-before-you-buy service
15. Newsletters, e-mail communications
16. Communities and forums through Web 2.0: website, blog, social networking, Twitter, Facebook, YouTube, etc.
17. Knowledgeable salespeople
18. Information online; printed format
19. Foreign language services to bridge barriers
20. Doing whatever your competition will not do to provide a better option

The list can go on, but you get the point. If successfully delivered, the costs of these kinds of services are easily absorbed by greater client loyalty, higher profits, and important word-of-mouth advertising, recommendation, and growth as a direct result.

Give it a season or two and watch the success and momentum build.

## Challenging Traditional Discount Strategies

It appears to me that quantity discounting has nothing to do with the cost savings experienced or the quantity purchased; it's merely a pricing strategy that the manufacturer or distributor conjures up and offers . . . and then violates regularly, in response to market demands.

It's an understandable power move on the part of the large chains and distributors that manufacturers and prime distributors cannot resist. Simply stated, chains and smaller distributors demand the lowest price possible in consideration of the potential for larger orders—not the promise, but the potential. What really happens is they test the product in a few dozen stores, having purchased at the truckload price, making a sizable profit. If it goes well, they repeat the order slowly, probably never reaching full distribution potential. They will not give you widespread forced distribution.

For reasons that remain difficult to understand, distributors take orders and do not pioneer new items with forced distribution . . . ever, despite success at the test-market level. They only want to stock traditional, long-term successful, well-supported best sellers.

The chains do the same thing. Buyers hedge and order minimal amounts of an innovative item, always afraid of getting stuck with inventory or slow-moving goods. They would rather miss a winner than get stuck with inventory.

So the demand for the lowest price is really an empty demand, as the buyers will order as little as they can to replace the product where it moves based only on what the market demands, never buying for greater distribution.

The real power is in the product itself, as it alone determines retail velocity while the buyers do everything they can to limit their exposure and risk. As they are certain the new product will either bust or peak and slow down quickly, they reduce their risk from the first purchase on.

So why should manufacturers and large distributors demand and get the lowest price possible price for very small orders as they test the market when there is no upside guarantee or promise? Good question, and I have no reasonable answer other than the likelihood that they will not place the order unless the lowest price is offered, irrespective of order quantity, and without real promise of support and greater distribution.

The point is that manufacturers or distributors must have a selling and pricing strategy to support their effort, or they will be forced to sell at the lowest possible price. Once you violate your own discount schedule, you may as well always offer the lowest price for everyone and accept that as your benchmark, as that is what the market will require.

Alternatively, if your product is good and sells off the shelf, grow slowly and prove its value with demand from the marketplace which will provoke many of the chains to buy at your appropriate pricing and quantity discount strategy and in volume. As now they see a winner, they do not want to be left behind. You need to be strong enough to say no in the early stages and develop sales where you get distribution support and sell at the right price.

Since the chains and distributors want you to pay for shipping, accept long payment terms, and accept returns for damaged goods, whether there are any damages or not, and on it goes, you had best hold your selling price to your schedule, or all the profits will be eroded before you get your check.

You are entitled to a larger price for smaller quantities, and the larger buyers are entitled to a discount based on cost savings of large orders. With a carefully designed strategy that rewards larger orders, you should hold yourself to your plan, ignoring the empty pleas and promises from distributors and chains.

> **You are entitled to a larger price for smaller quantities, and the larger buyers are entitled to a discount based on cost savings of large orders.**

If the product deserves it, why reward the distributor for adding nothing of value to your program? The obvious lesson is that lower pricing does not result in larger orders, so why offer it? If all the power comes from your product, why give in to the chains' demands? They are providing little assistance to your effort and are probably not worth the deal they are demanding.

Honor the smaller distributors and small chains that will buy at published prices. Honor the large stores that will also buy at normal wholesale, build profitably one store at a time, and soon the distributors and larger chains will come to you and be more willing to accept your published prices.

The chains and smaller distributors purchasing from manufacturers argue they must fit into the pricing strategy, allowing them to compete with the big guys and minimize their order. Do not believe this; it's untrue—it's a ploy to capture more profit from your sale.

If there is a mutually beneficial strategy that will support greater distribution, then I am all for it. But to automatically assign significant discounts to a modest order size when there is no cost benefit or no real distribution benefit makes little sense, and you are simply giving away the margin while hoping that larger distribution efforts will result. It won't. Every sale should be profitable. Do not get trapped in the no-win predicament where promises and potential get the best price; make them earn it.

## You Want Net Profit, Not Gross Revenue

Why is it that so many entrepreneurs focus on gross revenue and not net profit? The illusion seems to be the bigger the gross revenue, the better job we are doing, and the more successful we are.

If someone runs a multimillion-dollar company, apparently the person is smarter, better, and more successful than if he or she achieved $1 million in gross revenues. Does anyone ever consider that the objective is how much money we make after expenses, overhead, costs of goods, and labor costs, and not how much money we make before deductions? Too many people believe they will make more if they gross more, not evaluating the net profits.

Too often, I see companies develop gross revenues at the expense of profitability. They incur huge overhead by additions in payroll, inventories, advertising, debt, and most often reduced profitability for the sake of more sales by reducing prices. This is madness. Recently, I evaluated a business that had three retail stores and a warehouse. We demonstrated that by eliminating two stores and the warehouse, we reduced gross revenues from $4.5 million to $3 million and made a whopping profit on the one store because of a huge reduction in overhead expenses and payroll. In fact, we demonstrated that the additional $1.5 million in gross revenue produced no additional profitability because the increased cost of doing business absorbed it all.

An easier, more controllable one-store plan was superior in delivering a better quality of life as well as yielding more bottom-line profits, and yet the owner wanted to maintain the three-store operation. More revenue, he believed, must be better.

No, my friend, quite the opposite is sometimes true, but our fixation on the amount we gross is hard to jettison. Unfortunately, I believe it is all ego-driven, a numbers game, and the wrong numbers are being played. It's the net number, not the gross, that counts. I see this focus on gross revenue destroy companies every day; it usually comes with two strategies.

First, the owners, who want to increase revenues without concern for profit, will either lower the price to get the big order or set the price below market levels for everyone to pick their pockets in exchange for greater gross revenues. No, we do not make up for this loss by selling more; we lose more on every sale we make.

Second, the owners typically add salespeople and administrative middle management to manage the growing business without concern for the costs associated with the labor and related overhead requirements. So they sell themselves into oblivion, gorging on low-profit sales inadequate to cover the inflated overhead.

These are two direct paths to financial crisis and losses.

If only we were as focused on net profits and controlled overhead, making only profitable sales and leaving behind loss leaders and cut prices. Learn to say no to price gougers who promise you huge sales at ridiculous prices. Exercising sound business practices, we will experience reduced revenues but increased profits. Say no to low-margin sales.

When next discussing your business plans, look hard at the bottom line and explore alternative strategies with reduced overhead. Hold profitability with effective pricing that throws profits to the bottom line. We want net profits, not gross revenues.

## Gross Revenue and Cash Flow versus Profitability

Many entrepreneurs believe that first you fight for expanded sales, building revenues and cash flow (profit be damned), and then fine tune for profitability once you achieve the level of revenue you were looking for.

I have seen this theory practiced in many failing enterprises because business owners try to build the customer base first and then, if they manage to remain in business long enough, begin to raise prices, charge for shipping, trim internal overhead, adjust payroll, advertise less, and build in profitability. They usually fail to accomplish their goals as they choke to death from lack of capital, while trying to grow off the cash flow.

Some say they went out of business because they grew too fast. This frequently occurs, but the real reason is not just rapid growth but rapid unprofitable growth. They went out of business because they had inadequate profit to carry them. You cannot grow on unprofitable cash flow.

> **You cannot grow on unprofitable cash flow.**

Building revenue and then fine-tuning for profitability sounds like a reasonable approach, but on closer inspection it is fraught with inconsistencies and contradictions. It will result in cash starvation. Especially in a rapid growth curve, the cash flow will not save the day.

Since we are always chasing our dollars, between inventory, work in process, raw materials, daily and weekly overhead, and hard-to-collect accounts receivables, if we do not make a reasonable profit, there will be inadequate funds to run the business.

Assuming you have not started with an enormous bucket of cash, the only way to finance growth and development is with profit from each sale. It is a challenge, as accounts receivable represent a large amount of unavailable cash flow, especially in a growth curve. Thus, profitability is even more crucial to basic survival, let alone growth.

Why not start with profitable sales from the beginning and become more profitable every day, reinvesting the profit to fuel and support growth and development?

Further, what is the value of creating a customer base that is only willing to pay a below-market price? Is this a sustainable client base, a foundation? So I ask the rhetorical question, what possible reason would we have to sell anything at below an acceptable level of profit?

Recently, I watched a client lower the price for installing flooring to match a competitor's pricing, to meet a customer's budget requirements, and to grab the sale. The price was so low, it was very questionable whether even a very narrow gross profit would be earned; and with overhead, it clearly would not be profitable at all. Contribution, he said, keeps the employees busy; it's an in-and-out job, so why lose the business?

This is a good question and still gets the same answer: There is no reason to work unprofitably. Either charge a reasonable profit or do not do the business. If it's all about contribution to reduce the overhead burden, then change the overhead to have less burden, but the only thing that reduces the overhead burden is profit.

This may work for a while, but when the market declines, a receivable doesn't arrive on time, growth that demands investment requires more and more cash. A hiccup from whatever source occurs, you're not getting new dollars to replace the ones you used. Then—when you can't buy inventory or pay bills or payroll, despite growth in revenues or sales—you will understand the reason to work profitably and grow out of margin.

Think about it. There are three challenges confronting your cash flow:

1. Money needed to cover old unpaid payables that tend to build up when operating unprofitably
2. Money to cover current operations such as overhead and payroll
3. Money to invest in growth and development such as additional product or workers

Don't forget that a large percentage of your usable cash is trapped in receivables 30 days or more away. So how do you grow when you have to cover the old, cover today, and build for the future while waiting for your cash to arrive in 30 days … *impossible* in a word.

The only possible answer is to grow out of profits (or new cash investment). Every job, every day must be run profitably regardless of gross revenue. Growth comes from investing new capital from either sales or investment but not from cash flow. Resist this old, unsupportable tale of revenue first, profit second, or it will be written on your businesses tombstone.

> Growth comes from investing new capital from either sales or investment but not from cash flow.

## When Increased Gross Revenue Nets Less Profit

I was with a business owner the other day who exclaimed quizzically, "When I was doing $750,000 annually, I was bringing home $150,000. When I grew to $1.5 million, I brought home $125,000. When I went to $2 million, I brought home $100,000. Now that I am doing $2.5 million, I am still bringing home $100,000. What's the deal here? The more I do, the less I earn!"

How true, how potentially devastating. Here is what's happening to growth curves for many small business owners: The more they do, the less they earn.

The reason? A business not run or controlled effectively, with no key indicators or financial reports to support management decision making, is a runaway train headed for a crash.

Simply stated, the larger an out-of-control business gets, the more waste, the less profit, and the less cash there is at the end of the day. Despite the reality that the gross volume is increasing, the net is decreasing just as rapidly when a business is out of control.

Greater revenue can cover a multitude of sins, but the day of reckoning soon comes when there is not enough profitability or cash flow to continue the juggling act.

What happens is more waste, defects, and returns, lower pricing through giveaways by the salespeople to attract more sales, greater advertising that brings in more business but erodes profit, employees hired to support growth but productivity is low, and the cost of materials is growing rapidly but pricing is typically coming down just as rapidly; it's no surprise that the mantra of the business—the driving force—is more revenue, not more profitability, rather than what it should be.

The small business owner speaking earlier was better off doing $750,000 per year and taking home $150,000 than doing $2 million annually and taking home $100,000. His business is screaming for management leadership. He needs financial reports and a deep evaluation of his operation to correct the problems.

With financial reports he can see what his real earnings are. With an analysis of his productivity, he will learn he has far too many people doing too little work. With his analysis of his cost of goods, he will learn he has not adjusted his pricing for years; and while his costs have crept up, his pricing has crept down. He will see his average invoice is smaller and his margins are decreased; he will learn his sales force is lowering prices with giveaways, long terms, returns, and so on, just to increase sales revenues. He will see his advertising budget is too high. He will learn he has too much inventory and has too many losers on his sales sheet. He has too many salespeople selling too little and earning too much ... and on it goes.

Here is the answer: Less can mean more. Less gross revenue can contain greater profitability in percentage as well as in actual dollars. Get smaller and more profitable is frequently the answer. Undo the sloppy management style; insert appropriate controls and analysis; then grow with control.

Clean up, tighten up, and make the changes that will result in a cutback of revenue but an increase in profit—especially important in a down economy. Jobs are being lost; industries are shutting down; overhead is rising; people are spending less. Respond appropriately: Tighten the ship, prepare for declines, and focus on profitability ... sell less, make more, and manage correctly.

## Rent to Your Business and Reap the Benefits

A few reasons to support the strategy of purchasing the real estate your business occupies and then renting it to your business for the fair market price makes sense.

Here's why business owners should use this strategy. Income generated through a distribution or from profits, if it's taxed as a partnership (within an LLC or as a partnership) or even an S corporation with pass-through profit, with a portion resulting in taxable income, requires the self-employment tax, as much as 15 percent collectively from all sources, a sizable amount worth avoiding if possible.

If instead of this taxable format, you substitute rent income for self-employment taxable income, then you avoid the self-employment tax, saving approximately 15 percent, which is a significant saving.

This also works if the business owner already owns the property. Instead of *not* renting it at all, *not* taking cash to save the cash flow for the business, rent and reinvest the capital if necessary, but exchange taxable self-employment income for rental revenue. Save 15 percent in tax and then reinvest if you choose; it's a better deal.

In addition, rent is an expense to the business, allowed as a deduction that reduces taxable income for the business.

The real estate is then out of play, protected from claims against the business, as it is no longer a business asset that creditors can reach or attach in a lawsuit.

Further, by adjusting rents within fair market constraints, according to the availability of taxable income for offset, this allows for some valuable tax planning opportunities. Considering the depreciation, the interest write-off, and the additional deduction for insurance, maintenance, and repair, it may be a valuable asset for the owner.

Thus, for stability purposes and protection from possible claims and lawsuits, it makes additional sense for the owner to purchase the real estate from which the business operates. It should be purchased by the owner directly and rented to the business with full deduction of all costs by the owner.

The same applies to expensive equipment; rather than being owned by the business and vulnerable to attachment, as well as wasting potential tax benefits, it too can be isolated in a separate LLC owned by the business owner and leased or rented to the business, safer and more valuable for the owner.

New autos also work in this scenario, especially with the 2010-year 50-cents-per-mile business deduction. Better the owner should own the car and take the mileage deduction; it will pay for the car in one or two years if you have adequate income to absorb the write-off available.

It's about maximizing the potential tax benefits and protecting the property from attachment.

## Expand the Invoice ... Improve Your Bottom Line

The pursuit of more business is universal to everyone in business. Finding another great client, the next big order, is what's on everyone's mind, and we go to all ends to succeed.

Adding goods and services to the invoice is a great way to create additional revenue and profit without having to create or find additional customers.

> **Adding goods and services to the invoice is a great way to create additional revenue and profit without having to create or find additional customers.**

I was at the cleaners the other day and noticed a rack of snacks, some sewing kits, buttons in a small bag, collar stiffeners, and a host of other impulse items, and I asked, "Do you sell much of this stuff?"

With a large smile and a beaming face, the owner said, "I sell something to nearly every customer that comes in by offering them some item they appear to need."

He further responded to my inquiries, exclaiming he earns a sizable profit from add-on sales and plans to expand the opportunities for his clients to buy more.

More service-oriented, an electrician client always sells add-ons to every job he visits, like a full-house surge protector for just under a thousand dollars. They go like hot cakes, or a house lightning protector, or an outside motion detector light; these are reasonably priced add-ons that make a tidy profit, says my client. He sets up swimming pools with the electrical work required and then sells additional lighting or other electrical fixtures.

Every business can think of ways to add products or services to increase the invoice. It may be making pure impulse items available or simply expanding the service or business you currently offer with some creative ideas.

> **There is no better prospect than a satisfied customer, so find a way to expand your offerings and increase your profits.**

Once you have the attention of a customer, it is easier to add to the invoice and sell another service or product than to create another customer. Repeating this process often enough will expand revenues and increase profits. The idea is, however, to add opportunities for your clients to purchase more from you, be it important major items or services or small impulse items.

There is no better prospect than a satisfied customer, so find a way to expand your offerings and increase your profits. It's not about creating new business; that's another task altogether. It's about increasing the invoice to include goods and services beyond what the customer originally had in mind. That's added value.

## Are You Focused on the Wrong Part of Your Business?

Small business owners have a huge job. This is because they fail to organize appropriately by splitting the management duties into the three basic components: production, finance, and sales and marketing. They spend their days hopping between the three divisions, paying attention to the squeaky-wheel issues that are screaming for attention and the issues that appear most important, typically finances and production. That leaves sales and marketing to happen on its own.

After all, there are just so many hours in the day, and small business owners infrequently ask for help, less frequently allocate responsibility, and seldom organize effectively. As long as they are busy, they must be managing, and thus they are satisfied they have done their best every day.

Typically, small business owners specialize primarily in putting out fires and babysitting their people. The next priority is spending time and attention on the most important clients, the ones providing most of the revenue. These areas certainly seem like the right use of their time and energy. It is, however, the wrong priority. The above frequently repeated, common scenario is a cycle that prevents progress, growth, and development. What should business owners be focusing on? Sales and marketing.

We all know that nothing happens until something is sold. We all know that the single most significant and most frequently stated issue preventing growth and development is inadequate funds to support overhead, payroll, and, of course, growth and development. But do we ncrease our focus on sales and marketing? No, we ignore this division and allow it to do whatever it does on its own.

The first budget cut is always in the sales and marketing area, be it advertising or staff. The least amount of effort, time, and energy spent is on sales and marketing. Most sales and marketing programs are based on allowing potential clients to find you and ask you to sell something to them.

Most people argue they do not have the capital available to effectively advance the sales and marketing programs they can conceptualize if only they had the money to do it.

Why wouldn't this division be the first and most important aspect of your business day? Increased sales means increased revenue, which means freedom to develop your business successfully and profitably.

Make the sales and marketing responsibility your primary focus, and your financial worries will be over. Make sales and marketing your primary effort, and production issues will disappear, as you will always have adequate inventory, materials, equipment, and so on.

This does not mean you have to spend yourself into oblivion and buy more ad space. No! Sales and marketing efforts do not have to have a significant budget; they can be done on a shoestring; it's simply that they must be done.

## Horizontal or Vertical Expansion

There are a number of alternative strategies supporting profitable growth and development. Two alternatives are vertical expansion and horizontal expansion. Both work; it depends entirely upon your goals and resources.

Vertical development follows the natural chain of value-added commerce: importing or manufacturing, wholesale distribution, retail sales, and then direct sales to the consumer. Follow the line of development, the natural flow of a product from the original source to the end user through all the various channels. Each channel is a vertical step.

Horizontal development, in general, is more about growth by expanding more of what you are currently doing, such as expanding manufacturing in other locations, creating more distribution outlets or expanding the territory, adding more stores geographically, or expanding internally creating greater and more diverse capacity and capability, more machines, more product, more locations, more warehousing capacity, and so on.

With the evolution of the Internet, and the effect it has had on the direct market as well as the wholesale market, the business-to-business market is completely open and accessible. Manufacturers, wholesale distributors, and even retailers have the opportunity to sell direct to anyone who has access to the Internet. For the cost of an effective website, you can expand vertically.

A manufacturer can begin distribution and even retail and direct sales to the market. A retail store can sell direct through the Internet, can open more stores, and, with enough margin, may even create a wholesale distribution network. Horizontal and vertical expansion—one feeds off the other. Both are natural development paths; both can be successful.

Clearly, another important and limiting factor is the amount of capital and other resources required to support your expansion plans. Do the cash flow pro forma and plan the expansion based on the cash required and what is available.

In vertical expansion situations, clear separation between the stages is sometimes necessary, as competing with your own customers and suppliers can be tricky. However, it can be very successful if each layer of vertical development is operating independently and separate from each other.

The old real estate adage, the three most important factors are location, location, location, applies to both vertical and horizontal expansion, as location can determine the likelihood of success. It is not that there are specific winning factors that define success when determining what location is best; it depends on your marketing program. Discount Flooring, a national chain and online store, made its mark by locating in remote, low-rent areas, offering low price and no frills. The entire marketing program and strategy supported horizontal expansion all over the country.

Outlets bring factory cost to retail pricing, an opportunity for deep discounts and sizable profits. When you locate in a discount mall that attracts a huge population, the overhead is expensive; yet with large traffic the location creates significant revenue potential.

Locate distribution channels where your competition is not doing a great job or where there is a large client opportunity. Almost any growth plan can work if it is integrated with the location and supported by a comprehensive marketing plan Here are the three most important location decisions you need to consider:

1. How do you want to expand?
2. Where will you site your new location if you require one?
3. What is your marketing strategy to support your growth plan?

If it's all tied together and well thought out and implemented, you will succeed either way you choose to go: vertical or horizontal or both.

Look at your industry, competition, client base, and available capital. Then determine what expansion path will work best for you. Design you expansion by matching your resources to the plan, over time.

Horizontal or vertical? Both work, it's a matter of preference, strategy, and opportunity; market dynamics; and the availability of capital.

## No Growth Without Capital

I believe this issue is the cause of many failures of small business entrepreneurs. They commence a growth program without new capital infusion to support it, believing the growth will be fueled by revenue from new sales.

This is an impossible dream and will result in frustration, losses, and eventual failure. Yet so many attempt this strategy.

Here are the three issues controlling this phenomenon and preventing success:

1. There is inadequate cash from current sales revenue to cover current operations.

2. There are typically past sins that require debt service that also must come out of current operating revenues, putting more demand on the scant cash flow and profitability that is already stressed.

3. Any strategy to increase revenues by launching a new product, service, ad program, or other strategy requires some investment for production of inventory, marketing expenses, additional overhead, all coming out of operational cash flow.

Now the table will collapse since some available cash was applied to the growth program, leaving payable and operational overhead in default. In fact, what happens is this: If the new program is successful, creating new orders and new additional revenue, the cost of production, work in process, inventory, and so on will choke you before you get off and running. There is never enough cash to support all three areas.

Current operations, past obligations, and fuel for growth cannot be funded out of current revenues. Yet despite this virtual rule, many bet the farm on their latest and greatest innovation and effort, believing that increased sales from new expansion will solve their issues when in all reality, it will implode.

Why, you ask?

Cash flow, profitability, those are the reasons. Here's why. Receivables are always 45 to 60 days away, and so right off the bat you are not seeing your cash for a long time. Payables like payroll and taxes come weekly and are unmerciful—demanding payment—and typically increase with growth and development.

Cost of goods, work in process, inventory, and marketing costs—all the extras required to launch new efforts—must be paid for, which puts greater pressure on the cash flow.

However, lest we forget the reality of cash flow versus profitability, the only excess capital you really have to spend is the elusive increased profits from additional sales. Considering the nature of any new innovation or new launch, how much additional profitability can you really expect and collect in the short or medium term? Certainly not enough if you consider the time it takes to collect receivables.

There simply will not be enough additional profit available to fund the growth, as existing cash flow is far too demanding to allow room for expansion. The answer most people offer is, "Sell harder and create more immediate revenue." Wrong, it will all be absorbed by overhead, work in progress, inventory, receivables uncollected, and marketing efforts. It will not work.

> **The only excess capital you really have to spend is the elusive increased profits from additional sales.**

The only workable answer? A growth and development plan requires substantial investment and additional working capital. A cash flow plan will reveal this reality. Do one and see what it says for you.

Growth and development must be separately and additionally funded. Plan accordingly. Do not fall into this trap, as so many do. The three problems listed earlier will eat your plan up: current overhead, past payables, and cost of development, coupled with the inconsistencies of accounts receivable collections and accounts payable payments.

## Beware the Dangers of Merchant Cash Advances

So many businesses are in need of cash and because of poor credit issues cannot get the support they require from their bank, so they are easy prey for various nontraditional sources for new capital.

One easy source that more businesses are accessing is the merchant cash advance (MCA). Based solely on the revenues generated from business credit card machines, it works like this.

Depending on the dollar volume of your credit card business, the lender (not really a lender because it is better described as accounts receivable financing) advances an amount of capital, usually less than $150,000, to a business and is paid back automatically out of the revenues the credit card machine generates.

The so-called fee is approximately 25 percent of the *advance*, but when calculated as if it were *interest* on the *loan* can amount to hundreds of percents, even as high as 400 to 500 percent annualized. The MCA is unregulated because it is not technically a loan.

MCAs are compelling for the following reasons:

1. An MCA is quick and easy. You can have your cash within a week, with little paperwork and no credit issues.

2. Payback is automatic and daily, and so you pay less when business is down and more when business is up.

3. The debt is unsecured and not personally guaranteed by the business owner and only paid if the credit card machine generates capital. If your business fails and you have done everything correctly, there is no personal obligation to pay the money back, nor is there any additional collateral.

Here is the trap. The advance is typically designed to be paid back within a three- to six-month period; thus a 25 percent fee when recalculated as if it were interest and annualized can result in a comparable annualized interest rate of hundreds of percent.

If you happen to do well for a short time period and pay back more of the advance sooner than anticipated, the interest rate goes through the roof.

Keep in mind that the already contracted and typical credit card fees remain for the intended use of the merchant account, and so the 25 percent fee is above and beyond these fees!

It is unlikely that any business can afford such a financing arrangement for very long, or at all, as in the end not only will it absorb your profit, but it will create a larger cash flow issue than the one you were trying to resolve.

This is an easy source for capital needed by typically uncreditworthy businesses strangled by inadequate cash flow, low gross revenue, and slim profitability. Without other, more traditional capital-creating alternatives, the advance may appear attractive and eliminate some immediate problems, but this is not the way to resolve the real issues.

A decade ago there was one such merchant advance business, and it advanced approximately $10 million annually. Now more than 50 businesses offer this service, and the anticipated advances this year are over $700 million to $1 billion.

Think twice and reject the proposal when the high-pressure salesperson knocks on your door. Find another way to resolve cash flow, profitability, and gross revenue problems.

# Chapter 12

# Know Your Numbers

## Understand the Language of Business

**N**umbers are the language of business. Learn this language, understand what it is telling you, and be in control of your business.

Successful business starts with a vision, a plan to reach your vision, an organizational format to support your plan, and adequate financing to support your rollout, and off you go.

But that's just the beginning. For a business to be successful, it must be successfully managed; you must listen to its heartbeat, take its blood pressure, and track its pulse by monitoring its key indicator numbers in each department: finance, operations, sales, and marketing.

Track, monitor, and control the key indicators, all the numbers of doing business:

- Profit and loss statements
- Balance sheets
- Overhead
- Payroll
- Accounts receivable
- Payable aging
- Gross and net profit

Without tracking the numbers, your business is a runaway train, headed for a crash. Closely track, monitor, and control your business based on the key indicator numbers and financial reports, and it will soon play like a Stradivarius. You will make management decisions based on real information, not intuition.

Far too many say they are not numbers people, and so they skip this part of their business operation, preferring to focus on the vision, delivering the product or service they have passionately chosen to provide the market. I say, then get a job; do not consider small business ownership as an occupation, because numbers are the language of business. Without understanding them you are destined to fail, despite the quality of your product or service.

Business success is not just about the product or service; it's as much about the science of doing business, and that's controlled by numbers.

## Know Your Business Key Indicators

Review your key indicators every day, every week, every month. You can either hold the course if it's all working as planned or make adjustments immediately if there is any vacillation. Every day you wait before responding is more money lost, not taking advantage of opportunity, or allowing a small problem to become a costly large problem.

That's the beauty of small business, immediate responsiveness. It's like sailing a small boat; every adjustment you make and every tack you take immediately changes the direction of the boat.

If you are tracking, monitoring, and controlling your business, you want to read your key indicators and make adjustments as soon as possible. If you are holding the course no matter what your navigation is telling you or because you have no navigation tools, you are allowing the boat to steer you.

What does this mean? Key indicators are the pulse of your business. They report your condition and direction. Key indicators may include:

- Number of sales per day, week, salesperson, or product
- Length of time to absorb your back orders
- Time when you can deliver the next job
- Production figures (or ratio of employees to dollars earned)
- Accounts payable
- Cash in the bank

- Receivables
- Profitability
- Dollars per hour per service person
- Amount shipped (in dollars or number of widgets)

Choose the key indicators based on the type of business you run. A restaurant may count turnovers or seats served. A manufacturer may look at the production number, and a retail store might use its inventory turns. Some track gross dollars. Some track net dollars. The idea is to track relevant data, take note of changes, and then respond to what it means, especially if it indicates a trend.

Every business has four to six key indicators that, if tracked and monitored, will tell you the condition of your business and the direction it's going. Your job is to determine what the most telling key indicators are. What will alert you to impending success or failure?

> Every business has four to six key indicators, that, if tracked and monitored, will tell you the condition of your business and the direction it's going.

When tracking and monitoring key indicators daily, you can track small changes that predict trends, and you can make appropriate adjustments far sooner than without monitoring. Small changes can predict important trends before they become large issues.

Large changes force you to take note, and they point to issues that must be examined and interpreted. Something is either very right or very wrong. You will know both small changes that predict possible trends and large changes that indicate an immediate problem requiring attention.

Couple these key indicators with reviewing basic financial statements such as profit and loss by week, month, and quarter, and you are in a position to control the success of the business. If your business is job-oriented, wouldn't it be nice to be able to tell your profit and loss on a job-by-job basis?

That's the beauty of small business. You can see what's happening by the end of the day and make adjustments that reflect those changes the next morning. Key indicators support management decision making with real information, not gut feelings. Gut feelings are important but best listened to with the information to support them.

I hear business owners say they do not have enough time to monitor their numbers. You must. Reduce whatever else fills your day to implement this style of management decision making. Track, monitor, and control . . . it's the steering wheel, the compass, and the map of your business.

## Key Indicators and Accountability

Reading Rudy Giuliani's book, *Leadership*,[1] I found a section regarding how he turned his police department around and shattered national records for unprecedented, breakthrough improvement. He developed and then measured categories based on those used to grade police departments around the country. It's a terrific yet simple path to success and has direct application to many of you running small businesses.

Giuliani believes in accountability at all levels for all personnel. That means managers having goals and objectives and being held accountable for achieving them. He further believes that the way to reach the prescribed goals is by measuring success, by tracking and monitoring the key indicators, coupled with frequent challenges, reviews, and evaluations of the progress as well as problems. Then make adjustments in the goals when necessary. In other words, he is a believer in the mantra "Track, monitor, control," the three words I use constantly as requirements for managing a business successfully.

Giuliani did a few things to implement his own style of track, monitor, and control. He had his eight police districts track nearly every imaginable and measurable statistic. He asked them to track everything from the dozens of types of crimes that could be committed, where they took place, complaints, response time, accidents, even gunshots. You name it; he had it tracked. Then his assistants monitored the tracking, taking note of every increase and every decrease in every category.

Once every six weeks he met with his full staff and the entire management of each police district and grilled them on why some numbers were going up. He congratulated them on numbers going down and wanted to know why they were dropping, so others could learn about their successful implementations.

Not only was holding them accountable for both success and failure critical to the overall success of the turnaround, but having everyone responsible for the results attend the meetings prevented anyone from passing the buck or offering excuses. Someone was there who was personally responsible for the results and needed to answer for the why, what, and when.

What soon developed was a self-monitoring process that everyone involved up and down the entire chain of command followed, with managers taking responsibility for the improvements, holding themselves accountable for the end results.

As soon as the police executives in each district saw some of their numbers climb, they would be all over their forces asking why and making changes; then, when meeting with Giuliani, they had both improved numbers and good reasons for bad numbers along with a plan for changes to improve them.

It worked so well that the results made the New York City Police Department the talk of the country, and this program was soon being emulated by other major police forces in other large cities across the country.

This story, based on the importance of the role of key indicators and accountability, should serve as an example to every small business of the need to manage with a key indicator system: Track, monitor, and control; then reap the benefits.

## Managing with Key Indicators

Here is a scenario that shows how using key indicators is the way to take the guesswork out of managing and provide you with the systems to help you create and maintain a profitable organization.

My client has made a number of critical high-impact moves as follows:

- Closed a large warehouse, and now has materials shipped directly to the job sites
- Shut the remote office and reestablished his office in one of the stores
- Removed the deadwood, underperforming employees
- Rented half his space in one store to a complementary vendor, reducing overhead and increasing revenue with additional customer traffic
- Increased revenue by being present on the floor of the store where his office is and paying attention to his business

- Hired a workout specialist to rid him of his unsecured vendor debt, approximately $500,000, which removed the time drain and costs of attending to many lawsuits
- Entered into a 941 payroll tax workout, saving over a half-million in taxes

He did over $335,000 worth of business in August, and yet he cannot meet payroll, pay taxes, or pay necessary vendors. What happened?

He tells me he is working on a 30 to 40 percent gross margin, which should yield over $100,000 in monthly gross profits and more than enough to cover his operational requirements and leave a reasonable profit. It didn't. I asked him the following questions and began to break down what could be the problem:

1. "What are your actual gross percentage markup, margin, and gross profit?" He could not tell. I told him we could figure it out, but it would require some financial analysis.
2. "What are your payroll ratios to gross revenue or net profit?" Couldn't tell.
3. Can you compare current payroll with earlier payrolls to see if your payroll is creeping up?" Couldn't do that.
4. "What is your overhead burden?" Didn't know.
5. "How productive is your installation team? Are they finishing jobs as anticipated on time?" Didn't really know, but he thought he was OK.
6. "Are you training the employees?" No.
7. "Are you giving performance reviews?" Only to those he felt were doing poorly.
8. "How are your accounts receivables?" Seemed fine; he was on top of collections, although they are growing larger and older with many small problems collecting. Clearly a problem in the making.

So with $335,000 of monthly revenue, he should have been very profitable but was not. Something or some things were wrong, but he had no idea. He knew he could not make his required expenditures.

He asked me, "What's wrong?"

Here are my findings:

He was not tracking, monitoring, and controlling his business; thus, it was impossible to determine what was wrong with his operation.

We could not determine gross margin; we had no idea what the overhead burden was and whether or not it was growing. We didn't know how productive his installers were. We could not determine his payroll ratios. Without inputting information, he had no financial, no cash controls, no payroll or overhead budget. In essence, he was running his business in the dark without a flashlight.

I suggested that within a week or so of inputting data, I could tell him what his problems were and how to resolve them. Because I knew some of his business practices, I could guess that his profit margins were too low; I believed he was reducing price just to get a job, and so his gross revenues were up, but his net was way down. Upon further review, I knew his salespeople were very well paid but not with an incentive plan; thus, there was no reason to sell, as they already earned plenty.

I knew that there was no way to track sales to the individual sales-people nor to each store, and so we could not tell who was selling what. We did a quick review and determined that one store was tanking terri-bly, doing less than $45,000 for the month, while the other two were doing approximately $145,000 each. Something was very wrong in that underperforming store.

So what we have is a business out of control, with no way of know-ing what to do to correct it. Despite exceptional sales volume, the busi-ness was unprofitable, a fixable issue but impossible to deal with without information.

We will now spend the time and money to determine what key indi-cators to collect and provide the data to produce the reports we need, so we can determine what is wrong and what is correct. "Too busy," he said. "Too busy to make a profit?" I asked.

## Where Is the Cash?

I hear this question asked over and over, We are doing five hundred thousand, a million, or even a few million in revenue (it doesn't matter what the revenue is), so where is the cash? When I hear owners ask the question, I know they are not reviewing the key indicators. Here is where it is all hiding.

- **Accounts receivable.** Do not forget you always have a significant amount of cash owed but not paid. It may be the single largest source for find-ing your cash. There is always one-twelfth of your annual cash or more, perhaps one-sixth, owed to you but unusable until it arrives.

- **Inventory.** How often are you turning your inventory? Some items may be going quickly and turn many times per year and thus are producing cash, not hiding your investment. If you look carefully, you will find lots of inventory that does not move or turn frequently enough. That's where your cash is locked up—in your cost of materials, labor, and so on, waiting to be turned into cash after it's sold and the receivables collected. This can result in a huge cash drain.
- **High overhead.** This is a difficult analysis but must be done. As an example, perhaps in a generous spirit, you have committed to provide 100 percent medical benefits for employees and even for their families. Perhaps your offices, factory, or warehouses carry too high a rent load; or possibly, you have too many employees, too much vacation time, too much everything. That may be where your cash is going.
- **Productivity.** What your employees are producing in a given hour or day or a week—their productivity—might be very low, and thus you are paying more for your inventory than you imagine.
- **Profitability.** Are you selling your items for the right price? Check out your profitability; you may be surprised how little cash you have available because you are not profitable enough. Are you charging enough, or are you just spinning dollars? Most business owners have no real idea what their profit is and thus are driven by what they believe they must charge to sell products or services to either be competitive or satisfy a presumed market requirement.
- **Gross revenues may not be adequate.** You may need to increase total sales to yield adequate cash and profit to run your operation and yield the profit you want. Do a cash flow analysis.

Review key indicators to monitor the above issues and control your profitability, cash flow, revenue, overhead burden, productivity, and so forth. That's where your cash is hiding. Understand what is going on and fix the problem areas; make it all work together.

## Budgets ... a Mystical Concept

I believe it starts when we're kids and develops fully in adulthood; people universally despise budgets. Most refuse to use them as management tools in their lives or in business. "Why?" I ask.

As a kid when we get our allowance, we decide how to spend it. Aha! The beginning concept of budgeting. Frequently, however, the kid spends impulsively until it's gone then waits for the next disbursement, similar to how many of us run our businesses.

Some kids will budget for lunch money, bus fare, and of course "stuff," the beginnings of a real budget. Good, but this usually does not last long, as all too often the cash goes to whatever is most important at the moment.

> As a kid when we get our allowance, we decide how to spend it. Aha! The beginning concept of budgeting.

As we grow older, we do what I call partial budgeting—saving specific amounts of cash for specific items such as rent, car payment and insurance, and other expenses—but the overall concept of a budget is an underused tool and ineffective when it is a partial budget for specific purposes. It works for the purpose you are budgeting for but does not satisfy the overall planning function.

We budget for payroll, which is really a matter of hoarding all the cash that comes in until payroll is covered, and then we apply additional cash to whatever is next most important. This is a priority-list budget, not a true budget, as there is no planning involved. The entire picture is not budgeted, only a few high priorities.

Even business owners who have adequate cash tend to budget on a weekly basis, allocating cash to whatever is owed or required and seems most important at the moment. As there is enough cash to cover it all, there is no real need to budget, right? Wrong! So why budget at all? Budgeting done properly:

- Protects your bottom line by preventing overspending and depleting profits
- Makes certain there is enough cash at the right moment to do everything required in your business
- Reduces stress, increases stability, and allows for orderly growth and development

Those are three good reasons for budgets.

If you create budgets for all repetitive or known single payments and create line-item budgets such as advertising, employee payroll, and inventory, you can determine and control the use of cash and the amount of retained earnings. Everything you spend money on will be identified and controlled, fitting into the overall operating equation. It assures you that you are on course and heading to achieving your goals and objectives.

Here are two ways to determine budgets:

1. Look at last year's spending in each area and add a few dollars to the budget for this year, repeating the same expenditure and program.
2. Use "zero-start" budgeting; this means starting each line item with a zero. Do not look at last year's numbers, and try to redetermine what may be needed or desired for any particular line item. In other words, rationalize the budget for each line from zero to whatever is required based on the next year's business plan ... a much better process.

Budgeting protects your year-end profits and assures every dollar spent is well spent. It may not be sexy, but budgeting is an important business strategy. It forces strategizing, planning, and reviewing. It requires a business plan, written and executed as the budget indicates, which in turn controls the direction the business will go. A budget is the ultimate control and the best way to assure profits at the end of the year.

## Projections ... Your Crystal Ball!

I always create a full business spreadsheet with every income and expense item all loaded onto one equation-backed, all-encompassing spreadsheet. This may be complex with many sections or a simple one-page Excel spreadsheet.

A spreadsheet is a fantastic tool, as it allows you to see an entire business in one look. That's the objective, to have an all-encompassing view. Here is some of the information a spreadsheet can show you:

- The breakeven point, overhead burden, gross profit, and net profit
- Monthly movement of all the numbers so you can see well in advance peaks and valleys, loss and profit
- If there will be temporary losses, how much you will experience and when they will occur, so you can make the appropriate adjustments to smooth out the wrinkles
- If you are going to hit a wall, require cash, inventory, and so on, it tells you well in advance

Best of all, it allows you to plan. It's your crystal ball, a peek into the future. Most important, however, it is extremely detailed and gives you the information you are looking for and frequently reveals many surprises, both good and bad.

Of course, since we are projecting, once you see the results, you can change your reality, even if only illustratively, with the strike of a key. See what happens if you do it another way, asking the question "what if," making whatever changes you may want to see. Plot a new path based on your interactive numbers and see what will happen.

Then refine it, make further adjustments, and continue to see what effect the changes you make have on your business reality. It's a guiding light, a view into the possible future. It is a valuable tool that every business owner should review and use to make adjustments monthly at least and weekly if possible. Track, monitor, and control.

## Making Accurate Revenue and Expense Projections

Be brutally truthful with your estimates. I frequently see people artificially increase revenue projections or understate expenses to project a hopeful result. Conversely, others decrease revenue projections and overstate expenses to be conservative. Do not editorialize in your projections. Tell the truth, be as accurate as you can, or the tool will not provide you with the information you need. This is the place to be unflinchingly candid, entering exactly what you believe will happen.

But being right is a good thing. So often the well-intentioned entrepreneur does what he believes he must: cook his projections. Business owners who use artificial assumptions guarantee a commitment to achieving lower objectives. This practice builds in an escape hatch so they do not have to perform to a higher standard. These business owners intentionally create and support a business plan only capable of delivering to the lower projected standards—more costly, less efficient, and less productive plan, an intrinsically flawed plan.

> **Business owners who use artificial assumptions guarantee a commitment to achieving lower objectives.**

They do this believing that if there are additional revenues and fewer expenses down the line than projected, they will have more profit, and that's good. If they project lower revenue and higher expenses, they will more likely beat the projections and look good! All it does is create a business plan that is designed to perform at the worst level, as opposed to doing everything possible to reach higher expectations and achieving greater goals.

Here is why they do it. "To be safe," they say. They do it believing the best way to effectively project and plan is conservatively. I disagree 100 percent. Let me tell you the right way to project: accurately.

I understand projections are part vision, part experience; part art, part science; part reality, part fantasy; but we still have the responsibility to project as accurately as possible, neither overstating nor understating revenues or expenses. The numbers proposed should truly be the numbers you believe will occur, so you accurately support likely results and have the right number of employees, the proper inventory, appropriate infrastructure, the right supplies, and a suitable sales and marketing system, with adequate financial support and capital to implement the plan you want to deliver.

Accurate projections is a skill the entrepreneur must develop. It can be done; it takes time, focus, and the correct guidelines.

You may need to adjust the projections if an area of the business plan requires development over time, a ramp-up that was not projected correctly. Ongoing evaluation and reevaluation with adjustments based on reality is a natural part of the process, but that still requires an accurate original presentation as a base point.

It's a guide, a work in process, which never stands still and is always changing. Therefore, misstated projections will yield a different plan than intended, a worse plan, perhaps a failing plan, but all in the name of conservatism, as if that is a benchmark or a goal.

Let's state the projections as accurately as possible and adjust as required along the way, so we can manage the business we want and not the one we designed being conservative.

Be accurate, not conservative. Achieve greatness; plan for it. Be reasonable but not safe—safe creates instability and leads to failure. Projections are a planning tool. Let them do their job, as a projection will only work if the numbers tell an accurate story, the one you believe.

## What Should Your Business Be Earning?

This question is basic, but seldom asked or answered. Most entrepreneurs simply believe they will succeed, that they will earn more than they could in any other employment situation while enjoying the luxury of self-direction. Those rewards are good, but you still need to answer the question, "What should my business earn?"

I believe it is an important question, as there are ways to improve earnings if they are inadequate. And there are other uses for your time, capital, and expertise if this business is not yielding adequate return. A company must have goals and must be measured for its success, and the bottom line is just that ... the bottom line, the ultimate measuriement.

The answer to this question is partially controlled by your vision, which evolves into your mission statement, which is where you state your objectives, goals, and aspirations. This is where you establish the foundation that will determine if your business is going to be local or national, small or large. The other side of the equation is your implementation of the strategies and plans that support your mission.

## Earning Equation

It is worth developing a formula that shows what your business should be earning. Here is my equation; yours could be larger or smaller. The business must be able to:

- Retire debt as well as operate. This includes investor's debt, bank debt, credit card debt, whatever.
- Pay the owner a reasonable wage based on the industry and community standards. This should certainly be as much as one could make in other employment contexts.
- Earn enough to set aside 5 to 10 percent of its earnings for a rainy-day fund, cash flow peaks and valleys, new equipment acquisitions, and so on.
- Make a 10 percent profit at the end of the year ... or what's the point?

I talk to many business owners who pull a paycheck and are satisfied, to which I say, if you liquidated all your capital investment, collected your receivables and shut the door, what would the capital earn for you while you find a better way to earn a paycheck?

I see many business owners who barely get by, taking as little cash as possible, and continuing their time and cash investment in the growth of their business, which is admirable and acceptable if the curve tells you that you are growing and will reach profitability in the defined future. But this is not acceptable as a long-term plan.

Unfortunately, many small businesses are barely able to support their owners and can reserve nothing for the future. This is a challenge, as the owners want to operate, have made the investment, and, with all their cash tied up in the business, want to succeed. It's probably impossible to close out successfully, so they are trapped, tied to this weight pulling them down for a long-term commitment with no blue sky at the end.

So I say, do something else; it's a business, not a hobby. Invest in a program that will pay you your wage and earn you a return on your investment. Too many entrepreneurs spend far too much of their life chasing imaginary success, investing their time and effort but receiving little in return.

There are better uses of yourself and your investment, but you must have the guts to measure your success and make viable business decisions about whether this is the best use of your time, money, and effort.

> Too many entrepreneurs spend far too much of their life chasing imaginary success, investing their time and effort but receiving little in return.

Can every business achieve these goals? Probably not, at least not without more capital and a larger share of the market; and thus individual business owners are free to make the decision themselves about whether the business they have chosen is able to provide them with enough to satisfy their needs.

In this downturned economy, many businesses that were once profitable are now marginal or worse. The owners have a difficult time acknowledging that their business is no longer worthy of supporting, and it should be sold, liquidated, or shut down. It is an important decision and must be made without emotion and based on a realistic evaluation of the earning potential.

## What Is Your Business Worth to Sell?

Another measure of your company is how much it is worth on the market. This question is asked every day all over the country, "What can I sell my business for? Of course, the glib answer is, "Whatever the buyer will pay," but there are basic business principles that control, or at least support, the answer.

The biggest issue for determining worth is the intangible value called *goodwill*. Often a business will sell for more than its current assets minus the liabilities because there are other values the company has, such as market share, reputation, or client base.

A buyer is buying an opportunity to make money. The money that the business has been producing is evaluated as the:

- Amount devoted to operating the business
- Amount the owner withdraws
- Amount of profit the business books
- Value of its hard assets
- Special value from proprietary aspects, something special and valuable
- If profitable, the value of its goodwill

Depending on the industry and other factors, the amount of profit is subject to a multiplier anywhere from 2 to 10, and that's the price a buyer will typically be willing to pay for the goodwill of the business.

The next areas of focus are the value of the receivables and the inventory, and then other capital assets such as machinery, vehicles, and computers. These all have values and are typically sold for fair market value.

The focus, however, is always on the goodwill, as whatever the profit may be, the multiplier effect is where the real cash will be. If there is no profit, then how do you evaluate the goodwill? Simple, when there is no profit, there is no goodwill, and all you are selling are assets.

**When there is no profit, there is no goodwill, and all you are selling are assets.**

There is another lesson here. It might be tempting not to report cash payments for goods and services and decrease your business taxes. Keep in mind that not reporting cash sales is illegal and should not be considered. However, the value of the company's goodwill also diminishes. One must ask, "Is the tax reduction worth the value of the goodwill deduction?" The answer is always a resounding no! Yet business owners frequently do not report all their earnings—to their own dismay when they eventually decide to sell the business and get less than they hoped.

You will not be successful convincing a buyer that the revenue is really more than what you've reported on your tax return because you have additional cash receivables you didn't report. The revenue is what the tax return says it is, period. The major reason someone buys a business is to make a profit. If there is no profit, then there are only the assets to buy. When a business is not functioning as a moneymaker, there is no intrinsic value, no goodwill, to the business itself.

Maybe there is an opportunity to make money if an additional investment is made for advertising, inventory, or capital equipment, but that will be up to the new investor. Buyers will not pay for the opportunity; they will only for the past performance.

If you have a profit, then you begin to look at the percentage of profitability to extract the multiplier value. The question you ask is, "What would an investor be willing to spend to earn the profit the company generates?" If the profit is $100,000 per year, would an investor be willing to spend $500,000 to earn $100,000 per year? Possibly.

The multiplier depends upon many aspects, some intangible and some real, such as:

- There is latent opportunity to expand the profit if the investor adds capacity or does something else to the equation.
- The real estate is valuable and can be sold off eventually.
- There are a few long-term contracts from large, stable customers that add security and remove risk.
- There are patents or exclusives that strengthen the company's position.
- There is a strong likelihood of being bought out by a larger company once the sales are improved.
- Buying out a competitor can mean the selling business gets a premium because the combined businesses are worth more than the value of the two separate businesses.
- There is a clear, hidden, unexploited advantage or opportunity that will dramatically increase profits or gross revenues.
- The buyer has an ulterior motive, a hidden agenda, inside information, that adds value, and thus he may be willing to pay more.
- A noncompete agreement can add value by preventing the old owner from reentering the business and competing with the new owner.

All these tangibles and intangibles add value to the potential and thus increase the multiplier of the goodwill. In the end, it's arithmetic: the value of the assets, inventory, and receivables—and the goodwill if there is profit. The multiplier is where the negotiation focuses. Prepare your sales presentation around these factors, and you will have a clearer idea of what your business is worth.

Of course, there are always market conditions to consider, as well as industry standards for your specific industry. All these factors and more influence the selling price of your business, but in the end ask yourself, "What would an investor be willing to pay to earn this amount of annualized return?" Then you will be closer to knowing your true value.

## Note

1. Rudy Giuliani, *Leadership* (Hyperion: New York City, 2002), pp. 69–97.

 # Essential Financial Systems

## Important Invoice Terms

**H**aving a well-written invoice is one way to prevent your cash from hiding in receivables. An invoice is a contract. It includes the terms and conditions of the sale, usually stating the date, price, quantity, and description of what was sold as well as the terms of the payment, net 30 days or whatever it may be.

In addition, it includes any other information or terms you desire. It is unilateral and self-serving, as it does not require a signature or a response and is binding on both parties as long as the product described was ordered, delivered, and accepted in merchantable condition.

So what more could you add or what is missing from most invoices?

**Late or Nonpayment Terms.** The consequence for failure to pay as agreed is a crucial part of the invoice that many forget to include or never think about it in the first place. This is an essential part of your collection process and can be an expensive omission. It's the condition that says:

> Payment not received within 30 days of date billed will result in an
> additional charge of 1.5% per month, and in addition, the customer
> is responsible for costs of collection including reasonable attorney's
> fees incurred in the collection process.

Be sure to state the amount of interest due on a late payment; state it or lose it. If this phrase, or something like it, is not included, then you may *not* receive payment for the costs of collection, including legal fees. A court of law will *not* enforce repayment for these additional expenses.

Considering the high fees that collection agencies charge and the expensive costs of the legal process, this is a costly omission. If you are forced to pay collection fees out of pocket, then you will probably be unlikely to use collection agencies and lawyers because so often their costs are prohibitive compared with what is being collected.

Even if the invoice is large enough to warrant the collection process, why would you want to eliminate recovering the costs if by merely adding this line to your invoice allows you to include the costs plus interest in your collection?

You can also use the statement as an additional collection strategy, explaining to your late-paying customer that if payment is not received and you are forced to use the expensive collection and legal processes, the customer will incur the costs of the collection process in addition to interest and the actual invoice amount. On the other hand, many savvy business people will notice the absence of such language on the invoice and take advantage of the situation.

**Return Requirements.** Binding return requirements are another important concept to spell out for the purchaser. There are many other terms you can add including a restocking and return fee if goods are either returned or sent back without permission. Shipping costs could be added, and anything else deemed part of the deal by the seller.

**Warranty or Guaranty Rules.** Warranty or guaranty rules could be printed on the back of the invoice, where there's more room. But no matter whether you have it printed on the back or added to the front, as long as it is on the invoice, you're covered.

## Setting Up a System for Collecting Receivables

Successfully collecting receivables requires a systematic approach. Receivables are your lifeblood. You have prepaid by investing in the production and your overhead costs, and so you had best collect your receivables as rapidly and as effectively as possible.

**Defining Payment Terms.** First check your invoice; make certain you include specific language adding interest for bills unpaid over the terms of the deal and, most important, requiring the customer to pay the reasonable costs of collection including lawyer's fees. This now allows you to collect the expenses for collecting past due receivables.

Obtain credit card authorization in advance, which is usable on the thirty-second day after invoicing, by agreement on the credit application. Acquire a personal guaranty if possible.

File Uniform Commercial Code (UCC) forms and a security agreement if the deal is large enough and you are extending credit for it. Becoming a secured creditor is a powerful guaranty. If appropriate, file a mechanics lien as soon as you can; it is released with payment.

Have credit ceilings so no one can open credit and then expand it dramatically without someone reviewing the deal and making certain the client can handle the bill when it is due.

Get and check credit references. Make the first order or two payable in advance, until credit is established. In the end it is far better not to ship than to ship and not get paid.

**Have a Collection Plan.** It is critical that you create an overall credit and collection plan. Everyone involved—salesperson, customer, credit manager, owner, whoever is in line to help collect—should be included in the process, be it daily, weekly, or deal by deal. The information must be shared and acted upon in a timely way for appropriate response.

Consider these three precollection steps first:

1. The sooner you get the invoice out, the sooner you get paid. Best is to include the invoice with the shipment if possible, so it gets there simultaneously. If this is impractical, mail it as soon as possible. Mail, fax, or e-mail a copy anyway, as it may not get to the payable office from the shipping department.

2. Depending upon many circumstances, you may want to consider calling the customer a few days prior to the bill coming due and not only remind the customer, but begin to discuss details and possibly provide any missing paperwork necessary for paying the bill. Another purpose of the call is to find out as soon as possible if there is a payment problem; the sooner you know, the sooner you can begin resolving the issue.

3. Everyone, especially the customer, should be aware of the terms and conditions of doing business and the consequences of breaching the agreement. Your customers must know exactly what the rules are

and what can be expected for any variety of breach issues. You must do exactly as you've described the consequences.

Follow-through, reliability, and reputation must be consistent. I strongly recommend a quick-justice approach. Begin in 32 days after payment is due. How to begin brings me to the point of collection agencies. A waste of time from my perspective, as all that happens is an exchange of information and then an acknowledgment that the customer cannot pay what is due.

So let's get there as quickly as possible, skip the collection firm, and go directly to the pursuit letter from the law firm. Either it will get you immediate payment action, or the collection becomes more expensive for your customer, and you get paid in a while, maybe a long while, but you get paid. Write, wait, and then file suit if no response. That works, and the customer pays for the expenses.

If your strategy is to work with your customers and design customized payback plans, you are begging for problems. I do not recommend it. In the end, you will lose far more than by following the path I describe and recommend. Sometimes, however, it is a reasonable response. This should be a case-by-case decision, and there should be a process, a system for considering a customized payback plan.

Avoid shipping again to a client whose invoice goes old, over 32 days. An overdue invoice should signal a shutoff. Shipping a second time while holding an old invoice happens all the time, and then predictably the second invoice gets old and we now have two collection issues. The client should have been shut off immediately on the thirty-first day of not paying. Why ship again?

When the bill is due, someone should call the account immediately. If payment is in the mail, it's going to be late, and you are entitled to commence the collection process, and you should. If it's not in the mail, it's going to be later, so let the games begin.

Include the members of your sales force at some point in this process, as they are the first and best to explain your credit terms to new customers. Furthermore, since they are making a commission, they need to know exactly how to qualify a customer for terms and explain what happens if the customer goes more than net 30 or 60 days late.

The salespeople will be motivated to make good sales because their commission and relationship with their customers are at stake if the deal does not work out. Be careful, however: Keep in mind that they are working for their commission, and so they will do everything they can to keep the sale intact.

Other than explaining the credit terms to new customers, do not let the salespeople get involved in the credit side, but definitely include them in the collection side. You may want to use them extensively until you go to the lawyer. This works if managed well and if everyone knows the rules in advance. The salesperson must take responsibility for a bad sale and help collect. Commissions must be charged back if already paid to the salesperson or canceled if not yet paid. Train your staff to avoid any negative emotion, and rather, to be consistent, evenhanded, courteous, and respectful but committed to professional standards of effective collection.

> Train your staff to avoid any negative emotion, and rather, to be consistent, evenhanded, courteous, and respectful but committed to professional standards of effective collection.

Make certain you have an excellent paper trail, or at least documentation on computer that you can print out, such as invoice, purchase order, contract, shipping manifest, packing slip, and proof of delivery.

Someone must manage the legal process as well and work with the law firm as closely and effectively as it works the outstanding accounts receivable. Follow up, demand reports, and insist upon consistency and action, and of course, results. Have an established plan and flow of information, and do as much of the work for the law firm as possible.

The key to success is consistency of process and action and professional, respectful demeanor. Invoice quickly; call in a reminder; collect promptly; go to legal quickly; track, monitor, and control all information. Read the reports and inquire about every over-30-days client.

## Bill-Paying Strategy and Cash Control System

Many small businesses simply pay bills when the money is available and have no real plan or strategy to assure the right payments are made or allow for cash controls. This is not the way to go, and yet is the rule rather than the exception.

Yes, even paying bills requires a strategy that provides adequate opportunity for cash controls and decision making, putting you in control of your accounts payable, not the cash flow. Here is how it works, and it is how large corporations handle their cash control and payment strategies. Especially with declining revenues, a cash control system is critical.

First of all, there must be an opportunity for the manager of the department incurring the expenditure, that is, the person closest to creating the obligation, to accept the invoice as ready to be paid. This means the manager signs off on satisfaction, indicating all is correct with the invoice and the delivery of goods and services. This means checking the price, the accurate delivery of the goods ordered, and the quality, shipping charges, and so forth, all areas frequently filled with errors or dissatisfaction but billed and often paid anyway. Before a bill gets paid, a manager must check it and sign off.

Then, of course, there is the wait-for-the-cash game, which is typically how and when bills get paid in small businesses. Instead, try this.

Why not pay bills every Monday, or even every other Monday? This may take a while to arrange with your vendors, but they will understand the need for a system, and you can always blame it on the accountants and the requirements of doing business with you. It may help to change your payment status from COD to net 7 or 14 days, but you should be able to work it out.

During the week, you cut checks, but do not send them; instead stack them up in a pile ready to be sent out the following Monday, so the previous Friday the check run is concluded and waits for a Monday order to mail. Meanwhile, all week you are building cash in your operating account, spending little, and waiting to evaluate the check run and decide which checks to mail on Monday.

On Monday, you evaluate the balance in your checkbook and compare it with your check-run balance. Then you make decisions and manage your cash, paying out the most important first until the cash runs out. Of course, payroll is first and then payroll taxes, and shut-off notices for important utilities also move to the top of the list. Based on the cash available, you then determine which of the checks must be mailed.

If your requirements are greater than the cash available, you hold the check for another week, not Tuesday or Wednesday, but the following Monday. You get to decide who gets paid and who does not—a practice you cannot do as easily or at all if you disburse as you go during the week. You may find yourself out of cash waiting for some cash to become available, with an important bill requiring payment such as payroll or payroll taxes.

Then you go another week, without disbursing until the following Monday, and do it again, writing checks all week but building cash and waiting until every Monday or every other Monday to disburse. This gives you control over who gets paid, in what priority, and when. Of course you can always make exceptions during the week, but the fewer the better. This process also allows managers adequate time to review invoices.

Take control of your checkbook, and you are controlling the heart of your business. Cash controls allow you to include budget controls and other systems that are all controlled by this bill-paying strategy. Once utilized, you will begin to see how this supports all your systems and the general flow of effective business management and decision making.

## Presenting Financials That Tell the Right Story

Some believe that the numbers are the numbers, and thus there is no art involved in disclosing financial information.

Not so.

Presenting financial information in the hands of a skilled technician is an art form and can help tell the story you want, honestly and appropriately, and I emphasize honestly. There is no reason to lie, ever.

For example, a basic and very important disclosure for so many purposes is expressing the real estate evaluation. First of all, real estate always has a range of value: high, medium, and low. Depending upon your purpose and the comparisons you chose to use, you can express the value high or low within the allowable range.

Other factors can adjust the value dramatically. For example, deteriorated features, be it the roof or heating system or anything expensive, necessary, and in need of repair or replacement, will reduce the value proportionately. On the other hand, an extra building lot, which may be part of your front or back yard, can increase the value dramatically.

Receivables, another important aspect of a business financial document, can also be misleading. Leaving over-90-day receivables on the document increases value, taking them off decreases value, and both are viable decisions, as over-90 are considered noncollectible and should be written off. You may have over-90-day terms, or the industry may simply pay over-90 so the receivables are good.

Here are some other financials open to interpretation and presentation choices:

- Equipment, inventory, and work in process are all subject to high optimistic evaluations or low liquidation valuations, a huge difference with great impact. When evaluating any asset at fair market value, liquidation value, or replacement value, all three work and all three tell a different story.
- Owner's draw on payroll; the paycheck is obvious, but borrowed money from the corporation may not be. Expense money, cars paid for by the business, insurance paid by the business, personal travel paid as a business expense, and so on can be reported as owner's income or business expenses, a big difference either way.
- Wife or kids on the payroll may have nothing to do with production but is another expense issue that has flexibility in its reporting.
- Home office ... the same; it can go either way depending on what you are trying to accomplish.
- Have you invested money or lent it to the business and intend to be paid back? It could be either, a big swing.
- Bad debt write-offs provide another area that can affect the presentation.
- Cash or accrual accounting demonstrates large swings in reality.
- With repeating contracts, for monthly delivery, you can report that which is shipped or report that which you expect to ship in the future and book it as a sale. Either interpretation is true.
- Pending lawsuits, for or against, valued or not, valued high, low, or medium range, can be reported or not reported, as it is all conjecture.
- Management consulting fees—you might choose to add them in or leave them out.
- How you report contingent obligations or receivables, guaranteed sales, product on consignment, services on consignment, will change the picture accordingly.

On a personal level, it is a little harder to adjust your financial picture, as there are fewer opportunities; but the largest asset most individuals have is their home, and this can reflect a huge swing. When the real estate market is depressed, we can assess home values a corresponding percentage lower if we choose. If we choose to ignore the temporary market swing and hold on to historical values, we can fall back onto higher appraisals.

If we are not intending to sell but just valuing, there is no reason why we cannot use an older appraisal done prior to the market decline since we all know it will return to previous values in due time; thus reporting it artificially low because of a temporary decline in the market swing is a decision one can make either way.

Environmental issues, buried oil tanks, a swelling brook running behind your home, asbestos shingles, can destroy value if evaluated and reported, and on it goes. The skilled craftsman will probe, ask, and uncover the various issues and choices one can make and deliver either the higher, lower, or mid-range financial picture you may want, depending upon your goals and the purpose of the financial presentation.

The question is to whom are you presenting, what is the purpose, and what must you accomplish in your presentation. Then disclose in your best interest.

## Hold Your Accountant Accountable

Many business owners seem resigned to the fact that their accountant is a good guy but a little behind the times. Not very aggressive, does not provide any tax planning, gives little instruction on financial issues, provides no business advice. Your accountant is really nothing more than an old habit who does your tax return annually. The first you know anything about your financial condition is when you pick up the tax return and look at it, not really understanding what your accountant did, which was precious little anyway.

Typically you look at the gross revenue line and the tax owed and mutter a few thoughts and that's it. When I ask a potential client what annual revenues will be and am told, "I dunno. I find out when I pick up my tax returns from my accountant," I know that person has problems.

This is not everyone's experience, but it is probably that of many small business owners. Hold your accountant accountable for the services you need.

Here are just some of the services your accountant should provide to you:

1. Understand and recommend company legal structure. An accountant should understand your business and determine what the best form of organization is for you and your business, whether or not it is an LLC, an S corp, a C corp, or a simple proprietorship.

2. Recommend all available tax deductions. All available deductions should be taken including home office, travel and entertainment, and so on. When your accountant does not want to take that deduction for you because it's an audit flag, fire him or her immediately. If Congress provides you with an opportunity to take a deduction, take it.

3. Implement cost-savings tax strategies. Adding family members to your LLC to spread out income, making certain that IRAs and 401(k)s are implemented and money is being saved efficiently and cost effectively, and a plethora of other tax saving strategies must be considered.

4. Conduct periodic account reviews. Most important, a good accountant would want to review your books a few times a year to make certain that loans by principals are being paid back without payroll tax deductions, rather than being ignored, and to head off issues before they become problems.

5. Provide business advice. If you're losing money, an accountant should be able to advise you on how and where to stem the losses.

6. Always pay and file taxes on time, unless it's unavoidable; if that's the case, file proper extensions. An accountant should never allow the client to not pay or file taxes. While this may not be a factor the accountant can control, he or she should make every effort to advise the client appropriately and urge compliance.

7. Provide monthly or quarterly reports and explain what they indicate about the business. An accountant should ask for or prepare for the client financial reports monthly or quarterly and review them with the client, explaining what they mean and what is happening with the business.

8. Audit the checkbook for proper business use only. An accountant should make certain that the corporate checkbook is not being used as a personal checkbook and that spouses or secretaries are not deemed responsible parties for tax purposes.

9. Provide expert counsel when dealing with the IRS. Your accountant should lead you through the resolution process with the IRS should you fall into default, taking you to the meetings, protecting your interests, and filing the appropriate forms required to resolve and reduce tax debt.

10. Protect personal assets. The accountant should make certain personal assets are protected from the high risk of being in business.

11. Prepare and present loan applications. Your accountant should help you prepare and present loan applications to banks for lines of credit and borrowing.

12. Advise and assist in preparing a business plan and cash flow pro forma. Your accountant should help you create the business plans and cash flow pro forma required for management as well as for the banks.

13. Make certain that adequate cash controls are being implemented.

14. Advise and assist with closing your business. If your business is failing and is unable to respond successfully and meet the challenge head-on, your accountant should lead the way to liquidating and shutting it down, properly and effectively protecting the owners from additional losses.

15. Advise you on partnership relationships.

And on and on the list can go.

If you see your accountant once a year to pick up your taxes, that person is not doing what he or she should be doing and thus you need a new one. There are many excellent accountants willing to do the job the right way.

Too expensive you say? How much is success worth versus failure? Pay little, get no support, and go out of business . . . that's expensive. Have an accountant who will guide you to success—that's a bargain at any cost.

## Why Are You Paying So Much in Taxes?

Here is a statistic that will make you mad: 55 percent of the big business corporations in this country pay no taxes at all. Did they make a profit? Well, that depends on how you look at it. The real question is whether they make taxable income. The answer for these tax-avoidance companies is decidedly no! Worse yet, if you look at what corporate America contributes to the tax collector, the statistics are amazingly low.

They pay large fees for expert tax advice that saves them a fortune, while we at the lower end of the ladder, the small business owners, pay far more than our fair share.

Another factor involved in this unbalanced situation is that frequently it costs money to make money. Beyond merely paying for expert advice on how to organize to pay less of a tax on earned income, many sophisticated maneuvers that result in lower taxes are costly to implement and thus are out of reach of the average small business owner.

Having discussed this matter with many small business owners, I believe at the heart of this issue is the reluctance of accountants to be real tax advisors and to help their small business clients arrange their business to take advantage of strategies that would allow for a lower tax bill. I see many, many accountants merely take the numbers from the client off their QuickBooks files and dump them into a tax preparation program and out comes the bill. No planning, no real review, no reconsideration.

I still see accountants who are afraid to advise their clients to take home office expenses and other traveling and entertainment allocations. They say to their clients that they do not want to trigger an audit, and so their clients overpay. Their rationale does not make sense, yet I hear this all too frequently.

> **I still see accountants who are afraid to advise their clients to take home office expenses and other traveling and entertainment allocations.**

When asked, the accountants usually say something about keeping their bill affordable because their clients really do not want to pay for tax advice and planning. Small business owners say they want to pay as little as possible to get their tax return done, and so they shop price, not service.

In the end, it is the responsibility of the small business owners to achieve the best bottom-line results they can. Paying a larger-than-necessary tax bill is not conducive to that goal. In short, there is no reason to stick with your accountant even though he or she has done your taxes for 20 years, knows you and your business, and charges little for the service. It is time to get smart. Shop and pay for competent tax planning advice, not after the year is over but in the beginning of the year when you can implement strategies to yield the best results.

You work far too hard and risk far too much to end the year paying a larger percentage of your profits to the government than you are obligated to. Let's take a lesson from the big guys: Pay for and enjoy the benefits of sophisticated tax planning. It works, it pays for itself many times over, and it is not about stretching the code and living in risk; it is about using the code and paying less.

## You May Not Have to Pay Taxes on Your Paycheck

Here is one common piece of advice often overlooked by accountants who fail to provide their clients with the level of business, accounting, and tax advice they require. Some accountants say their clients did not ask for the advice. Too few seem to understand the responsibility an accountant has to consult meaningfully and provide their clients information and strategies that would lead them into safer, more secure business practice.

Here is a very common practice that I am certain many accountants see and choose not to comment on.

**When You Lend Your Company Money.** Many business owners invest sizable amounts of cash into the business. Sometimes the loan is one major investment, or frequently it is many smaller ones; other times it's a slow but steady flow of personal capital into the business to prop it up when required, covering low spots in the cash flow, investing in inventory, covering payroll, or whatever the emergency may be.

This may be categorized as a loan from the owner to the business and should be accompanied with a note with interest and an attempt to pay the note back. Yet, instead, during the ensuing months, the owner takes out payroll, which is taxed heavily and paid for by both the business and the employee, in this case the owner.

Instead, the accountant could have classified the paycheck as a return of borrowed money, which is a nontaxable event and not subject to payroll deductions or contributions by either the individual or the business, a huge 15 percent savings at least. Filing a 941-X can repair this issue, but is infrequently done.

Better yet, when things get tough, cash is scarce, and the owner has invested, for example, over a hundred thousand dollars and has taken out a hundred thousand dollars in payroll over two years, the accountant could file the appropriate paperwork to reclassify the payroll and have the sizable amount of taxes paid returned to the employee.

Why would an accountant fail to instruct a client that a better way of accounting for loans from the owner to the business exists, which follows the code exactly and converts a heavily taxed transaction, payroll, into a nontaxable event, a loan payback? Make sure your accountant knows you expect this kind of advice.

 # Payroll
# Essentials

## Designing an Effective Commission Rate

It is a huge stumbling block for many business owners to determine the right commission rate for a particular job. The objective for establishing an equitable commission rate is as follows:

- Generate the most revenue possible for the business.
- Allow the employee to earn an appropriate income without overpaying.
- Provide the employee with the opportunity to earn well beyond if performance is exceptional by using incentive-based compensation.

Many business owners throw up their hands in despair over this issue, exclaiming, "I have no idea how to figure this out," and so they don't. The worst thing you can possibly do is have a sales force paid by salary and not earn by commissions. Such a plan is guaranteed to yield the lowest possible result at the highest possible cost. Paying salespeople less than the going market rate is folly; paying them more but based on sales is a win-win. Paying employees based on their productivity is the best and only way to go. Here are some thoughts that may make it a bit easier for you to create a meaningful commission rate that works for both employees and the company.

All salespeople should be on commission. However, a base pay frequently accompanies the commission to support cash flow during dry spells when sales are scarce, which can happen. Providing a base pay also shows that the company is investing in its salespeople and that the salespeople are, in fact, employees, not independent contractors in business for themselves. It also gives the company the right to control the salespeople's time and effort and the rules they must abide by.

Set the base pay first. It should be bare subsistence—just enough to hold someone together. Thus, $18,000, $24,000, and $36,000 are good base salaries, depending upon what the anticipated annual compensation will be. This base pay entitles you to require certain cooperation that is slightly outside of direct selling but within an employee–employer relationship, such as training others, completing paperwork requirements, responding to complaints, and attending sales meetings.

Determine what the high-end earning potential should be, for example: $78,000, $98,000, $150,000, whatever you deem reasonably possible for the job, but high. Create a commission rate based on 3 to 7 percent of gross sales that will potentially yield that range of income. Only pay commission on the net, not on shipping costs or taxes.

If invoices are on high-priced products or services, then commissions can be lower. If low priced, then the opposite may be true. Of course, even when the item price is low, if gross sales are large, then again lower the rate to yield the appropriate results. You should also look hard at your profit percentages, and based on how profitable the pricing is, you may have to adjust the commissions up or down.

Make certain you pay commissions at least monthly, not quarterly, and let the sales force ripple with energy and commitment in anticipation of receiving valuable commissions. Presumably the salespeople will achieve greater productivity, more new sales, and higher invoice sales based on their desire to earn more commissions. It works amazingly well. Most important is to make a significant part of the paycheck the commission, so that the employees get it—they are working for success, not for hours spent, and are rewarded for success, not time.

You can require minimum sales volume, and the sales projections will be reached, and the company will run well with adequate cash and profitability.

If you are setting pay for production workers, sales managers, or any other jobs other than direct sales, then consider a higher-percentage salary and a lower-incentive pay, which should be based on the particular part of the business. Find a way to measure productivity within the respective departments and then peg the commission rate to that key indicator.

It could be production figures or whatever is most relevant and easily measurable and applicable to a person's job. When at a loss for a specific measure, peg the commission rate to production, sales volume, profitability, or other business ratios that make sense to everyone.

The best business model has everyone on commission-based income that is based on gross revenue or production goals, and then the whole workforce will pull together to achieve the overall goal ... success for the company and success for themselves. That's the goal, not individual performance but the whole team pulling together to achieve company goals. It's a great thing if everyone earns more than industry standards as long as it's based on success.

> **The best business model has everyone on commission-based income that is based on gross revenue or production goals.**

Gone are the days where everyone earns a paycheck based on hours. Earnings must be based on productivity. Once you commit to it, however, you cannot go back, and there is a transition period that may be difficult. It may cause established employees to leave, and new people will enter, which is OK. It is the best thing you can do to increase revenues and profit simultaneously.

## No More Overtime ... There Is a Better Way

To many business owners, overtime is a badge of success and points to a smart businessperson. It says, "We have so much demand that we will resolve this huge demand for productivity by paying our help time-and-a-half to work over 40 hours ... aren't we successful!"

This makes no sense at all. It is bad management and results in low productivity. Now there may be a time and place for overtime, but I am just not sure where and when that may be. You should be increasing productivity or hiring additional help, but not paying overtime to complete orders.

Let me define overtime: rewarding your employees for not producing enough during the 40 hours allocated, which is both possible and a reasonable expectation. It means paying your workers extra to work slower.

Productivity is the issue, not how little we can pay the employees. Paying people more to produce less is not a way to increase productivity. It's a way to give your employees more of your profits than they deserve. I have visited too many businesses where the owners adore their employees, claiming they are the best. However, they could not produce an additional widget if they tried, and, yes, frequently resort to overtime to get the job done. They argue, "That's to be expected, and it's better than overemploying, having too many workers."

I have done so many productivity studies that I can tell you the results now, without having to do one more. Most of America works at the productivity rate of 30 to 45 percent. At best you are getting 20 to 30 minutes out of every hour in meaningful production.

> **Most of America works at the productivity rate of 30 to 45 percent. At best you are getting 20 to 30 minutes out of every hour in meaningful production.**

This is not to say your employees are purposefully working slower than they could or producing less than possible. It is to say, however, that with concepts such as overtime and hourly wages, you are training them to work slowly and rewarding them to produce less.

What does work? An incentive-based reward system. It works well for increasing productivity and has more advantages.

First, if properly designed and implemented, productivity will increase by one-third or more. This means profits increase dramatically, and some of the increased profit is returned to the employees as a reward for outproducing the stated objectives or current standards. Both the company and the workers make more.

Second, improved productivity occurs without investing an additional dollar, an additional employee, or additional machinery, and without overtime. In fact, if you can trim the payroll by reducing the number of employees and then, at the same time, hit the accelerator with incentive rewards, you will find that you can outproduce prior benchmarks with fewer employees. Now, that works ... with everyone onboard, pulling together, earning more when extra profit is made and less when it isn't. That's fair.

Third, you have the opportunity to detail a number of additional directives into your incentive-based reward system, such as quality workmanship—all of which contribute to your bottom line, better quality of life in the business, and greater employee retention and longevity of your business.

Other benefits include less absenteeism, increased skill, better attitude, more peer training, a happier crew, better customer relations, fewer mistakes, higher-quality workmanship, cleaner, and whatever you want your business to be. When enforced by the requirements of participating in the reward system, it will happen. When your work requirements become part of your incentive-based reward system, you will achieve them. It's a career path, not a job. It is also a team effort if incentives are designed properly.

But many prefer to pay overtime, proudly, believing it is a mark of excellence that you have that much business that you must overpay to have it completed.

## How Much Revenue to Allocate for Payroll

This is a critical evaluation that any business owner can figure out and understand. Payroll tends to be one of the largest line items on your expense side, and is a payable every week or every other week, with taxes to contribute and sometimes other add-ons such as insurance, vacation pay, and sick pay. It frequently is the Achilles heel of the overhead side of the business, the single item that can make or break a business operation.

Since operating profiles of businesses are all different, there is no one correct number that makes or breaks a business operation. In fact, the degree of profitability and other functions of the business will help determine the correct ratio of payroll to gross revenue.

The percentage of your employees' productivity is the most important number and is the amount of production your employees give the business per hour, measured by the output divided by employee cost. Productivity is a variable that can be influenced by management efforts.

The gross percentage of payroll as compared with the gross revenue is the ratio that will begin to tell you if you are in trouble or on the right path. A great place to be in that ratio range is 20 to 30 percent.

For example, if you have 20 employees and your gross annual payroll is $500,000, the gross annual revenue for the corporation is $1.9 million. Dividing the gross annual payroll by the gross annual revenue yields 26 percent. So the ratio of employee output to revenue is a healthy 26 percent.

I see many businesses that tip the scale at over 50 percent, and, yes, this is a business that is always in trouble. Businesses that run in the 20 to 30 percent range tend to be successful, at least from the payroll point of view.

I see many business owners fooling themselves because either they do not include themselves in the equation or they take no paycheck and thus the payroll numbers are artificially low. Another trick business owners use to fix the numbers is they define their personal revenue as owner's draw and thus do not count it in the payroll equation, artificially lowering the number.

The ratio is only an indicator. The real issue is what the business owner does about the number. Most have no idea how to reduce their payroll and maintain or increase productivity. Therein is the real secret for success: reducing payroll and increasing individual and, thus, over-all productivity. There are a number of ways to accomplish this, but first you need to learn how to identify the red zone and then figure out what to do about it if it is higher than 30 percent.

Take the test and compute the ratio of your payroll cost—the real cost, including yourself, the taxes, and all the add-ons—against the gross revenue. If the number is high, you must correct the ratio or fail-ure is likely. Too high a payroll is one of the most common reasons busi-nesses fail.

## What to Do When You Can't Make Payroll

So you can't make payroll. This happens. Payroll comes every week or every other week, relentlessly. Along with payroll come taxes and other contributions, which often include medical insurance and 401(k) accounts.

Missing payroll is a horrible experience.

So many business owners fight all week to make payroll on Friday and sometimes must ask the employees to wait until Monday or even wait another week to cash or deposit. It happens far more frequently than you might guess.

When our economy is melting down resulting in rapidly reducing revenues, receivables being stretched out, and costs increasing, many business owners who have never confronted it before will be forced to deal with this most difficult matter of not making payroll.

So what can you do to best handle this situation?

If done appropriately, you will not experience a mass walkout, as many business owners fear or believe will occur. Most employees will understand and will work with you, if the matter is handled properly.

Communicate, as soon as possible. Reduce the stress and the waiting from the employees' minds, as most certainly they will know before you tell them. They will be waiting and watching to see what you do and how you handle it. Earlier notice allows their pain and anger to subside a bit, and they can prepare as best as they can.

This will also reduce the pain and frustration you are experiencing and reduce the matter to a workable situation with information and communication, a plan that outlines the solution, the response, as soon as possible.

Do it yourself. *Do not* assign this responsibility to a manager or staffer. As the owner, you should stand before your employees and tell them the situation. You must accept the responsibility for the failure; it's your problem, your job.

> **Tell them that you are most sympathetic and appreciate their sacrifices and the issues this creates for them and their families.**

Tell them why the payroll is late; tell them when it will be good. Also explain to them that you're not taking any cash out. Tell them you are doing everything you possibly can to alter this situation. Tell them what they can expect in the future even if it is not good. Tell them that you are most sympathetic and appreciate their sacrifices and the issues this creates for them and their families.

If possible, take whatever cash is available and divide it out, $50 or $100 per person, with everyone getting the same amount, gas money to get home or whatever priority need, and do not deduct the amount from their paychecks when it is time to distribute them. Ask your people to work with you and help overcome the issues, and tell them how much you appreciate their sacrifice. Pay everyone the same amount of pocket money irrespective of normal differences in paychecks.

If you do this, a few things will occur:

Most will cooperate, and the few that you lose will probably be best for the company as they are identifying themselves as expendable, non-team players. In fact, it will reduce the next payroll without having to fire one more person.

If you tell the truth and keep all the employees informed, demonstrating respect and concern as well as sharing the appropriate information for them to understand your predicament, in the end your employees will be more loyal, more empowered, and more satisfied with their job. They will accept any immediate changes that are required, including downsizing, removing perks, lowering pay, forgoing bonuses.

If you make the visible and immediate moves and have an impact on your bottom line, your employees will be more accepting, cooperative, and supportive. Even firing their friends and coworkers will demonstrate your commitment. Most of your employees will stay and work hard to help turn the business around.

> If you make the visible and immediate moves and have an impact on your bottom line, your employees will be more accepting, cooperative, and supportive.

If it happens again, your employees will be better able to deal with it. As long as you make progress and change is clear and you tell them the truth as soon as possible, your employees will remain loyal and will work for a promise.

Make certain you keep your word; make no promises that you cannot keep. If you do break your word or promise, you will soon see massive abandonment because trust will be gone. Do this and you will survive missing a payroll, or more.

## Are You Taking a Paycheck? Why?

Sounds like a silly question, but it's quite serious. Are you taking a paycheck? Most of you will say yes, others will say occasionally, some just draw cash when they need it, and some say they take nothing now but will some day.

I further imagine that all small business owners invest in or lend some money to their business, be it cash, through credit cards, or even borrowed money. Even those who say they did not invest or lend any cash, if challenged, admit they dip their hands into their pocket for gas, supplies, business lunches, and so on and never get repaid; after years it may be many thousands of incidental investing or lending.

So here is the choice that your accountant forgot to tell you about.

If you inject some cash into your business, say $50,000, you are entitled to classify it as a loan, not an investment. Especially if you expect to get it back, which you probably do, you are entitled to be repaid, which is not a taxable event. Thus, the businessperson mentioned above who lent $50,000 can withdraw $50,000 without taking taxes out, saving about 15 percent in payroll taxes, which is $7,500, a sizable expense or a meaningful saving.

I recommend that you create a paper trail, including a note to you from the company, that you record paybacks as they happen, and that you add interest so it appears to be a legitimate lending relationship. A board of directors vote, noted in their minutes, makes it totally supportable and defendable if audited. This is important, because if the IRS claims that it's an investment, not a loan, you lose the tax-free opportunity, and it becomes a taxable event. Document the lending even if it occurred years ago. Do not back-date; just record the event and date when executed.

This principle also covers immediate family—your children and spouse. So if they lend, you can repay any of your immediate family members and declare it a payback of a loan and thus nontaxable.

# Chapter 15

 # Partners and Franchises

## 50-50 Partnership Structuring Strategies

I counsel those contemplating a 50-50 partnership on how to structure the design to avoid the natural pitfalls that will occur in such a relationship if entered into unprepared. I also advise them on how to protect their interests.

Here are a few strategies that will work when confronted with such a proposition:

- Using an LLC as an organizational format, which I highly recommend, as it offers quite a bit of flexibility, you can allocate the beneficial interests in a different proportion than the ownership interest split. In other words, you can have a 50-50 ownership split and split profits by another ratio, favoring the money investor or the managing partner or any partner you prefer. This can also be changed quite easily and as frequently as desired. In all other organizational formats the beneficial interest parallels the financial interest and cannot be easily changed or changed at all without changing the 50-50 ratio.
- You can allocate the distribution of losses in an LLC differently than the distribution of profits. This can also be changed at will.
- One partner may be the managing director, but the minority partner or partners can control the vote for all management decisions. This

can be modified to apply to specific types of decisions made by vote, or the partners decide without the manager voting at all, and thus protect a specific matter that one party wants to control. The reverse is also true; you can vest the power in the managing director, taking any decision making completely away from the members. Once again this can be changed easily and frequently by those with the power to vote this type of change.

The answer is all in the design of the entity. Careful design can create an organizational format that satisfies everyone involved; even a 50-50 partnership can be controlled successfully by these strategies. If this fails to satisfy some party to the deal, a proxy controlling one's right to vote can be transferred, effectively changing the voting power.

You can design any result into the organizational format; it's a classic matter of form over function, or is it function over form? Take your pick.

I believe function over form is the way to go, especially in designing unique organizations that satisfy the needs of the individuals investing and working in the business.

## The 50-50 Recipe for Disaster and What to Do About It

I see this issue frequently on both ends of the spectrum, before there is a problem and after. Two friends enter into a business agreement and decide to share ownership and decision making 50-50, and herein lies the foundation of a problem.

Most of the time, the potential pitfalls of such a decision are not even considered; it is just believed that 50-50 is the fair way to go without seeing the trap this creates for the unwary. Further, even if there are internal feelings regarding who should have more say, it's easier, as it seems fairer, to resolve these issues with little or no confrontation by settling on an even split. Who can say it is not fair, we all think, and this decision avoids difficult discussions.

No two partners can ever agree on everything, especially important issues. I urge you to design a more sophisticated organizational format, one that will satisfy everyone's needs and allow for reasonable problem solving and decision making when the time comes.

First of all, this issue should only occur regarding material decisions, the sell, buy, borrow, merge, and close issues that affect the value and mission of the business, the really important matters, those that should be resolved at the highest level, the board of directors' level. All operational matters should be broken into departments and decided at that level. The make-or-break issues, which cause lawsuits or liquidation, are for the co-owners. It may be easier to resolve this matter if the partners recognize that each is responsible for, and thus in control of, his or her department area on an operational basis. This will typically focus power struggles on the larger issues and an easier agreement to make and support.

I understand the respect demonstrated by and ease of entering into a 50-50 ownership and decision-making relationship. It seems like the right thing to do, mutual hard work and respect, doing it together, sharing the good, the bad, and the ugly equally. It's a great concept, but it seldom works well in real life, as it is unrealistic to expect that every important business decision will be agreed on.

Marriages are 50-50, and look how difficult it is to keep one going. Partnerships share this same quality. Certainly, different issues are involved, but there is something to be learned through observation. A business needs to have a clear decision-making procedure; there needs to be a tiebreaker or final decision process when disagreement exists—especially disagreements about large, important decisions that really matter—or nothing will ever get done.

> Most often it's the cash that is respected the most, and the one who brings the most cash into the business is typically given the control of the final decision, 51 to 49 percent.

Frequently, there is a disproportionate investment of time, capital, credit, assets, or skill by the business partners. No relationship is ever exactly 50-50. Most often it's the cash that is respected the most, and the one who brings the most cash into the business is typically given the control of the final decision, 51 to 49 percent.

When push comes to shove regarding important material decisions, decisions that both partners should have input into, one partner, the money partner, can vote his extra 2 percent, the controlling factor presumably affording that partner an opportunity to protect his investment and resolve the issue to his satisfaction, protecting his money interest.

This path respects the importance of the cash investment, without which no business entity would ever be launched. I understand the value and power of sweat equity; but in the end, in today's business environment, cash is king.

Therefore, point one, 50-50 business ownership relationships should be avoided. Someone must have the ultimate final word, tiebreaker status.

In fact, the law has terms and procedures for resolving this situation as follows: In a 50-50 relationship of ownership interests, when the partners disagree on material issues, if the business is incapable of moving forward because of this material disagreement, it is therefore at an impasse. In such situations, the court decision will be an orderly liquidation of the assets for the benefit of the shareholders.

This is always a disaster for everyone, the worst possible conclusion, to be avoided at all costs. But this can become inevitable if the power and authority are shared 50-50 and there is no agreement about important matters, as the business can no longer be effectively run.

What about fairness and equity, I hear you ask?

One of the advantages of organizing under the laws and operating agreement of an LLC is that profit and loss as well as capital gains can be shared differently from decision making. You could have a 50-50 profit split but a 51-49 decision-making split. The agreement can be structured in many different ways, but the result is that one person has final control, and so there will be no deadlocks, as there will always be a tiebreaker. While not a complete answer for the frequently implemented 50-50 deal, sharing profit equally and decision making unequally is the best compromise one can make.

## The Danger of Co-Owners Comanaging

There are many bad habits that frequently evolve out of partner relationships in the business environment. One of the worst is the issue of shared decision making. Another aspect of this unsuccessful strategy is the frequently usurped decision-making authority, done when convenient. Both management styles must be identified and rooted out, as they will surely lead to disaster. I see it in two specific situations.

First, when a husband and wife team or other co-owners decide to run a business together, as co-presidents, co-CEOs or co-anything, even cosignatories on the checkbook, it's all very dangerous.

Second, sometimes two equal partners run a business with clear organizational boundaries, but they choose to jump their boundaries and usurp authority to make random decisions outside of their pre-scribed organizational authority, because they are a partner and can.

Here is what happens: Because of the concept of co-ownership, or shared leadership, there is this sense of equal empowerment. After all, he is a half owner, co-CEO, and the husband, or partner, so he can jump in and make whatever decision he may feel is appropriate at the moment.

You'll find yourself in endless discussions trying to reach a mutually agreeable conclusion. When the co-owners have different views, they may force compromise, which waters down the right decision into something inappropriate as well as deliberating far too long. Usually, the decision making is far too public with no clear leadership. To the employees it feels as though the company is run by ad hoc committee meetings to work out simple decisions.

This leads to inconsistent management, inconsistent orders, a change of directions midstream, and confusing communications, leaving employees in a quandary about what to do and whom to follow. So they do nothing, or worse, they play one boss against the other; nothing productive gets accomplished.

> There can never be a co-owner in a coleadership position under any circumstances, as it will not and cannot ever work.

This must not be allowed to happen; there can never be a co-owner in a coleadership position under any circumstances, as it will not and cannot ever work, especially if there is an outside relationship such as a marital one or a relationship of any sort; there always needs to be a clear definition of who is in charge, who makes what decisions regarding what areas of responsibility. There cannot ever be two authority figures equal and available.

The solutions are obvious although implementation is sometimes difficult. Despite partnership relationships or ownership sharing, the organizational lines must be clearly established and intensely respected. A usurping of authority or co-decision making cannot be allowed. It will only cause a breakdown in leadership and a destruction of the business process.

There can and should be manager meetings during which differences of opinion can be explored, but in the end the lead manager's decision must be respected at all times.

This sets the stage for a divide-and-conquer action by mischievous employees who would exploit this management weakness for their own benefits. It further creates competition for control of the decision-making process and wreaks havoc with the company.

> **There can and should be manager meetings during which differences of opinion can be explored, but in the end the lead manager's decision must be respected at all times.**

It goes back to effectively designing the management organizational plan and committing to it, so the partners have clearly defined positions and work within the boundaries of their job description, deferring to the other managers who are responsible for other decisions in other areas of the business. If anyone is taking action counter to this, stop it immediately.

## 50-50 Partner Buyouts

Most frequently, partners in a small business are very close friends or family or are in long-term, trusted sweat equity business relationships. Perhaps one of the most difficult challenges confronting this relationship is how to break it up when the time is right. There are always many emotional issues to work out, but you can find the right balance in how you accomplish the buyout and determine the price and terms. If they are fair, the relationship and the business have a chance of surviving. If they are not, more than likely, either the buyout will not occur at all or the relationship will end, with a long-term, very negative air and a huge personal loss as well a strong likelihood the business will suffer or cease to operate.

Partnerships break up for many reasons—some personal, some financial, some ego driven. When breakup happens, two important goals must be achieved:

1. Preservation of the business
2. Preservation of the relationship

Here is a way to resolve this difficult transition safely and respectfully for both partners in a buyout situation.

The deal must be fair for both sides. If adequate consideration is paid and the process is not injurious to the players, and if the terms of the payoff are agreeable to both sides, then everyone will survive even if there are a few ruffled feathers.

The devastation and destruction so frequently associated with partnership breakups can be overcome if a buyout plan is established in the beginning of the relationship, as long as everyone agrees on it at the onset. When a breakup occurs and the plan must be used, all the parties will remember they already agreed to this process, it was fair when they agreed, and so it must be fair now, which means disagreement is less likely to occur.

I have a strategy that either partner can invoke, knowing the potential consequences; thus it is only utilized if the partner is truly ready. Here is the deal, simple and honest. Everyone wins, but no one knows who will be the surviving partner until the strategy is played out.

First, it is important that both partners have a full grasp of the numbers: the asset value, goodwill value, accounts receivable, accounts payable, an income statement, and a balance sheet.

Then the partner 1, who wants to buy out partner 2, makes an offer. The offer had best be as high as is reasonable because if partner 2 chooses, she can turn around and use that offer price to opt to buy out partner 1, who tended the original offer.

Partner 1 can up the ante and offer more, but the game is over. Partner 2 has now exercised her option and made a turnaround offer with the same number that is now binding on partner 1. Partner 2 may, however, now choose to either accept the new counteroffer so partner 1 gets the company or demand that partner 1 accept her turned-around offer at the original offer price and be bought out. This process creates equality, is respectful, and assures fair value for the partner being bought out, whichever one it may be.

In addition, at the beginning when this plan is agreed to, the terms of the deal are also agreed to. And since no one ever has cash, and to make certain the two partners can both implement the buyout, the agreement further states that the bought-out partner will accept a note for 5 years at 8 percent interest payable monthly, or whatever terms were agreed to at the inception of the plan.

This works. The offering price by the first partner is high because the offering partner knows if it's too low, the other will buy him out for that price. If the offer is high enough, the other partner may accept it; either way it's respectful, affordable, and a win for both.

The business and the relationship can be spared the destruction, which so often occurs. If you have a 50-50 relationship and have not considered exit strategies for an individual partner, add this strategy at your next board meeting.

## Joint-Venture Magic

There exists an excellent path that will deliver additional revenues and greater profitability as well as improving your visibility, client list, and long-term viability and with minimal cash expended. It's called a joint venture.

Think about it—not a long-term partnership, although it could be, no legal entanglements and protracted contracts, no inventory increase, no additional advertising necessary, although it may help, and lots of potential new business and new customers.

Consider creating joint ventures with companies that are symbiotic to yours, providing an add-on service or product to sell to your existing clients while your joint-venture partner provides all the development and inventory to support your additional marketing efforts and sales.

> **Consider creating joint ventures with companies that are symbiotic to yours, providing an add-on service or product to sell to your existing clients.**

For example, let's say you're selling bicycles. Why not create a joint venture with a clothing company or retail store to put in a line of clothing suitable for a bicycle rider that would attract sales without additional investment? The joint-venture partner has already made the huge investment and has inventory ready to sell.

The joint-venture partner could be either vertical or horizontal; it makes no difference. Just so long as it is somehow associated with the same customer as you currently service, you can attract increased sales without additional investment or risk.

Better yet, your joint-venture partner is doing the same thing with your line of goods, adding your line to its marketing program with you providing product and resources for them. It works two ways: Both expand each other's market, client list, and gross sales with a higher net profitability, and neither costs much additional capital, development time, or effort.

If it works for you, continue. If it fails, you withdraw. No profit split, no equity split, no issues, just mutually beneficial alliances that yield greater profitability and additional gross revenue.

Each adds to the other's advertising and marketing efforts, and both get a real hit without it costing each other one penny more. By using the same ad space with additional product, it doubles the impact at no additional cost—another win-win for both joint ventures.

All that is required is imagination to figure out what works together and whom to work with, what products and what business; then put it together. Use each other's inventory and sales efforts and away you go.

It may sound complicated, but it really isn't. Have your lawyer draft a joint-venture agreement before you start, just to make certain everyone is on the same page, and then try it out. There is no reason why you cannot have many joint ventures going at once. It works.

## Franchise Not Working? Get Out!

Unfortunately, I talk with far too many disappointed franchise operators, but *disappointed* is far too soft a word; how about *decimated* franchise owners. Disappointed and financially wiped out, they've been preyed on by one-sided agreements that only work for the franchise company.

I see from 5 to 14 percent of gross revenues as royalties! This is irrespective of whether or not the franchisee is making any money and even if it is experiencing major losses. The franchisee is forced to pay a huge amount to the franchise company every month. It's not right.

Often the franchise company's promises are unfulfilled, broken, or unable to be performed. I see no advertising support, and the projections and promises that are made are grossly inadequate and hardly likely to be fulfilled; yet the franchise company gets its royalty check every month, no matter what.

I also understand that franchise holders are afraid to break the contract, believing they are impossible to break. Not necessarily so. I have broken numerous one-sided agreements, which were supported by teams of their lawyers.

Yes, the impossible-to-break contracts can be severed, sold back, transferred, or ceased. You need the determination, experience, and know-how to do it. Hire a professional to break the contract and free your business from this tyrannical yoke.

 **Protection Strategies**

## Are You Protecting Your Customers' Deposits?

After a customer pays to buy a product, many companies purchase the product to fulfill the order but then hold it for some time rather than shipping immediately. The reasons vary. For example, some businesses base delivery on other production schedules or cannot deliver until they install another product first. Perhaps the item must be ordered but that requires payment first. So the business holds the customer's deposit and orders the product. If your business has such a relationship with customers, then you need to know how to handle the situation.

I talk about this because there are many businesses going under. When the IRS, banks, or vendors attach a business with liens, the question is, what happens to the customers' deposits and products they paid for but have not yet received?

This issue is important because a creditor seizing customer deposits on a product or products not yet delivered could lead to breaches of law. Here is what you must do to protect both you and your customers:

1. When you receive the customer deposit, do not deposit it into the general operating cash fund. Segregate it into a specific customer

deposit account held separately and not used for anything other than purchasing the product it was intended for. This begins to establish the rights of the customer beyond those of the business, the bank, the IRS, or whoever may be making claims against your general cash fund.

2. Once the product is ordered and arrives on site to be held for the customer until it is appropriate to install or deliver, the item should be segregated from the general inventory area and held in the "customer-owned product area" clearly labeled with appropriate signage.

3. The specific box or item must be labeled with the customer's name and specify that it belongs to the person, for example, "owned by customer Joe Brown."

Then if you are defaulting on a loan, the customer's product will be protected, as you have done everything appropriate to isolate and identify it as a customer product. So even if the IRS or another creditor is levying or placing a lien or attachment, or you go out of business and close your doors, the creditors who sweep in looking for anything to liquidate to cover their defaulted receivables, or note payment, or tax payment, will not be able to touch the customer's deposit or product.

This plan will afford you the best possible defense to protect your customer's deposits or product against being considered part of your general fund. It protects you, your customers, and the product from inappropriate seizure and liquidation, and it eliminates a dangerous and costly defense against a customer's claim of theft or larceny.

Contractors and stores of all sorts are experiencing downturns in their businesses and may face liquidation while holding customer deposits or product. Yes, it is more work to label and segregate the product, but it should be done. It's one thing to lose your money; it's another to lose someone else's money or product.

## Put It in Writing

I recently visited a business with 20 years of successful history, doing much of its business on a "handshake," with an occasional contract typically provided by the other party. "This worked for years," the owner said. "And now as we attempt to collect over a half million dollars from a handful of different contractors," he reluctantly admits, "it does not work anymore."

What is it that's going on? Are people becoming crooks? Are they purposely taking unfair advantage of subcontractors, who do the work and rely on a person's word and handshake? Why do they then refuse or fail to pay based on some trumped-up reason? Is there a trend of excuses, such as misunderstandings, broken communications, intervening circumstances, that somehow makes it OK to break one's word and change the deal after the fact?

I believe the reasons for this happening are probably irrelevant. What is important is that this frequently occurs. While it is possible to reduce and control this problem, eliminating it altogether is difficult although not impossible.

Here is something we all know that works well in protecting one's interests: Reduce every agreement to a written contract. It does not have to be an expensive and lengthy proposition involving lawyers every time. Having a lawyer draft an all-purpose contract that you can use over and over, changing the facts but not the format, will work well enough. Even a simple self-serving memo outlining who does what for what compensation and what terms is adequate to work from and protect your rights, even if it is unsigned by the other party. It's still a memo outlining what you believe the agreement to be at the time it was made and is valuable and could possibly be controlling evidence of the relationship.

This clarifies disputed details, unstated terms and conditions, price, and so on. It's an important act of business preparation and, irrespective of why the problem exists, the best way to prevent many issues from arising. It amazes me how much business is done without a contract or written agreement that outlines commitments and terms. No wonder people end up with different perceptions of what was agreed on.

> It amazes me how much business is done without a contract or written agreement that outlines commitments and terms.

This may have worked before, but it is no longer a viable way to do business. Everything should be reduced to a written document, everything by contract, especially change orders and adjustments to the original deal.

Stop work and create a written document signed by both parties. Do not proceed until all the details are agreed on, especially price, terms, and specific obligations.

There can be no exceptions. Written contract first, change orders before additional work, in writing with terms and conditions and specific obligations in detail.

It keeps honest mistakes from occurring, prevents simple miscommunications, clarifies issues, makes certain there are no misunderstandings for any reason. It assures both parties are in agreement of basic facts.

Unfortunately, dishonest businesspeople will not be controlled by a written agreement, as they will find a way to dispute something indisputable. How to protect against this? A written agreement removes wiggle room and allows for more aggressive collection and possible recovery; without it your case is lost before you start.

Be careful with whom you do business; check history and references; limit your risk to affordable losses if all goes bad. Do not let the debt grow uncomfortably and unaffordably large.

> **Be careful with whom you do business; check history and references; limit your risk to affordable losses if all goes bad.**

When confronting default, jump on it as quickly as possible with counsel, not a collection agency, and not many months later. Respect your terms, and if it's net 30 days, on the thirty-first day you need to be in contact and determine if it's a collection problem. If so, go directly to your lawyer and resolve it. This does not mean you cannot work it out with your client as long as you are attending to the issue. Hopefully, you have added the costs of collection to your invoicing and contracts so your contractor will be paying for the lawyers, not you. The sooner you act, the safer your receivable and the most likely you will be paid.

If your business requires such exposure, then consider internal organizational strategies. In New York City, each taxicab is separately incorporated because of the high risk and likelihood of an accident and ensuing lawsuit. That way, only one cab and its medallion are exposed to risk even though one owner may own a thousand cabs and a thousand medallions. This may not be the best strategy for you, but some attention must be paid to limiting, controlling, and absorbing exposure and potential losses.

Put it in writing and then collect aggressively and promptly, know whom you are doing business with, and limit or control your losses.

## File Your Homestead

Things happen. Businesses going bust, sickness, and divorce are among the many possible unexpected occurrences. Things happen that may result in large debt and an eventual attack on your home equity. It's part of a business owner's life, taking risk, and losing sometimes.

When unexpected events occur, it is important to be prepared. While there is much advice and many strategies are offered on how to deal with these issues, there is a simple way to protect much of the equity in your home, with little effort, and the cost is well under a hundred dollars.

Yet so many have not taken this step. It's called a homestead, and it's a statutory provision that all states have enacted to provide protection of the equity in one's principal place of residence from creditors' attempts to liquidate your home to pay debt. Here's how it works.

You have to file a homestead. Completing this simple document requires you knowing your address and the book and page location of the deed in the local registry of deeds. Your lawyer can find this out quickly and easily, or you can go to your local registry of deeds and a clerk will assist you in finding the information you need.

Here is the good news; it protects $500,000 of equity in Massachusetts and varying amounts elsewhere in the country. No one can penetrate this barrier. Keep in mind it works only against debt acquired after, not before, you file the homestead form.

If you are refinancing your home or acquiring a new home with a new mortgage, the mortgage company will usually require you to either wait to file your homestead or remove your homestead until after it files the deed, and then you can. This way the mortgage company comes before the homestead and thus has full access to your equity in case of foreclosure.

All after-acquired debt is barred from penetrating the homestead, protecting up to a certain amount—for example, $500,000 of equity in Massachusetts. That's it, that's all you have to do. You do not need a lawyer to accomplish this, although most lawyers will handle this for you inexpensively. It's almost free and protects a huge amount of your equity.

## Do Not Operate as a Sole Proprietor or Partnership

This is simple, and yet I see business owners over and over that are operating out of a sole proprietorship or partnership form of organization.

It is so easy to organize as a limited liability corporation, called an LLC, or if you have good reason, as a corporation. Creating an LLC can be done online. You can be protected by this organizational decision in half an hour. Still so many remain unaware and unprotected.

## Benefits of a Corporation Organization

If your partner is your spouse, you are begging to lose the equity in your home and carry debt with you well into the future if the effort fails. It's simple to organize under the protective shield provisions available under either LLC or corporate organizational status. It costs relatively little, and while it requires an additional tax filing, it is worth the protection offered.

Here is why. As a partnership or sole proprietorship, you are personally liable for any debts of the business, including tax liabilities for unpaid payroll taxes, lawsuits—anything. If you have a home and if there is equity in it, the equity is available to your creditors for paying off the business debts.

Since small business is so risky and so frequently fails, it is foolhardy to risk the equity and security provided by a corporate shield or LLC protection. Why assume such additional risk when an organizational decision will protect you?

If you need additional reasons, tax workouts are far more difficult as a sole proprietorship, where many winning strategies not available. In addition, other workout strategies for debt owed to vendors, banks, and so forth are also more difficult. When you are personally liable, all your debts are personally guaranteed, as opposed to them remaining business debts.

## Become a Limited Liability Corporation

Go online and follow the directions: First get your EIN, which is a federal identification number assigned to each business on request, and register as an LLC. Choose taxed as a partnership, and you have the best of all worlds—the tax benefits of a proprietorship or partnership and the protection of a corporate shield. You can have your lawyer or accountant do it for you if you feel uncomfortable doing it yourself..

You will have to change your business identity to announce the existence of an LLC or corporate format. Thus, your stationery, invoices, website, business cards, and so on will all have to be reprinted and changed to reflect the entity choice. You will have to create a new checking account, and since you get a new tax ID number, you get to start your credit history all over again. The insurances and leases must be changed, but in the end it's all worth the effort and additional expense.

## Custom-Designing Bylaws and Operating Agreements

There is a prolific use of standard forms for designing corporate entities. Yet there is a need for more detailed provisions, more personal strategic input of specific requirements, and more control over basic material decisions and procedures beyond the standard forms that many lawyers use.

These standard forms in no way deal with the vast array of specific and detailed requirements a deeper analysis demands. Many business organizations end either because the business failed, or one owner wants out, or one owner wants the other owner out, or the partners reach an impasse over basic disagreements of material issues. At some point, everyone finally looks at the controlling language in the bylaws or the operational agreement to see what it has to say about resolving the issues and realizes, when it's too late, that the issue was never dealt with ahead of time.

The controlling documents should specify specifying how to settle the assets and how to value, pay for, and exit the partnership.

### Issues to Address

Talk to your lawyer about what to include in the bylaws or operational agreement when both owners can agree and no issues exist to distort their vision, when both parties are working toward what seems fair. When an issue arises, the rules are binding, and because everyone has already agreed and deemed them fair, they need not be discussed, reconsidered, or revisited. Thus, you have a path for resolving issues.

Here are some of the issues you and your lawyer should consider:

- How should the invested cash be handled? Will it be debt or equity for all parties or possibly a little of both? Will the debt be convertible to stock if the business takes off and the equity convertible to debt if the business busts? When and on what terms is it repaid if it's debt?
- If there is going to be sweat equity, describe the process that determines the conversion of sweat to equity, including time and values.

- How does one get out of the partnership, and how does the remaining partner buy out the exiting partner? How are the value of the assets and the goodwill of the business determined?
- If there is a buyout, how will the payoff be structured? Will the remaining partner provide financing to the exiting partner?
- What are the majority requirements for various decisions? Will it be by super majority, unanimous vote, or simple majority, which helps minority positions control important votes and decisions?
- What are the restrictions for a partner selling stock to outside parties, including rights of first refusal or even outright restrictions?
- How will you issue stock? How will you handle watering-down-stock issues and decide about issuing and distributing new stock or different classes of stock?
- How will you handle capital calls? What if one partner does not contribute and the other does?
- What are the requirements for agreeing to any material financial decision such as buying, selling, borrowing, or merging?
- What is your agreement for restricting majority management control?

In addition to addressing the above issues, the bylaws or agreement should:

- Ensure that employment contracts with working owners specify term, salary, benefits, and termination policy
- Include specifications for voting rights, proxy rights, and rules to call a meeting to vote on a material issue
- Spell out dividend distribution rules
- Stipulate noncompete rules
- Document the structure of the board of directors and who controls

It's an important concept for all involved, protecting one's rights and installing appropriate systems in advance of issues to support the business's continuity and operation.

The bylaws or agreement also protects individual rights of both the majority and minority owners.

It makes sense to eliminate confusion and prevent avoidable issues and problems. It is cheaper and more efficient than litigating differences of opinion after issues develop that the bylaws or operating agreements could have resolved. Unfortunately, lawyers all too frequently rely on the standard forms. It's easier and cheaper rather than discussing the merits of a more detailed set of agreements.

It will cost more to develop these agreements, but it's worth it in the end since it avoids larger issues and supports logical well-thought-out relationships. Consider this a must-do, and be careful, as the lawyer you use may have loyalties to one owner over the other, and thus, this may skew the technical discussions of corporate design.

> It simply makes sense to eliminate confusion and prevent avoidable issues and problems.

## Litigation Bluff as a Business Tool

Many business owners misunderstand the successful and efficient use of a lawyer when confronting a business problem, say a breach of contract or some other business issue. Many believe you go to a lawyer to litigate. If left to his own devices, that is exactly what the lawyer will set you up to do. At the same time, he will probably tell you results are always unpredictable and charge you a lot of money.

Unfortunately, both the businessperson and the lawyer have missed the potential for a cost-efficient resolution for most business problems. It's called the "litigation bluff," and it works most of the time—not all—but it's worth a try.

The bluff is based on the idea that nobody wants to sue or be sued for many reasons. Here are just four:

1. It's expensive for all parties, the plaintiff and the defendant.
2. It's time consuming.
3. The damages and results are sometimes devastating to either or both parties.
4. It takes way too long to resolve, and you have to pay along the way before anyone knows who the victor will be; the price is very high.

As said so many times, the only winners are the lawyers. It is true that some issues are appropriately resolved through litigation, but most are not. Since it is clear that most, if not all, businesspeople believe the above-stated four realities, we are primed to use the litigation bluff. The bluff works because people know the pitfalls of litigation.

You go to your lawyer with a problem; perhaps your vendor mis-shipped and yet is billing you anyway, or a contract has been broken, whatever. You review the facts with the lawyer, who then recommends a lawsuit. He asks for a $10,000 retainer and tells you to be prepared for another $15,000 prior to trial and an additional $25,000 or more for the trial, and so on.

You say, "All I want is the sternest, nastiest letter imaginable sent to the would-be defendant restating the facts and the likely outcome should you be forced to litigate. Include a strong suggestion that if the defendant's lawyer calls him by Friday with the intent to settle, we may be able to work this out. If no call, litigation will commence without further notice or discussion.

This letter should cost $500 to $1,000 plus the interview time. If all works out, the entire job will be affordable and a resolution will be in hand within 30 days.

So the would-be defendant gets the letter and the following occurs. He calls his lawyer and makes an immediate appointment. He goes to see his lawyer, who is now ready to prepare for litigation. She discusses with the defendant the cost of retaining her services, the likely costs going forward, and the slim chance of victory.

On the other hand, the defendant soon begins to see the light and with or without the suggestion from the attorney is beginning to think about the merits of resolution, as one way or another he is going to spend some money, maybe lots of it.

So he makes the right decision and authorizes his lawyer to call your lawyer and engage in a resolution discussion. With luck it will be over in a week or two, and while the parties may not get what they want, the problem is resolved and with the least possible cost and quickly. This allows both to return to the better use of their time, focusing on profitable business. A single letter can replace years of litigation and a fortune in legal expenses.

Now, let's say the "defendant" does not bite at the bait. The next step is to pay for the suit to be filed, maybe $2,500 in fees, but done without the intention of ever litigating, as that is where the huge expenses are outlaid. You have just upped the ante and forced the defendant to hire a lawyer and be prepared to spend a small fortune without a clue as to the outcome.

This provokes another chance to settle although the settlement is now more costly because you spent more on litigation. The deal is then resolved, and everyone goes home. You have invested an affordable amount of time and money and have achieved your objectives, though compromising your desired result to some degree.

That's using your lawyer effectively and cost efficiently.

In the end, over 95 percent of all suits are never litigated, but are resolved. Most people are not using the litigation bluff strategy but are intending to litigate and end up resolving because the reality of the time and money to be invested eventually sinks in. Many walk away from the lawyer's meeting and do nothing. They do not want to support a litigation strategy but are told there is no alternative.

The point is, manage your lawyer; use your lawyer effectively. You can always pull the plug in advance of actual litigation if the strategy fails to produce the results you want. The important point is, a lawyer's letter gets the attention of your defendant.

Using the litigation bluff, you will win most of the time. Be prepared to settle and not get what you would have asked for and maybe gotten if you litigated and won, but it's now and without the investment of time and money. It's a better conclusion, and most frequently, the letter works.

## Using the Noncompete Agreement

Are noncompete and nondisclosure agreements worth it or not? How can they protect you? What is their value? Business owners use them, and employees sign them all the time. Here is a nonlegal evaluation of an important and useful business strategy.

Please recognize up front, this discussion is not meant to provide specific legal advice; that should be done by your lawyer. It is, however, important to discuss and consider the business merits supporting the logic of using these agreements as a protection strategy.

There are many aspects and implications of such agreements, which are frequently found in today's hiring practices and must be better understood from both sides of the deal, employer and employee.

What can be protected? Generally speaking, only something that can be considered proprietary, a secret, a special application, a unique strategy, a mailing list—not general business practices.

For example, without specialized training and a unique application, a secretary cannot be restrained from being a secretary in another office by a noncompete clause. However, if the secretary handled sensitive information, had unique contact with secret sources, or went through specialized training, it may be possible to restrain the secretary from working in the same industry for a brief time period to prevent damaging disclosure of confidential information.

To make such a claim and for the noncompete to be enforceable, the groundwork must be laid. Additional efforts would have to exist, such as the business exerting efforts to protect this information and treating it as confidential.

Also the time period and geographical area are narrowly construed, with a typically acceptable time being two years or less and with distance, unless it's an industry issue, being quite narrow, a few miles, 10 at the most.

When narrowly applied to a specific situation for legitimate reasons, as intended by the statutes, it provides reasonable protection to employers who must share their secrets with their employees. When issued merely to restrict competition and remove the opportunity for an employee to gain work elsewhere, it is deemed a restraint of trade and seldom enforced.

While neither employee nor employer wants to pay the legal bill to enforce the principle, it acts as a barrier to employees who leave an employment and want to work in the same field in the same market.

On the other hand, savvy employees know all too well that they are unlikely to be chased; and if chased, the court will narrowly support the contract, if at all. But because of the fear of such action and the cost if required to defend, employees frequently voluntarily follow the letter of the agreement, not wanting to create a legal battle. Also, believing that since they agreed, they need to do the honorable thing and follow through with self-enforcement.

If it's one of a minority of situations where an agreement is appropriate and it is narrowly written, so it will be upheld, it is just as true that there is a natural inclination for some employees to directly ignore it and breach the agreement whether enforceable not.

Thus, what is the advice? Write it if you must, enforce it if necessary and appropriate for your circumstances, and act accordingly while operating your business. Anticipate general acceptance and support by employees who leave your employment, so long as it is reasonably written regarding time and distance.

It works more by self-control and personal commitment than by court enforcement. Use it if you need to, have your lawyer draft the cease-and-desist letter, inform the renegade employee you intend to defend your claim, and then see what happens. Or spend the cash and try to enforce it.

At its best use, it is a reasonable barrier most of the time. Whether self-enforced or supported by a lawyer's letter, most people will respect the requirement, especially as a job requirement, and act appropriately. This is what makes it a viable and important strategy to use.

 # Lender and Other Workouts

What was anticipated occurred. Christmas 2008 and 2009 were similar to each other, and it looks like Christmas 2010 will also be similar. In 2009, the valuable fourth quarter was a disaster, hitting a 38-year low. Retail sales were down 5 to 8 percent on average; many businesses did much worse. Considering that for many businesses the fourth quarter represents 40 to 50 percent of annualized gross revenue, the season was a disaster.

Many small businesses are drowning under excessive debt, worsened by diminished revenue, and will not be able to continue without some form of relief. Thus, they contemplate bankruptcy.

## Consider the Workout Alternative

A well-orchestrated debt workout program can preserve your assets and rid you of most of your debt, leaving you in control of your destiny and the results, as opposed to court-ordered receiver, and foreclosure and liquidation by auction, who earns from your demise and liquidation.

There is no reason that secured debt cannot be reduced to minimal paybacks and that unsecured debt cannot be eliminated completely. Personal guarantees can also be reduced to nominal payments. Even unpaid payroll taxes and SBA-guaranteed loans in default can be reduced to small, affordable losses paid over time. The business can be preserved, although reorganized, and you can get the second chance you need and deserve.

In view of declining real estate values, you are better off entering into a workout negotiation with the mortgagor, your lender, than going into bankruptcy; bankruptcy may preserve your home but also preserves your debt, thus only postponing the inevitable by providing a reprieve from liquidation for a brief time. Ultimately, when the debt is simply too much to afford and more than the house is worth, you are likely to lose your home.

### Reducing Excessive Debt

The issue is the excessive debt—it must be significantly reduced or eliminated, not adjusted or modified. Paying only the interest is meaningless. Even a reduced interest rate is ineffective since the debt is the killer; so unless it is reduced dramatically, there is no real relief available.

Under our legal system, in which the banks and creditors are completely protected, the only option is a bankruptcy, and it always results in a win for the secured creditors and a loss for the borrower. If the battlefront is moved to a business negotiation, a workout strategy, the results can be stunning ... for the defaulting borrower.

If your core business is viable and it can operate profitably after removing the excessive debt, then you must evaluate the workout option. It could be your salvation, as it delivers the second chance you truly want by reducing the debt.

## The Pitfalls of Bankruptcy versus the Workout

Bankruptcy is not the best answer for resolving debt. It is costly, time consuming, and dangerous, as the results, which can be devastating, are out of your control. With the new bankruptcy act, the trustee can and will order you to repay substantial amounts of credit card as well as other unsecured and secured debt. It is no longer a quick path to ridding yourself of all your debts.

Here is a brief analysis showing the pitfalls of bankruptcy:

**Loss of Assets.** The bankruptcy trustee can absolve you of much of your debt, but not all, and at the cost of losing your assets. This may seem like a fair deal under certain circumstances, but think of the alternative: losing most of your debt and keeping your assets. In bankruptcy, you will lose your business, the key asset, as it is the income producer.

**Expensive.** Bankruptcy is not cheap. Paying the lawyer, the trustee, and the court-ordered debt service, you are in for an expensive ride that does not end quickly but carries on and on, with costs out of your control. Every month you must pay the trustee and the court-ordered payments to unsecured and secured creditors, as well as your lawyer's bill.

**Time Consuming.** Time is another issue, as you will be endlessly involved in frequent motions, filing monthly reports, and responding to other issues that the opposition, the secured or unsecured creditors, may want to explore while looking to liquidate your assets for their own best interests. Each motion and report requires lawyers as well as the trustee, and you are responsible for paying the bills for their services. You may even be required to support the services of the various creditor committees' lawyers, as those services are appropriately charged to you ... costing more all the time.

**Stress.** The stress of fearing what may happen and what does happen— again outside of your control—is arduous, hardly a walk through the park. It is possible for you to lose your home and business, depending on your equity position and cash availability. Too much equity with not enough cash, and you may lose your house for the benefit of the creditors. It is also possible you may have to bring your spouse, as a co-owner of assets and a guarantor of debt, into the bankruptcy.

**Public Embarrassment.** There is the public embarrassment as well: public notices and liquidation of assets, not fun at all for you or your spouse.

**Operating in Their, Not Your, Interests.** Remember, trustees earn in two ways: First, they earn a percentage of the cash collected, and second, they earn their fees. They are definitely working against your best interests, as your liquidation makes them money, and the longer you remain in the system, the more money they earn.

A well-designed workout is painless, private, frequently far less expensive, and usually far more effective in achieving your goals of debt relief and asset protection with a speedy conclusion.

**Bankruptcy versus Workout Benefits.** The business and your home are really the issue. Wouldn't it be a great conclusion to lose most of your debt, all the unsecured and much of the secured, in exchange for a reasonable and comfortable payoff, while keeping your home and business assets intact? This is the objective of a workout.

Additionally, IRS tax debt cannot be absolved through bankruptcy proceedings, so if this is an issue, a workout with an offer in compromise is far less painful and less expensive and can reduce your debt to the IRS without bankruptcy.

In my entire career spanning over 30 years of practice, I seldom recommended a bankruptcy, and only on few occasions has a client decided it was the best method of resolution. Hundreds of other clients have taken the workout route and remained in business with less debt and a renewed opportunity for success. So before you take the bankruptcy plunge, get an opinion from an experienced workout practitioner.

> In my entire career spanning over 30 years of practice, I seldom recommended a bankruptcy, and only on few occasions has a client decided it was the best method of resolution.

One important consideration for selecting a workout over bankruptcy is the amount of time and cash you have for implementation. There are 24 business health symptoms and indicators, listed below, you need to be alert to, so you have the option of taking workout action before it is too late.

## Debt Workouts Are Not a Get-Rich-Quick Plan

Debt workout is not right for every circumstance. It's not a way to dodge responsibilities. Here are some of the situations where it isn't the right strategy to pursue.

Some small business owners with significant debt want to do a workout to reduce their payments. Upon evaluation, however, their finances do not add up; they don't justify a workout. Instead, we see a successful business, possibly with reduced revenues, but the business is still profiting. A workout for the sake of reducing debt cannot be employed just to avoid paying a loan that a company can and should repay.

Another issue we confront is when business owners have sizable wealth accumulation. This, too, presents a challenge. Under those circumstances, you can strip debt off an underperforming business, preserving it from foreclosure; but during the workout for the personal guaranties, you cannot hide existing wealth. For business owners who have paid off their mortgage, their valuable house becomes a blank check for the banks. The owners must pay more than if they still had a mortgage and the house was in disrepair. Their exposed equity becomes a basis for payback.

A third issue that we confront from time to time is when the business is doing well, but the business owner takes cash out before depositing receipts and thus makes the business look as if it is underperforming while the owner is building up cash reserves under the mattress. Yes, this happens.

Debt workout is not for small business owners who are misusing the system, whether it is to get rich or to cheat. Debt workout is for small business owners who are drowning in debt and cannot survive otherwise.

## 24 Workout Indicators You Can't Ignore

It is critical for the business owner to recognize the need for a workout as soon as possible. The condition your business is in when you commence a workout strategy will significantly affect your ability to accomplish workout goals. Typically, as you contemplate your options, the adverse business conditions steadily decline.

Here are the 24 symptoms to be aware of:

1. No retained earnings
2. No credit terms, everything COD
3. In default of payment terms to vendors and subject to collection efforts
4. No product inventory
5. Office supplies understocked
6. Late or in arrears on bank lines, credit cards, mortgages, and so on
7. Defaulting on loans
8. Credit cards shut off
9. Abandoning benefits for your employees
10. Missing an occasional payroll or spending every week aggressively collecting receivables just to make the weekly payroll. Covering payroll on Mondays for checks distributed on Fridays
11. Not taking a payroll check yourself
12. Abandoning marketing plans and canceling advertising and other marketing efforts

13. Canceling trade show appearances
14. Losing important vendors and service providers, such as your lawyer, accountant, or product suppliers
15. Dealing with utility and phone shutoffs
16. Postponing repairs and maintenance
17. Downsizing in various ways and forms
18. Morale plummeting
19. Employees leaving
20. Reducing insurance coverage or being canceled for failure to pay
21. Business owner working endless hours
22. Depression moving in
23. Vacations canceled
24. Health insurance plan allowed to lapse

These are the 24 signs of impending destruction. But the good news is that if you recognize these symptoms early enough, the patient is still breathing, still in production, still has receivables, and still has some economic power remaining to fuel a workout. If you wait until you crash and burn, will no longer be able to ship product, there are no receivables, and you are eroding your cash; the upshot is that you will have limited or no resources remaining for a workout or even a sale of the business.

**You Need Cash.** Here is the point. Workout requires some cash to save you lots more. It requires the ability to retain professionals to assist in the process. Without cash to support the workout, you will have no ability to limit the damages or create your exit plan. Eventually, you will simply shut the doors and go home penniless, unable to reduce or pay off the enormous debt. Explain that to your family as your creditors repossess your cars and foreclose on your home. After you have been forced to close your doors and stand there without any cash availability, you will be unable to contemplate, let alone implement, a quality workout plan that limits or eliminates debt and provides enough fuel to start your next venture. That's what happens when you ignore the workout indicators.

**You Need Time.** So here is the action plan. As soon as you find these symptoms present, begin planning your workout strategy, hiring your professionals, and securing a safe exit strategy that reduces or eliminates debt and allows for adequate cash for you to make a safe transition into your next income opportunity.

# Why Not Ask the Bank to Reduce Your Loan

Banks simply will not reduce principal, so do not bother to ask. You are asking banks to bid against themselves; they will not do it. In fact, you really cannot ask any creditor to reduce your debt, and yet it is the most common approach small business owners attempt. It's as if borrowers believe the banks want to be fair and will deal evenhandedly and respond to such an inquiry with a reasonable compromise.

There is little reason for them to fall into this strategy. You will get a laugh and a rejection. They expect every penny of a loan to be repaid, of course; that is the deal. Banks will not willingly participate in a unilateral reduction of debt to satisfy your cash flow requirements. This same principle applies to any workout. However, vendors or any non-bank creditor may negotiate against themselves, but here is a better way.

The optimum way to negotiate with a bank for a discount of principal is with a specific bona fide offer in writing with a specific time to close. This action results in a response and a resolution. This kind of offer to compromise requires much specific information and an effective presentation, but it works—and a request to reduce principal does not.

Unfortunately banks are reluctant to provide debt reduction. Think about the ramifications: If they willingly reduce debt on a request, every borrower in the country will line up and expect the same treatment; this will cause the banking system to crash.

# Speedy Decisions and Rapid Implementation to Avoid Losses

Workouts require speedy decisions and rapid implementation, or you can suffer huge losses while you contemplate your course of action. It's understandable that business owners want to take time to consider their options. Workouts require major changes, most of which are very difficult and heart wrenching and require serious consideration. Given the nature of a workout situation, the smart business owner recognizes the need for immediate response and action: thinking clearly but acting quickly.

A lot of resources, cash especially, are wasted while the borrower contemplates what actions to take. Frequently, these wasted assets are critical for future survival if only they were available now.

**Thinking and Acting Quickly.** For example, if the business situation includes a tax lien and the IRS is telling you it intends to levy, its actions could include a levy to all your customers for receivables; or it could mean a levy of your bank accounts, stripping all the available cash irrespective of floating checks, and it could also include seizing your business assets.

The operative point here is that thinking and acting quickly can have a dramatic effect on your outcome. By quickly filing an IRS offer in compromise,[1] for example, all collection activities cease while awaiting the outcome of the offer, which could take nine to 12 months, an eternity. During that time, you could implement many strategies to change your situation favorably. Here are a few examples of other ways of thinking and acting quickly to prevent losses:

- Collect your own receivables with deep discounts, if necessary, but get the cash in hand rapidly. Even if discounted, having the cash is a whole lot better than allowing the IRS to take it. Ceasing payments to creditors, as soon as possible, creates the basis for a workout. Making payments postpones the workout and depletes your available cash.
- Remove overhead, let employees go, stop payment on rent obligations, and so forth; all must be done as soon as possible to preserve cash and set the stage for the workout negotiation.
- Liquidate inventory rapidly and for discounted prices to create cash and prevent seizure.
- Sell assets rather than allow them to be placed under lien, seized, and liquidated.

> Ceasing payments to various creditors, as soon as possible, creates the basis for a workout.

The alternative is waiting allowing creditors to sue you, and then you get judgments that convert unsecured debt to judgment liens. You waited too long.

Yes, it's all difficult to contemplate, let alone implement. You must trust your workout specialist who is guiding you, or if you are attempting to do it yourself, make your decisions and take action.

**Taking Control.** To successfully navigate a workout situation, it is imperative that you take control of your assets as rapidly as possible and implement whatever strategies you deem most advantageous rather than allowing other secured creditors to take control and implement their strategies, which are definitely not in your best interest.

There is a subtle point here: If you allow your creditors to control your destiny, you have lost. Once in control, they will liquidate you to their best interest, not yours. Worse yet, in the end, you will still be liable for the shortfall debt after liquidation. In a workout, in exchange for a settled payment, you are released from additional debt and collection, a huge benefit. If done correctly, you will also retain use or ownership of the business assets.

Yes, a workout typically requires significant changes, but if planned effectively, in the end all that happens is you lose the debt and have a new chance to go forward without the debt holding you back. This is the objective, and it requires deft implementation of a clearly defined strategy, which forces your creditors to deal with your plan instead of your creditors forcing you into their liquidation plan.

The number one rule is act quickly. Unfortunately, there are many business owners that find it difficult and follow another path. The sooner you act, the more power you have. The longer you wait, the fewer resources and options you will have.

## Protect Your Liquid Assets

If you are in default and have a personal guaranty, your liquid assets are available for the taking by the defaulted bank, especially including bank accounts, insurance policy cash values, and other caches of liquidity. The best advice is to move all your accounts out of the bank with which you are in default.

However, defaulting borrowers overlook this strategy more frequently than you might expect. Banks will empty joint accounts, sometimes of the borrower's children, elderly parents, or any other family member.

"Heartless," you say. "How could they do that?" Easy, this is not about doing good. There is no moral perspective, no judgment involved; it is about collateral, default, and collection. They do what they must. Likewise we must defend as appropriate. If you leave cash available, the bank will take it.

## The Danger of Negotiating One Issue at a Time

There is a general tendency for business owners in deep economic trouble to approach the myriad of issues threatening them one at a time, addressing the most pressing issue first and then moving on to the next one that screams the loudest.

It may be a natural approach, but it is not in your best interest of your debt workout issues. The best workout plan deals with all the issues at once and resolves them all simultaneously.

Who knows or even considers which one is truly the worst or the most dangerous? The problem you choose to address may not be the most strategically correct one to deal with first for many possible reasons. It is vital to look at all the issues confronting you and determine the best way to resolve them all, which may require a specific order or progression to yield the best results for you.

Remember, each creditor is only concerned with collecting his or her own debt, but you are concerned with all of them; thus order is important matter to consider. You must realize that as you work out each problem, you get stronger and more valuable as layers of priority debt protection are peeled away from you, revealing more and more value for the next workout creditor. Negotiate all at once and remain in control.

> Each creditor is only concerned with collecting his or her own debt, but you are concerned with all of them; thus order is important matter to consider.

**Working on All Debts Simultaneously.** A workout strategy must work on all debts simultaneously to make certain all the debts are effectively handled while you are in the worst possible condition and at the lowest possible liquidation value. Use one debt against the other to reduce the payoffs and secure releases, demonstrating a lower likely return to the creditors should they attempt anything other than working with you in the manner that you offer. It's a win-win situation under the worst possible conditions. An effective workout strategy takes all the issues and uses the secured creditors to fend off the unsecured and then the highest-priority secured to fend off the lowest-priority secured.

Of course, there is nothing better than a priority tax lien to bring fear to and cooperation from most creditors' collection efforts. On the other hand, imagine being the last workout creditor in a long line of workouts and realizing all the previously unpaid debt has been cleaned up and all the assets are once again vulnerable ... what a huge opportunity for the least likely creditor getting paid because he or she was the last one to be confronted and thus ends up getting paid in full! The assets have become vulnerable and exposed without any other barriers between the collecting effort and the valuable assets.

The key to success is designing a plan that takes all this into consideration and with one overall strategy and a number of substrategies; all the debt is worked out simultaneously and within the same context and at the same time frame, yielding the best results for the debtor.

This is just one kind of issue that needs to be handled in conjunction with a total workout plan. Here is another.

## Avoid Turning Forgiveness into IRS Debt

Debt forgiveness converts to ordinary income and is taxable ... beware!

The forgiveness of debt is considered ordinary income by the IRS and could leave you with a substantial debt now due to the IRS, instead of to the bank or whomever the original debt was with.

This is a lot like the proverbial jumping from the pot into the fire. Owing the IRS can be a daunting experience and very expensive, as the interest and penalties can be huge and compounding rapidly.

Also, if several borrowers are guaranteeing a loan, say for $1 million, and they negotiate forgiveness for the entire amount, the IRS holds each guarantor liable for the full $1 million forgiven. Each person is liable for the entire amount; *individually and severally guaranteed* is the term. So each borrower guarantor could be looking at $300,000 to $400,000 of IRS debt. Ouch!

What can you do to avoid this? A number of strategies do exist that eliminate the threat of debt forgiveness being converted to ordinary, taxable income. While difficult strategies to implement, they work well and must be considered. There is a significant exemption from this situation in the Mortgage Forgiveness Debt Relief Act of 2007. As stated therein, any debt forgiveness associated with your principal residence is *not* subject to 1099 ordinary income treatment. This includes debt forgiveness from refinancing or selling your principal residence and is an important exclusion.

There are additional exemptions that are broad and on point, as the law further states that if the borrower in default is insolvent when forgiveness is granted, the conversion to ordinary income for tax purposes does not occur. A simple form will demonstrate this, and your CPA will be able to easilyhandle this matter. The issue is no longer a barrier to most defaulting borrowers.

If you're unaware that the IRS considers debt forgiveness as income, unless exempted with the appropriate forms, you will find out about it in January when you get a 1099 for the amount you negotiated.

## Understanding Secured, Unsecured, and Tax Debt

There are two types of debt, secured and unsecured. Unsecured debt is typified by traditional vendor debt, no personal guaranties, no collateral, and no security for the creditor. Secured debt is different, typified by mortgages or other Uniform Commercial Code, Article 9 (UCC 9) security filings that provide a means for a supplier of goods on credit to secure payment.[2] Specific collateral is attached to the loan, meaning that if the debt goes into default, the creditor has the right to liquidate specific collateral to recover the debt and the costs of collection. The UCC can be limited to the car against which the loan was secured, the piece of equipment, or whatever may have been signed by the debtor as collateral for the loan. Sometimes, the UCC includes a blanket filing that covers all assets such as accounts receivables, inventory, equipment, auto, cash on hand, and future assets to be acquired.

The tricky part is when you have multiple security interests all covering the same total of all your assets. In this situation, which is quite common, the order of priority determines what a creditor gets after the assets are liquidated. The order of priority is dictated by the date filed. Thus, the first secured interest gets everything he is owed until he is paid in full. Then the second priority secured lien holder gets what remains until she is paid off. In turn, the third and fourth get paid, and the process continues until the cash is gone; everyone remaining gets nothing. The unsecured creditors come after the secured creditors are paid in full. The unsecured shares have no real collection right, as the debt is without collateral. They are paid at the discretion of the debtor.

Unfortunately, the debt does not go away for the secured or unsecured parties who were not paid if they have personal guarantees. If a secured or unsecured lender or creditor has a personal guaranty, the debtor remains personally indebted to the lender or creditor for future collection, and the lender or creditor must be included in the workout.

In fact, this concept of personal guarantees requires its own workout, one for the business and one for the individual who has typically multiple personal guaranty issues.

> **Understanding the positions of your creditors, the quality of their security type, and the order of priority will help you determine your workout strategy.**

The unsecured creditors have no specific rights against the assets of the business, as they are all funneled toward the secured creditors. Thus, when a business closes, the assets are liquidated for the benefit of the secured parties in the order of priority of their filings. Unless there is some cash remaining, which is highly unlikely, there is usually nothing available for the unsecured creditors. Clearly, the first security lien holder is in the best position and will receive the most and perhaps all he or she is owed.

Understanding the positions of your creditors, the quality of their security type, and the order of priority will help you determine your workout strategy.

Even the IRS must respect the priority of filings and thus may fall behind other creditors with higher priority, although the IRS has the ability to trump higher-priority lien holders under certain circumstances and over specific assets such as accounts receivable and inventory. The priority for the IRS and the state taxing authorities is determined by the assessment date, not the filing date.

## You Must Be in Default to Begin

I am confronted frequently by people who want to do a workout but still keep current with their payments. I know it makes little sense from the borrower's side to make the decision to default when, if necessary, you could continue to pay, but consider the logic from the lender's point of view. Why enter into a workout negotiation if the customer, the borrower, is paying? It doesn't make sense for them to support a reduction of principal if you are demonstrating the ability to pay currently.

I realize people bend over backward, depriving themselves of a paycheck and juggling other payments to stay current on any number of secured debt obligations including mortgages and credit cards. They are truly in need of a workout and are prime candidates since the cash flow cannot support the overhead and debt service requirements, and yet they manage to stay current on most of their obligations out of a sense of duty and commitment while their business continues in decline and erosion.

However, the truth is there can be no workout negotiation while you remain current with your payments. In fact, you must be at least 90 days in arrears in most situations to be considered a candidate. Thus, if you are headed for trouble or realistically are already in trouble, review your debt service commitments and plan to default as soon as you make the decision to enter into a workout negotiation so you can proceed as soon as possible.

> **If you have the foresight and skill, however, it is possible to begin a workout even before you default on your payments.**

Furthermore, if you are not taking a paycheck and juggling your payables to stay afloat, you are really kidding yourself. You are already in need of a workout and have simply failed to recognize the symptoms.

It may seem backward thinking, but the entire world of workouts is backward, and, yes, you must go into arrears, default, and fail to pay before your creditors will negotiate a workout. If you have the foresight and skill, however, it is possible to begin a workout even before you default on your payments. I call it a preemptive workout.

## Preemptive Workouts, the Secret Path to Survival

A preemptive workout. I believe I have coined this concept, inventing it out of necessity! And I believe its time is here: When the facts line up, it's the way to go. I've done preemptive workouts for a number of clear-thinking small business owners, and the technique works ... assuring the survival and emergence of a business capable of navigating these difficult economic times, with prospects of lasting well into the future.

Who is a good candidate? If a business with significant debt, deeply declining revenues, and sharply reduced valuation of its assets continues on its financial path, it will self-destruct. When the revenues dip too low, the business will no longer be able to service its debt. The requirement for survival is reduced debt ... a workout before the business is crushed.

It requires an evaluation to assess your current and future condition and to determine if you are carrying significant debt. In an industry hard hit by the 2009 recession, with reduced revenues likely to be the new normal and to last a long time before they return to previous levels, if ever, you are ripe for either a preemptive workout or a going-out-of business sale.

You must explain to your lender that, while you have demonstrated your capability to service the loan in the past and that you may even be able to support it today, next month or the month after, you will *not* be able to support the loan. So now, before you crash and burn, you want to do the workout, so you will survive and be able to pay off some of the loan rather than none of it.

Wow, can you imagine that discussion with your banker? "I am OK now; I am paying the monthly debt service now but experiencing severe pain and watching my business decline and begin to die. So let's do the workout now, so I can survive and pay you less, but that's better than going out of business soon and paying you nothing."

That's advanced. That's like closing the barn door *before* the horse gets out.

**Convincing Your Banker.** The problem is that bankers are not quite there ... yet. Most are not in tune with the clarity and appropriateness of preemptive workouts and thus will look at you in a funny way and restate your position as follows: "You mean you can pay me today and are current at the moment, but you believe you will have difficulty paying next month, so you want to renegotiate the loan now? That's a good one," he will chuckle.

It is unlikely that your lender will understand or be able or willing to explain this concept to his or her superiors and committees. They may be willing to reconsider restructuring your debt, allowing interest only for a short while, lengthening payback, reducing interest rates, but are unlikely to even consider reducing the principal.

**Selling the Workout.** How do we engineer a preemptive workout?

We just do it. We reorganize, redesign, reimplement, and explain to the bank that this is what is necessary to support ongoing business under different terms and conditions in this changing economy, different from when we originally made the loan. Thus, the loan must be rewritten.

It's a tougher sell, but worth doing when you see the writing on the wall and know your revenue will be down, unlikely to return for a while. Thus, the debt is too high for your business to support and must be reduced to survive and pay the bank something more than liquidation value.

The trick is in the skill of implementing the plan and the effectiveness of the presentation of fact and projections. If done well, the results will be stunning, as you still have the necessary capital to survive and emerge as a smaller, tighter, more effective business with less debt and the ability to service it.

You will need to deal with the situation as a business issue rather than attacking with a legal defense.

## Business Negotiation, Not a Legal Issue

As I talk to so many people who believe the answer to foreclosure is a legal defense. Not so. It doesn't work, it's a trap, and if you go this route, you're falling into it, head first.

You owe money, signed notes and mortgages, defaulted on the loan, and are now being sued, with the banks intent to foreclose and liquidate your collateral. Then they will pursue your personal guaranty, liquidating your personal assets, possibly your home. Now you know what's going to happen, so why wait to see it happen.

It is a trap because it forces you to respond, so you believe, to the lawsuit as directed by the legal process and to your lawyer who must answer for you. This is the first step in the legal process, which you enter into and will not get out of whole.

It's a battle you cannot win because you have no defense. So why allow them to take you down a path that you cannot possibly succeed at?

The real answer is to resolve this matter with negotiation, compromise, and resolution. Come to a business conclusion: a business workout, not *litigation*, which in the end is just another word for *liquidation*. Of course, there is always bankruptcy, which we discussed earlier in this chapter, an expensive form of liquidation.

> Come to a business conclusion: a business workout, not *litigation*, which in the end is just another word for *liquidation*.

So why does this happen? It's simple. The bank or the Small Business Administration or the IRS simply wants to close the case, liquidate the assets, and write off the loss, moving on to other deals. The organization sues to accomplish its goal. You respond by going to see a lawyer, who tells you she must answer the suit, or you will default, and you're hooked; you swallowed the bait.

Then your lawyer must continue in the legal process until she has siphoned all your remaining cash, and now the bank liquidates your assets.

One note on lawyers: It's like going to a bakery; you will always get baked goods. Go to a lawyer, and you will litigate. Go to a bankruptcy lawyer, and you will go bankrupt; what else can you expect? There is a time and place for lawyers, litigation, and even bankruptcy, but it isn't in a foreclosure setting. That's my opinion.

If you open the doors to a negotiated settlement, you have a chance of winning. Depending upon your plan and skill, you at least have a chance. I've seen many clients succeed with workouts by ignoring the legal game, where you will lose, and instead forcing a business discussion that you can win.

This applies to any loan, whether from the SBA, banks, or secured or unsecured creditors. Negotiate; do not litigate. This is a sophisticated approach requiring skill and experience. It is not a place to learn how to do it. Having a third party represent your position and conduct the workout negotiations is far, far more effective than representing yourself.

## Notes

1. An offer in compromise (OIC) is an agreement between a taxpayer and the Internal Revenue Service that settles the taxpayer's tax liabilities for less than the full amount owed.
2. "Securing Dept Payment through Use of Article 9 of the UCC and Construction Liens," www.business.gov/guides/finance/managing-finances/secure-debt-payment.html, accessed December 9, 2008.

# Chapter 18

# Workout Advice

## Lawyers Do Battle; Bankers Talk Business

When a prospective client recently called me, he was desperate for some help. His bank's lawyers had filed a motion for the court to appoint a receiver. If and when done, a receivership would end the client's hotel business, as appointing a receiver is a liquidation process that absorbs all available cash while it prepares to close the doors and auction the empty nonoperating building for pennies on the dollar. What a disaster for everyone, the bank and the borrower.

He had hired a bankruptcy lawyer who was fighting with the bank's lawyers, each staking out a position for the likely battle and bickering about every reasonable request each side had. The client's bankruptcy lawyer was refusing to produce documents and provide information that would be required if either filed suit or pursued legal action. Both sides were getting ready for the showdown; there was no cooperation, which served to propel them faster and faster into the courts.

The bank's lawyers were ready to pounce, expecting the receivership motion to be granted. The bankruptcy lawyer was waiting for a sizable retainer and would file to prevent the receivership from occurring for the time being. The client knew any legal action at this point would result in disaster, but what choice did he have?

No one was talking to the lender, because once legal action goes to counsel, it is lawyer to lawyer, and the banker does not get involved anymore. Therefore, there is no basis for resolution, no meaningful discussion. Just lawyers doing what they do best, spending their clients' money and squaring off for a fistfight.

Since I am not counsel, I have every right to call the banker and talk, which I did. On my first call, we agreed to pull back the lawyers, put the legal action on hold, and work this problem out along the lines I proposed—without squandering excessive cash on a meaningless legal battle, destroying the business potential of the asset, and reducing the potential return to the bank.

I agreed to send the bank all the pertinent financial information it had requested that our lawyer refused to deliver. The proposal: Reduce the loan from $1.7 million to $600,000, which keeps the business running. The next step was to submit an offer in settlement for the remainder of the personally guaranteed debt and walk my client out of harm's way for an affordable payoff, 2 to 5 percent of the debt owed. That's a happy ending to a story that almost culminated in disaster.

Lawyers do what they are supposed to do ... litigate. Businesspeople should do what they are supposed to: Negotiate, settle, work things out, compromise, and conclude safely and sanely for everyone's best interest.

## Do You Need a Lawyer?

No, unless the lawyer is experienced in handling SBA workouts; then you are hiring him for the right reason. An SBA workout is based on your financial position and net worth, your income stream, what the collectibility of the debt may be following the requirements of the SBA process, and so forth. These are not legal issues. After all, you did borrow the money, and you do owe it. There is no question about this; there is no defense; the bank did nothing wrong. You simply need a workout, not a legal defense.

There is little a lawyer's expertise can add to help you through the process other than unnecessary expenses. If you're hiring one to walk you through the paperwork, then the lawyer must have the SBA workout experience to project the response needed for your situation and the best strategy you should employ. There is seldom any direct face-to-face negotiation. It's all done with forms, and one must know the game to play effectively. I do not believe a lawyer's skills will help you navigate the situation more effectively.

If you are being sued by the bank's lawyers, you may need a legal response; however, this is a huge sign you are not following an effective strategy because, after all, you owe the money. Also, when you add a lawyer to the mix, it requires a lawyer on the other end to respond, and so your workout is now interpreted through two lawyers before it gets to the party who must decide the issues.

The more important person, who is in a position to help you, is the banker you borrowed the money from. The loan is guaranteed by the SBA but written and funded by the bank. The banker's opinion of you and how you are acting is important to the results. Better you should remain in contact with the banker and gain a favorable opinion than resort to counsel, which adds separation from the real player. Do it before you liquidated.

> **The more important person, who is in a position to help you, is the banker you borrowed the money from.**

## Bank Intimidation Without Representation

The credit card industry, leasing companies, and some banks have found a new way to intimidate borrowers in default into making payments they cannot afford. Knowing that the borrower is easier to coerce into submission, they staunchly refuse to talk to third-party representatives, only the borrower. It's a formidable strategy that is difficult to thwart, but absurd.

As an inalienable right, every borrower is entitled to professional representation, to appoint someone with a power of attorney and the authority to deal with the bank. The bank or credit card company that blocks professional representation for the sole purpose of intimidation breaches the borrower's rights.

When the problem arises, we've had success removing the barrier by retaining counsel to produce a legal memorandum on the subject. Currently, a minority of banks use this tactic, but I see the numbers growing as it works, so they think.

Because of the bureaucracy in many of these banks, it is difficult to reach the appropriate decision maker, and since this is policy created at so-called high levels, no one below is authorized to make changes.

I recommend to my clients when the bank calls insisting to speak only to them, simply state, "I am being represented, so please talk to my agent who has power of attorney." This will eventually work. The bank does not care if you end in default and then go to the workout department. It is there to intimidate you into doing what you cannot and should not do, pay more than you can simply afford.

> The bank does not care if you end in default and then go to the workout department.

It is unfortunate that the creditors feel that it remains in their best interest to rely on intimidation tactics rather than quality representation for a productive conclusion. They still do not get it, that this type of predatory action is contrary to everyone's best interest. It may have short-term positive results, an ill-conceived momentary spike, for their collections, but it has long-term negative results for all concerned. It will simply force people into bankruptcy, which is far more expensive and far less productive than debt workout.

## Beware the Bank's Advice When Defaulting

I continue to get e-mails and calls daily from people from all over the country telling me stories about the difficulties they have negotiating settlements with the SBA or their banks.

I hear more bad stories about banks misrepresenting the SBA work-out standards. Lawyers use the tried-and-true intimidation tactics they are so fond of. It is depressing to hear how people are being taken advantage of despite their attempts to do what they believe is the right thing: acknowledging their debt and their commitment and wanting to pay it off as best as they can.

Why do borrowers in default believe they would get the straight scoop from their lender or their lender's attorneys? Isn't it a bit naive to think that you will get reliable answers to your questions and reasonable responses about aspects of debt reduction and forgiveness that are not in the lender's best interest?

Do not expect your opposition to give you the best advice it can against its own best interests. It's counterproductive to even ask, and yet this appears to be the way people figure out what to do to work out their debt issues.

If you are naive enough to rely on your opposition for advice and guidance, then perhaps you deserve to get the beating you will get. In these situations, unfortunately, people misrepresent and intimidate. In short, they do anything they can to gain an advantage and get the borrower to pay back as much as possible. Do not take advice from your banker when in default.

Despite your willingness to come to the table in a defaulting situation with integrity, honesty, and a desire to work things out amicably and appropriately, your opposition is coming to the same table with one purpose, to extract the most it can to prevent losses. Your opposition's motives do not include giving you good, honest, or even accurate or reliable advice or information.

Worse yet are the hordes of people who do rely on their own, so-called expert counsel, their lawyers or accountants, who are general practitioners. They have little experience with SBA or bank workouts or any workout. They have no idea what works and what doesn't work and tend to go along with the bad or incorrect advice or information handed down to them by the collecting parties.

> Worse yet are the hordes of people who do rely on their own, so-called expert counsel, their lawyers or accountants, who are general practitioners.

I have said it before and say it again: Get expert advice from people who practice in the areas of your concern. You would not go to your family doctor, a general practitioner, for advice on cancer or brain surgery. Why would you go to a general practitioner or the opposition for advice and information about issues that threaten your financial life?

## Avoid Your Banker's Turnaround Referral

Here is the scene: You are in default on a loan to a bank, either in payment default or perhaps in noncompliance with loan requirements. The bank is getting ready to foreclose on you, liquidating your assets, calling the note, and demanding payment on your personal guaranty, as well. A complete and total loss, business and personal, is in the making.

So when your banker calls asking for a meeting, you reluctantly agree to go, hoping for the best but knowing that this is dangerous ground you are walking on.

The banker surprises you with an understanding discussion, although guardedly threatening. The banker explains that you are in default, technical or real, and must come back into compliance as soon as possible. The banker may even give you a time and a goal to reach, which she warns that you had best meet or her hands will be tied, and she may have to foreclose. Bad news, but she is very nice about it.

Of course, what she asks for is probably impossible to satisfy, including additional collateral, your spouse's guaranty, large and steady payments on the arrears, and more.

You must be polite and noncommittal, but never willingly give up what the bank is asking for since all it is doing is fattening its position so it can collect more in liquidation, which it is surely planning to do once it has all you have to give.

Never let your spouse sign, especially after the loan is in jeopardy. If you do, you are giving the bank your home. Never give the bank more collateral than it already has. Try not to agree to a deal you cannot deliver, because as soon as you breach it, the bank will liquidate you instantly, especially if it has improved its position as much as possible.

This may all seem obvious, but here is the tricky part. The banker recommends a turnaround expert to help you turn your company around. Danger! This person is your enemy. The banker will tell you that you need expert guidance. The bank will forgo immediate foreclosure if you hire a recommended turnaround expert who will guide you to solvency and improve your ability to pay the bank as required. It's a great idea, the banker suggests.

You will know the turnaround expert's true colors when he suggests that the bank will cooperate with extensions (but seldom gives you what you need ... more money) if you give the bank more collateral, such as your home or your spouse's guaranty. Fire him. The liquidators are on the way, and he is their advance man!

He is working for the bank, not for you, and he will deliver you on a silver platter if you allow him to. Frequently, the bank will give you a list of two or three of these so-called experts, feigning noninvolvement and allowing you to choose anyone you want (as long as it is someone on the list). The bank is trying to demonstrate to a future court that it is not interfering with your business and is not subject to lender liability claims later down the road.

This turnaround expert will charge you lots of money, but would never think of negotiating a workout with the bank to reduce the payoff to less than what your company owes. He will not recommend against giving up your spouse's guaranty as a cosigner or to providing additional collateral. He will find a way to add valuable collateral to the bank's position, while obtaining some presumably valuable concession for you. Do not hire or let a bank-appointed turnaround expert into your office.

If you are in danger of failure, the workout person you hire independently is intent on protecting your assets, reducing the payouts, and beating the bank in every way possible.

## Be Truthful with the Bank

We are all imperfect and can make bad decisions. When in default, we are forced into uncharted territory and do not know what to do. We sometimes keep poor records, miscommunicate with the bank, practice avoidance, breach our word, or hide. We are all human. In workouts with the bank, we tend to increase the damage by continuing these poor business practices. Then we compound the issue by promising the impossible and projecting unrealistic turnaround results. After failing again, we get more defensive and more apologetic. The cycle continues until we destroy our credibility completely and reduce the likelihood for a best-case workout.

I arranged a client discussion with the bank workout officer, who wanted to find out what had happened, the sequence of events leading to the business difficulties and the borrower's plan for payback and resolution. He insisted on interviewing the borrower directly.

My client had made mistakes, had communicated poorly, and was out of touch with her business. She was distracted by personal issues and, frankly, did not know what was happening, had no plan for debt payback, and was struggling with the reality of losing it all.

Coaching her prior to the meeting, I urged her to follow one simple guideline, and I assured her if she did this, it would be a more successful meeting as we would regain the trust of the banker. I suggested, "Tell the truth, no matter what it is. If you do not know the answer to a question, do not make up a response; tell the banker you have no idea. If you made mistakes, inappropriate or wrong decisions, admit it truthfully. If you have no plan or strategy, admit it."

So we had the meeting, and she treated the situation with candor, integrity, and honesty, telling the banker the truth instead of what she thought he would want to hear. No one was happy with what was happening in the business, but the banker appreciated the candor and rewarded us with cooperation despite the disastrous business losses. She needed the cooperation of the banker to enter into an effective workout scenario.

During my coaching, she wanted to make things up and sway from the hard truth; fortunately, I convinced her to come clean, and she did. The results were positive.

You will still want to arrange your affairs in your best interest and protect yourself appropriately. Yet it is better to face the music and deal honestly and candidly; it works out better in the long run. This is the only way to begin a successful workout.

 # SBA Workouts

## A Few Words

**M**ost high-risk small business loans carry an SBA guaranty, which reduces the risk to the bank and supports the bank's lending to high-risk small business borrowers that would not otherwise be qualified for a loan.

However, the mere fact that the loan is an SBA-guaranteed loan adds complication. It requires understanding that a debt workout must include the SBA with its requirements and procedures as well as the lending bank's requirements and procedures. Of course, there is no playbook, and you cannot rely on anyone to tell you what to do and how to do it. It is not in the lender's best interest for you to be armed with important how-to information for accomplishing a workout, or so the bankers believe.

Having accomplished hundreds of these workouts with SBA-guaranteed loans in default, we have evolved a strategy that works well with significant debt forgiveness as the result. In many instances, we can preserve the business, as well as reduce the personal guaranty to what we call affordable losses. Without bankruptcy or other legal proceedings and by incorporating the workout as a business strategy, we manage to create successful conclusions for all involved: the bank, the SBA, and the borrower in default.

It is tricky water to navigate and requires significant experience and knowledge of the SBA systems and the secured bank's requirements to conclude with a satisfactory workout with debt forgiveness.

Many businesses took out loans when revenues were high. The recession has resulted in massively reduced revenues for many who cannot afford to continue paying back their loans and are in default. Others are flirting with default by not taking a paycheck yet knowing deep down they cannot survive paying back these loans. With a personal guaranty, the losses will be catastrophic, with bankruptcy seemingly the only way out, a huge defeat for all involved.

The following insights developed out of experience performing workouts all over the country with hundreds of banks for over 30 years that may help shed light on this process.

With revenues down, the debt is too much to repay. The only way to survive the downturn is to have the debt forgiven, not modified. Even if modified so you can afford the payments, the business is no longer worth the debt it borrowed, as its revenue is sharply reduced.

Debt workout resulting in debt forgiveness is crucial for survival in recessionary times.

## Beware the Dangers of SBA-Guaranteed Loans

I have seen enough Small Business Administration loans to ponder the following three circumstances that are not in the best interest of the small business owner:

1. I cannot imagine how or why the SBA will guarantee loans that are far too large for the borrower to service under the most optimistic of circumstances, and thus default is virtually guaranteed. Be aware that the default rate for SBA loans is now approximately 15 percent. You are at high risk, and you have bet the farm, especially after including your spousal guaranty, as well. Remember, the banks are highly guaranteed and are unlikely to experience losses.

2. Many loans I see are simply ill conceived, as the business plan is grossly deficient and cannot work, let alone support the debt service. Because of the SBA guaranty, the banks agree to make loans that should not have been made in the first place. Interestingly, the SBA has this as its mission ... to support borrowers who do not qualify in the traditional marketplace. To make certain these people get

loans, the SBA guarantees the debt. So it acknowledges that it is starting off with high risk.

3. Often, a lender offers to give a business owner more money than he or she asked for, with the banker stating, "You qualify for another few hundred thousand. Why not take it?" If the SBA were not guaranteeing your loan, there is no way you would ever hear these words; but without any substantial risk, the banks have no problem giving more than you need. Sounds great until you have to begin servicing the debt and gag on the payments. Frequently, that is the reason for default.

What do we expect other than a higher rate of failure? This may be acceptable or even an appropriate objective when providing high-risk loans, but to add fuel to the fire by overlending, and then, upon default, tightening the noose and saying, "You had your one shot, and now we will extract what we can and leave you on the roadside," is not an acceptable conclusion.

This strategy is backfiring now that the economy is being challenged. Apparently, as long as the banks have both the husband and wife sign the guaranty personally, putting their home up for collateral, combined with the SBA guaranty, the banks feel they have so little exposure, they would agree to lend to anyone any amount for any purpose. Thus, they rationalize excessive lending, and the SBA goes along with it believing that the banks are underwriting effectively and prudently.

In essence, we lost the very important underwriting filter, where loans were closely examined and carefully reviewed, so those that passed stood a fair chance of success. The result is that high-risk, inexperienced business owners, and now higher-risk inexperienced borrowers, are borrowing too much money for questionable business plans and are facing a disaster.

If borrowers were not held personally responsible with their home at risk, it might be OK, but that is not the progression. I wonder if these issues are capable of supporting a lender liability suit, as some of the loans I see that are in default are questionable and should not have been made, and now borrowers are poised to lose everything, their home included. What was really accomplished?

There is also the issue of ongoing support through modifications to the loan, which are typically available to traditional borrowers but unavailable to SBA borrowers. For example, a small business that runs out of cash and needs more to finish a project or turn the corner into profitability and increased gross revenue will require a loan modification.

Because the ability to modify most SBA guaranties appears to be unavailable as a workout strategy, there is huge pressure on the borrowers to be right the first time, even though they may not survive early peaks and valleys of a project start-up without additional capital or other loan modifications. Second-round financing that may be required, while available with many traditional loans, is generally unavailable to SBA-guaranteed borrowers.

Borrowers opening new businesses or buying existing businesses are failing at a rapid rate because the banks and the SBA are not doing their jobs correctly. While it may appear they are helping by providing requested capital in high-risk situations, in reality they are hurting the borrowers.

How can you avoid getting into this situation? Prospective borrowers must not rely on the bank to determine if their loan application has a reasonable likelihood of succeeding. The underwriting function traditionally plays an important role in making certain only viable potential business plans are funded. This may not be the case with SBA-guaranteed loans. Here is what you should look for:

- Have your application for borrowing and your business plan checked by an experienced business consultant or accountant who will determine if your assumptions and parameters are reasonable and can be achieved with the amount you are borrowing. You will not get additional cash to help if you run short.

- When you see yourself heading for trouble, *stop!* Ask for help; seek an outside opinion, not the bank's, not the SBA's, but from someone hired by you to do an analysis. This step is critical. Seeing the potential disaster in advance allows you to make preemptive decisions while you still have options, while you still have some cash remaining to support a reengineering or even a workout, if necessary.

In short, you need an objective third party, such as an accountant, to support your loan application effort and not rely on the bank for such input. Otherwise, you may regret relying on the bank later on when business projections do not work out. Especially when the economy is depressed and business turns bleak, these loans are the first to fail.

## Beware of Cosigning a Note Guaranty

There is much misunderstanding about cosigning a guaranty for a note to the SBA or any secured lender. Here is what you need to know.

The information in the following sections is not a legal analysis and should not be relied upon as such but is a general description of legal concepts for your education and understanding. Seek legal counsel for answers to specific questions or for an analysis if you are in this situation.

A guaranty that is limited spells out its limited reach, for example, "Limited to include the undersigned real estate but not a general guaranty for the entire debt." This means the signor guarantor has granted a collateralized position to the lender only against your ownership interest in real estate. This position is frequently asked of a spouse.

If not limited by the language in the guaranty, you can consider yourself a guarantor of the entire debt, and the lender can reach into any of your assets, including your home, to perfect its position. It can liquidate your assets to get paid. That's what a guaranty means. (Please seek specific assistance from your attorney.)

> If not limited by the language in the guaranty, you can consider yourself a guarantor of the entire debt.

One danger is in thinking that if you are a coguarantor with someone else that somehow this means you are responsible for only half the debt … *not so!* A coguarantor, or every coguarantor, agrees to be individually liable for the entire debt owed, not just a portion. The lender can look to one individual and collect the entire debt and not even pursue the others if they are less liquid, and this is a legitimate practice.

Another misunderstanding frequently occurs when a guarantor leaves the business and receives an agreement from the other guarantors to hold the leaving guarantor harmless from the liability of the debt. In other words, the remaining business partners agree to make the payments in behalf of the leaving guarantor so the leaving guarantor believe he is off the hook. In reality, he is not. This agreement is between the two guarantors and not the bank. The bank has no obligation to honor this agreement and can still collect against the exiting guarantor and his assets as if the agreement did not exist between the departing guarantor and the remaining borrower guarantors.

Beware of the lender's demand for your spouse's signature; the lender's sole intent is to make certain it can reach the equity in your home. Make every effort to not have your spouse sign the note to protect your home from future collection efforts, even at the cost of not getting the loan. Small business loans are far too risky to put your home up as collateral.

> Make every effort to not have your spouse sign the note to protect your home from future collection efforts should they occur, even at the cost of not getting the loan.

Yes, a lender can take your home even if your spouse has not signed, and it may in some instances liquidate the home and then give the spouse his or her share of the equity. This, of course, reduces the value of the liquidation, and thus it may not happen at all, but be aware of the possibilities. (This rarely occurs, but can happen and is a negotiating chip used by the bank)

There are many instances when a guarantor does not know he or she personally guaranteed a loan because the guaranty is buried in some paragraph in language that is difficult to discern or recognize as a personal guaranty. This may be successfully challenged and requires a lawyer's specific analysis to determine your rights.

A personal guaranty requires a personal signature. Thus, when signing any guaranty language or documents, be certain to sign as your titled position, be it president, general manager, or vice president, indicating you are signing on behalf of the business entity, not on behalf of yourself personally.

When there is a second signature line and a request for you to sign both as a business entity officer and personally, beware you are accepting the risk personally, and you need to understand what that means and what that could cost you. If you sign personally, you may be held personally responsible. If you sign corporately as an officer, you may not be held responsible personally. This is a huge difference.

Simply stated, you should always have legal documentation reviewed by a lawyer who works for you or do not sign it. You will be held responsible for what you sign.

While many banks freely state they will not lend to you unless your spouse signs the guaranty, you need to challenge this, as many SBA-guaranteed loans are written without spousal guaranties. It is possible, they may be bluffing when they tell you no spousal signature, no loan.

The banks' favorite ploy in gaining spousal cooperation is to challenge the wife or husband with, for example, the remark, "So you don't believe in your husband? Well if you don't believe in his success, why should we?" What wife or husband can deflect that challenge? That does not mean he or she should guaranty the note. Beware!

## Modifying Your SBA Loan ... Not the Way to Go

I talk to many borrowers who obtain guaranteed SBA loans and then, because of the downturn, experience problems and cannot make the payments. Typically, revenues are down from the sharp recession, the business does not develop as projected, and cash flow is less than anticipated. The borrowers want to modify the loan to allow them to make smaller debt service payments. They expect the future to be brighter, and so when the modification is over, as it is most often a temporary request or allowance, they can then return to the original debt service requirements.

It is difficult to get such cooperation from either the bank or the SBA, and if it does occur, it will be short term, probably three to six months of interest-only payments, hardly the answer to your problems.

Second, it is unlikely that you will be in better shape when the modification period is over. The time will be too short and the modification too insignificant, and the business will not be generating significantly larger revenues in three to six months.

The problem may be perceived to be the business's inadequate performance, but I suggest the real problem is that the loan was based on higher revenues pre-recession and now the direct result of reduced revenues from the recession. It's too much debt and will not be serviceable by the business. The reality is, the business is earning as much as it can, and it is unlikely you will be able to adjust it meaningfully in a short time. Thus, the only answer is not to modify the note terms but to reduce the principal debt through debt forgiveness.

The problem is how, when neither the bank nor the SBA will willingly consider such a request. Even getting a modification is frequently very difficult and most often rejected. The real point here is if you find yourself thinking that all you need is six months at interest-only or a few months without any payment, stop. Do not accept the bank's meager offer of modification; it will only prolong the pain and will not solve anything.

You need a major adjustment. A large reduction of debt, not a minor tweaking of interest or a few months of nonpayment. It will take a sophisticated strategy carefully implemented to produce this result. Many new businesses have a false start, or fail to yield the results as projected as soon as expected, or are simply suffering from the massive recession we are experiencing. This is not unusual or unpredictable. The unusual aspect here is that SBA loans are far less flexible than standard loan relationships. You cannot expect cooperation.

## What Happened to Payment Deferrals?

Below is a press release from the SBA. It is interesting because I am working with over 50 banks handling defaulted SBA loans, and apparently, few have read the announcement. Few banks offer anything other than collection efforts. The only relief I am aware they offer is a three to six months of interest-only payments. Occasionally I see deferments, and occasionally I see the bank simply looking the other way for long periods of default, seemingly doing nothing.

I encourage you to print out this release and show it to your banker. Who knows? Maybe someone will pay attention.

**October 20, 2008 Release Number: 08-105.**

**In an Effort to Help Small Businesses, SBA Encourages Lenders to Offer Loan Deferment Relief**

WASHINGTON—In response to the financial crisis, the U.S. Small Business Administration today announced it is strongly encouraging its participating 7(a) lenders and Certified Development companies to work with business borrowers to provide them with the flexibility they need to keep their businesses running during these difficult economic times. As access to credit and capital has tightened, many businesses face increased challenges in meeting their financial obligations. This is especially true of small businesses hit hard by the recent economic slowdown that are now unable to make payroll, or purchase essential inventory.

SBA is reminding participating lenders they have the authority on a case-by-case basis to extend temporary payment relief for qualifying borrowers with 7(a) and 504 loans who are struggling to make their payments. "The SBA is here to help small businesses during these difficult economic times. We are encouraging our lending partners to follow suit by extending three-month payment deferments on their SBA guaranteed loans to qualified borrowers who need relief," said SBA Acting Administrator Sandy K. Baruah. "We recognize that small business owners are faced with challenging decisions right now."

By providing three-month deferments to qualifying borrowers who are struggling, our lending partners can help small business owners free up the capital they need to maintain their businesses.

If a deferment longer than three consecutive monthly payments is needed for a loan, borrowers can work directly with their lenders who in turn will work closely with the SBA to identify the best solution.

At the same time, the SBA is asking its lenders not to broadly call borrower loans due to changing financial variables, such as fluctuations in personal credit scores, declining collateral values, and reduced home equity, which are currently affected by the disruption in the financial markets.

The SBA has issued a notice that will be distributed widely to its lenders and 120 field offices encouraging them to look at these cases individually and to work with individual borrowers in order to facilitate the longer term success of these small businesses.

If only it were true . . .

## Defaulting on Your SBA-Guaranteed Loan

I talk to many small business owners who entered into SBA-guaranteed loans. And often I come up against borrower's remorse, a condition that most defaulting borrowers experience. They feel really bad about not fulfilling their obligation, not satisfying their commitment, and breaking their promise to repay. I have great respect for this belief that we should all fulfill our commitments, honor our word, and do what we say we will do.

Sometimes, however, circumstances beyond your control force a small business owner to fail. An economic meltdown is one example that no individual business owner could have prevented. Universally, I find that small business owners stop at nothing to succeed, including investing every penny they have, borrowing as much as they can from wherever they can, working without taking a paycheck, and putting in many long hours. They do their best to succeed and want nothing more than to be able to pay their obligations, but sometimes they come up short.

We know that when you go to the bank and ask for help, the answer is, "No deal. The SBA does not allow adjustment to the terms." Because the SBA requires the banks to exhaust their legal remedies to collect and liquidate the collateral to satisfy the note (under the threat of losing their SBA guaranty), the banks are not disposed toward making meaningful modifications. Thus, when things go wrong, you are in deep trouble with no opportunity to work things out safely. The most they will offer is three to six months of interest-only payments, no help at all. They will liquidate your home and everything else you own.

### Insurance—You're Covered

There is one aspect that the borrower is seldom reminded of and is what I consider the equalizer. You paid a significant insurance fee for the SBA guaranty—insurance for the bank to receive the guaranty to cover the bank's losses should you default. So when and if it happens, when circumstances occur that prevent you from paying, you have already paid for the insurance to cover the bank's losses.

So why do you feel so bad about being unable to pay? Why destroy yourself and your family's financial future to honor your word when you have purchased insurance to cover the losses? It is seldom your negligence or personal failure; it is typically the result of uncontrollable events. Since all those involved in small business loans are aware of the possibility of this happening, they require you to purchase protection for the bank. Despite this insurance, the bank is still be required to liquidate your assets as best as it can. Then the bank puts its hand out to the SBA for the guaranty . . . that you paid for.

## Shorter Default Period for SBA-Guaranteed Loans

In recent times, the benchmark for banks to call SBA-guaranteed loans in default has been 90 days. That's when the lawyers are engaged, the note is deemed in default and is called, and the liquidation of collateral by foreclosure and auction begins.

> Keep in mind that the banks' guaranty from the SBA depends on their exhausting their legal remedies to liquidate collateral when the borrower is in default.

Keep in mind that the banks' guaranty from the SBA depends on their exhausting their legal remedies to liquidate collateral when the borrower is in default. Once the process begins, there is no talking to them. You can only respond to the legal process, which leaves you little room to change their course of direction.

Now the banks are ratcheting up the default point. Some banks consider 90 days too long to wait, and in one instance we experienced recently, a bank began its process a mere 15 days after failure to pay a monthly installment.

The leash is shortening, and you must respond more quickly to the assault. Or else when you wake one morning shortly after failing to pay, you may find your business assets in liquidation, facing foreclosure. While this time frame is not universal, I anticipate it as a growing trend.

There is still a process to unfold requiring photographing assets, doing appraisals, making demands, and so on. However, the banks are beginning to awaken to the many months being wasted while nothing happens, including getting debt service payments from the borrower. They are beginning to eliminate this time of inaction. So do not expect many months to unwind while nothing is done. Those days appear to be passing quickly, and you can now expect the assault will begin almost immediately.

The lesson is, since you know well in advance that you will soon be defaulting, it behooves you to plan, to determine exactly how you are going to deal with the foreclosure and liquidation process and, of course, the resulting personal guaranty attack.

Alternatively, it is never too late to enter into a workout scenario. If you don't know how to develop such a plan, get help.

## An SBA Loan Workout Can Be Done

I frequently hear that SBA loans cannot be worked out: paid off short with a compromised conclusion and forgiveness of the shortfall. It ain't so.

It is difficult, as with any workout negotiation, and one must have a clear understanding of the SBA's rules and requirements. It can be done successfully if the timing and situation are handled correctly.

The SBA has its own offer-in-settlement forms, it has a committee that accepts and rejects, and it is even willing to, indirectly through your corresponding banker, negotiate a fair resolution for a defaulted loan. In fact, it is also possible to talk with an SBA representative, although not a decision maker.

That's both good and bad, as it's both the bank and the SBA that must be satisfied, and each has its own rules and requirements. In the end it's the SBA's decision that counts although it's the bank you talk with the most. That makes for some confusion, as frequently the bank or its attorneys are not telling you the truth.

The SBA does, however, have some strong requirements that are fast and hard and must be understood to avoid your being frustrated and wasting your time.

1. The SBA requires that the breaching business no longer be operational when an offer is made. This requirement is not cut and dried but is subject to many options. How to handle this requirement is also an important part of the strategy and must be evaluated very carefully to serve your own best interest.

2. All the business assets must be liquidated. This is another important part of a workout plan, which, when handled effectively, can be accomplished in your own best interests.

3. The bank must implement a significant legal effort to recapture any potential cash before an offer will be contemplated. In other words, all the collateral must have been liquidated. Many homes act as collateral for the loans, and yes, they can and will be liquidated if this issue is not handled correctly.

All the guarantors, including a spouse who signed the guarantees, must deal with an SBA loan default effectively and completely. If not a spouse, then each guarantor sinks or swims on his or her own financial merits. If the debt is guaranteed by both spouses, there are greater difficulties that must be worked out effectively.

All the guarantors, other than husband and wife, must file their own offer in compromise and create their own negotiation settlement. Frequently, this becomes a source for negotiation, as we and the bank want to resolve all the issues in one global resolution for all parties, which can be a challenge.

**Banker Support.** Keep in mind that the bank actually lent you the money, and the SBA merely guaranteed to pay back up to 80 percent. Since the SBA will pay the bank, it requires the bank, as its agent, to exercise all due diligence to collect as much as possible or the bank may potentially violate the terms of the guaranty and lose the payback. This is the source and reason for a tough bank collection practice and a no-compromise attitude.

Your lending banker's support and cooperation are important in developing a successful workout, and without a good banker relationship, a good workout conclusion is diminished, although achievable.

For an SBA workout, the overall principles remain the same: maximum collection under the financial circumstances of the borrower's situation. Clearly, however, this is subject to interpretation and effective presentation. It takes time, as the review committee is in Virginia and services the entire country. It is a political beast, and over the years, depending on various political issues, the committee can be easier or harder to work with in addressing loan shortfalls.

> **Your lending banker's support and cooperation are important in developing a successful workout.**

As of this writing, I believe the SBA is suffering many losses. It wants to stem the flow of loss, but its mission is to support the small business system and the borrowers, and so the results are mixed, mostly depending on the quality of the borrower's preparation and presentation, tough, but fair, I would say.

The SBA is very busy and reviews files in the order they are received. It typically asks for additional information, once under review, to better understand the financial condition of the guarantors, and thus the procedure can be extremely long, taking many months, even years. We average about 10 months to a year to completely resolve a defaulted SBA loan workout.

**Second-Wave Negotiations.** Once the workout has been reviewed, negotiated to conclusion, and accepted, I have had success in modifying the acceptance further, the *second-wave* negotiation I call it, adjusting the terms and conditions and even lowering the payoffs further than agreed, based on the realities of the refinancing or source-of-funds requirements (lenders' requirements if you are refinancing to support the workout).

This second pass is important and can yield extraordinary results.

My advice is to protect yourself as best you can with effective financial planning *before* the notes are called and *before* the business closes and the assets are liquidated. You want to be in control of this process, and in the end it will work out best for you. You know where you are headed before anyone else; thus planning is critical for the best outcome for the borrower.

**Avoiding Potential Tax Consequences.** For SBA workouts, just like those obtained directly from a bank, debt forgiveness is converted to ordinary

income and taxable. There are sometimes serious potential tax consequences, which can be devastating, and in the workout you run the risk
of solving one problem while creating another. Many exceptions are
made to this ruling, with some of the new legislation to be aware of, but
seek appropriate counsel before you work out your debt. Most borrowers in default have little to be concerned around this issue, but it requires
analysis to be certain.

## How Much to Offer in the Offer in Compromise

Business owners constantly ask me this question, "What is a reasonable
amount to propose for an offer in compromise for a defaulted SBA loan?"

I have a very simple answer: the combination of your income stream
and your liquidated value. The liquidated value of the business assets
does not include your personal guaranty.

Computing what that means is a bit trickier, as the liquidated value
of your net worth is frequently not easy to compute. Once done, the
number yields a relevant value, used as an important benchmark to
determine the right amount to offer. What you earn can support debt;
what can be realized by liquidation helps determine the amount the SBA
expects to collect from you. The combined value is the real number. The
skill is in presenting your offer in the best light, most beneficial for you.
This, of course, does not include fraudulent transfers.

While it can take a long time for the SBA to get back to us with an
acceptance or rejection, the SBA will ask for current information when
it sends out its rejection of your first offer, which it frequently will turn
down. Financial recovery or further business decay will require adjustment to your counteroffer.

> The largest area of error in computing your net worth and liquidated value is in
> overestimating the value of your home.

The largest area of error in computing your net worth and liquidated
value is in overestimating the value of your home. We all tend to believe
it is worth more than it is.

In presenting your offer, take these factors into consideration:

- If you live in a homestead state, such as Texas and Florida, your
  home equity is protected.

- If your spouse has signed the guaranty, this allows the bank to reach all the equity; if not, then only half the equity is available.
- Be careful of adding value for minority ownership positions in land or other businesses, as it can be argued that despite the inherent value of the underlying asset, there is little value in a minority position since it cannot be liquidated.
- Protected assets like 401(k)s or IRAs are exempt from your calculations.

There are many traps and pitfalls that must either be eliminated or explained adequately, and it may require a professional to assist you in developing your best possible presentation. It requires both experience and specific knowledge to design an effective financial statement. The idea of down-valuing your position is contrary to everything you have done in the past and creates a challenge to successfully deliver the right answers.

## SBA Disaster Loans ... a Disaster

Disaster loans for Katrina, the World Trade Center, earthquakes, wildfires, and other devastations, what a wonderful service our government provides! It acknowledges that these are events, which we are unable to control, devastate or even wipe out portions of our community. Coming to our rescue, the government offers emergency loans to provide stability, salvation, and even survival to the families and businesses severely affected by these disasters. People who are left without homes, possessions, cash, clothes, life's essentials, are given the support they need to survive and reemerge ... that is the hope.

Thank you, government. These are the types of services we need our government to provide, and apparently they are. If only the story had a happy ending, but there is a tragic flaw. Here is the disaster part of the disaster loans.

Once again, you had better recover, make a profit, and earn an income no matter how serious your situation and ability to recover, because in the disaster loan program there is no offer-in-compromise program. There is no way to work out your loan if you fail to recover and pay it back.

With a normal SBA loan, there is an offer-in-compromise program, and it is based on the clear need for compromise, recognizing that many

SBA-guaranteed loans will default. The SBA's own guidelines allow reductions of up to 80 percent of the loan, and in many situations we have helped business owners who need further reduction. So what could be wrong with this plan? It sounds appropriate and the right thing for everyone involved.

Yes it is, except for reasons that defy logic and challenge the credibility of the SBA, as it appears that there is no offer-in-compromise program for disaster loans. So the neediest people, who receive assistance when confronted by a disaster and have accepted money to survive, had better recover completely and profitably, because the loan has no offer-in-compromise provisions and serious penalties for default.

It gets worse. The Department of Justice acts as the collection agency and will jack interest rates on defaulted SBA disaster loans to as much as 42 percent. The SBA offers low interest rates for disaster loans. When businesses default on payback, it buries borrowers with insurmountable debt, crippling their opportunity to emerge and restart their lives.

When we challenged the SBA, through commitment and tenacity, we penetrated the system and uncovered a path to debt forgiveness. The SBA, however, does not advertise, admit, or even acknowledge it exists.

> **When we challenged the SBA, through commitment and tenacity, we penetrated the system and uncovered a path to debt forgiveness.**

In 2010, the SBA tacitly agreed to 50 percent forgiveness of disaster loan debt on review and qualification. This is not enough to provide any real relief, but it is the beginning of opening the window of opportunity. We shall see how this works out in the future.

## Workout Myths

Like so many matters, unless you concentrate in a specific area and thus have deep and broad hands-on experience handling the many variations of that theme, you cannot possibly provide the expertise required to do the best job possible. In other words, do not conduct your own SBA workout … get an experienced specialist. The knee-jerk reaction to having a troubled loan is to get a lawyer. Rethink this approach.

There may be ancillary legal issues involved requiring a lawyer, especially if you allow the loan to default and are involved in the foreclosure process; even then, I suggest the answer lies in a business workout, not a legal defense. After all, what possible defense could you mount ... usually none.

Like any other workout, overall, an SBA workout is a business problem, not necessarily a legal issue.

The objective is to reduce debt and preserve assets, not just to defend against foreclosure or try to prevent the liquidation of all your assets, including your business and home.

## Changing Rules for Offers in Compromise ... for the Good!

It used to be that it would take about a year to get a return response from the SBA after submitting an offer in compromise. The SBA responded with a letter with a rejection, a counterproposal, or an acceptance. You were never given an opportunity to talk directly with a decision maker. You could only attempt to negotiate through an intermediary message carrier. While it worked a little, it was time consuming and cumbersome.

Now the SBA is relying more heavily on the participating lending bank to handle most of the burden and certainly all the contact with the borrower. This is working out better. The banker negotiates with the borrower what the banker believes is an acceptable deal, and the SBA fairly quickly responds to the banker, who then relays the response back to the borrower.

> **The SBA is relying more heavily on the participating lending bank to handle most of the burden and certainly all of the contact with the borrower.**

The return time from offering to response is down to three to four months and in some instances much less, weeks even. And we get to discuss and negotiate a resolution with the lending banker; when the banker supports the resolution, it has a good chance of being accepted by the SBA.

While this may sound even more cumbersome, it is far better because we can negotiate with the banker, whose agreement is now important for the result. The SBA is now swayed and almost always accepts it, with few exceptions.

Unfortunately, we have also seen some abuse, as the banker is now the point person in the process and sometimes changes the deal presented to the SBA, or perhaps the SBA moves the banker to change the deal. As a result, we are seeing accepted deals being twisted and changed on return from the SBA. However, we still get to negotiate, although on the banker's terms, not ours; so it is working far better, if not perfectly.

## Fast-Food Service for Loan Workouts

Yes, we received an answer to our request for an SBA workout in an hour. It is hard to believe, as we usually wait many months for other responses to an offer in compromises to surface, and now, all of a sudden, we get a call from the banker in an hour with an answer. It was a rejection, but it was an answer! We adjusted slightly, and the offer was accepted a few days later.

How did this happen? Some banks are so strongly affiliated with the SBA, they are granted the authority to accept or reject offers in compromise on behalf of the SBA. They e-mail all the information to the SBA for review and rejection of or agreement to the bank's decision.

It takes time to do a workout. Figure on a year, but once in discussion, the hard collection tactics tend to cease if the bank is properly handled, and you work out the issues civilly and effectively.

# Chapter 20

# IRS Workouts

## Resolving Unpaid 941 Taxes

I t happens way too often, so you are not alone. It's not a good decision, but I understand why you fail to pay your 941 payroll tax, week
upon week.

The tax payment is voluntary, which makes it easier to skip this
week's 941 payment and pay the phone bill instead (or whatever bill is
most important to your survival at that moment). You rationalize that
without your phones operating, you are out of business. So you pay the
phone bill and not the payroll tax, hoping to make it next week.

We all know what happens. Next week never comes ... very deadly.
Why deadly?

**The Levy Warning.** Because not paying the 941 payroll tax creates an impos-
sible-to-avoid a trap for below-breakeven operations. You continue to
operate below breakeven and will probably not catch up soon enough to
avert disaster. Eventually, the IRS catches up, as it always does. After a
while, with a progression of notices warning you of the obligation and
the IRS's intent to collect the tax due, you finally receive a notice that
reads, "We intend to levy." That's like the noise from a rattlesnake warning you before it strikes, a warning you should not ignore.

**The Levy.** The IRS will sweep your accounts and remove everything in all your operational accounts. The agency typically chooses a Friday to catch your accounts since they are likely to be bloated with payroll. Unable to cash their checks, your employees become quite upset, and you cannot operate effectively, as every check that is floating will soon bounce. Now you have to replace the cash to cover everything you wrote checks for before you can write the next check ... oh yes, it is also possible that your account will remain inoperable for a while as you work this out.

Some banks take a levy action very seriously and will close your accounts. The levy becomes a permanent record on your credit history, and it becomes difficult to open new accounts because other banks will refuse.

Here is what you can do to alleviate the situation if you choose to handle it yourself.

**The Workout.** You must immediately call the IRS office handling your account and ask for an agent in the collection department. Tell the agent you have been levied and want to work this out. If you have difficulty, ask for a manager for assistance.

The agent will check a few things first, to determine what your situation is. The agent will also ask if you have filed the required tax returns due from the offending business entity. Hopefully, the answer is yes. If it is no, you will need to have everything filed before the agent can work with you, and the IRS will continue to collect until resolved.

Then you must be current for two consecutive quarters before it can work this matter out with you. If you are not, you have to figure out how to become current for the prior two quarters before the IRS will enter into a payment plan. That is the objective, a payment plan for what is owed, since there is no compromise procedure under the existing circumstances.

You must remain current throughout this entire process, or you will be shut down faster than you can blink. The IRS takes trust fund abuse seriously, and it will liquidate your assets, putting you out of business and possibly out of your house ... if you fail to resolve this matter and stay current during the entire process.

Now you must fill out Form 433-B for the IRS, the Collection Information Statement for your business, which will help the service determine how much it can extract from your business while you pay off the arrears. This form is available online, or your IRS office will provide it to you. The 433-B requires some backup documentation for what you claim are your cash flow requirements. Be careful; the IRS will ask for a list of current receivables, and if all does not work out to the IRS's satisfaction, it now will know exactly where to go to seize receivables, and it will.

It will determine the responsible party, presumably the person who signs checks or makes the decision about what is and what is not paid. However, your secretary, your administrative assistant, or your spouse, anyone in your business who is writing checks, could also be held responsible. You and every responsible party will be asked to fill out a 433-A, Collection Information Statement for Wage Earners and Self-Employed Individuals, for collection information to compute what the IRS can extract on a monthly basis from you and everyone else to clear this debt.

That's the good news: the IRS will permit a monthly payback program for what is owed . . . all of it, including penalties and interest and corporate contribution as well as trust fund money, everything you were supposed to pay and more. And it will probably be much more, as often the penalties and interest are more than the tax you failed to pay in the first place.

Keep in mind that you are accruing interest throughout the payback program, and every payment goes to past interest and penalties but current interest first, all before your unpaid tax is credited. If your debt is large or old, it could take a lifetime to pay off.

> Keep in mind that you are accruing interest throughout the payback program, and every payment goes to past interest and penalties but current interest first.

Depending upon your 433-B information, the IRS will permit a rapid payback of the unpaid, past-due payroll taxes. This payback schedule is negotiable but is also based on the information provided. Your business will remain under lien until the final payment is made.

Pay your 941 taxes, or shut the door. That's my advice . . . that's the law. Failure to pay never works out well. If you cannot afford to make the payments, you must consider your business plan as the problem, not the tax. The real issue is lack of liquidity, profitability, gross revenue, or all three. Solve these problems, and the tax issue goes away. The tax issue is merely a symptom of a deeper problem that must be resolved before the taxes can ever be paid.

## 10 Realities of IRS Tax Debt Payment

To start, it's helpful to understand what Internal Revenue Service agents experience every day. They often have to deal with cheaters, liars, scoffers, and procrastinators; and then there are the "professional" tax guys—lawyers and accountants. No wonder the IRS agent's attitude is frequently unfriendly or even aggressively.

There are probably far more people that want to do the right thing who would pay their taxes if they could, and want to pay the debt off but can't. These people expect a degree of cooperation to support working out their tax debt but often fail to get it.

In my experience, taxpayers who owe back taxes almost always break promises. What happens, I believe, is that the agents are so beaten up by the bad or tough attacking behavior of so many of the people they experience, where promises are so infrequently kept, that their prevailing disposition is often defensive, nontrusting, and uncompromising. Frequently the IRS will require a payback program that is impossible to agree to because it is too aggressive, one that the taxpayer will most certainly default on.

There are, of course, some fair and honorable agents. Then there are some tough agents who are difficult to work with, as their objective is immediate payment on the back taxes owed or immediate liquidation. Immediate performance is typically impossible, and liquidation appears harsh under any circumstances, but this is frequently the situation.

Most taxpayers believe they are being unjustly charged for the penalties and interest. The service believes the penalties and interest hold the same importance as the tax itself and must be paid. There are some statutory provisions for removal of the interest or penalties; however, in most instances the service will not tell you about this or how to do it. It wants to collect it all. So here are 10 realities you must understand before you state your case to the IRS agent:

1. People want to negotiate a deal, but it doesn't work like that. Everything is controlled by equations, applications with an accept-

ance or rejection process, with separation between agent operatives and workout decision makers, and with staged levels of authority.

2. People believe that the following argument is compelling and will yield results:

   "Let me stay in business, and I will earn the money to pay you. Shut me down, and I will not be able to pay."

   The service would rather shut you down than have you abuse the tax code. Its reasoning is that you will likely do it again, so the sooner it stops you, the better. It is not interested in your argument unless it is clear you are making money and can demonstrate an ability to pay the debt off.

   Another version of this argument is about all the jobs that will be lost. The IRS will not be moved.

3. People believe they can negotiate a payback plan that makes sense and is affordable while staying in business. Doubtful. Frequently, the agent will require a payback program that is impossible to agree to because the taxpayer will most certainly default since it is far too aggressive.

   Not only is it frequently too expensive, but since you must also stay current on continuing 941 payroll tax obligations in addition to the arrears, it is unlikely that you will succeed for long.

4. People expect forgiveness and a second chance after bouncing a check in a payment plan. The IRS will stop the plan and demand payment, not allowing you back into a payment plan.

5. The argument, "You will get pennies on the dollar at an auction," is ineffective, as the amount collected is unimportant; it's the process and the finality of the liquidation auction that matters.

6. The IRS will put you out of your home if there is enough equity and if you do nothing else to prevent such action.

7. It will garnish paychecks, including pension and social security checks.

8. It frequently makes errors, and it is sometimes almost impossible to correct. The agents will follow the computer no matter where it takes them and what it says, even if they know it's wrong.

9. You must be current for two quarters to enter into a discussion and either work out a payment plan or make an offer in compromise. Failure to be current for two quarters will prevent any cooperation and will result in seizure.

10. Anyone who signed a check or satisfies other general requirements can be held totally and individually responsible for unpaid payroll taxes. Be aware of your rights and do not allow the IRS to attach everyone in sight as responsible parties. This can be appealed and won if the IRS becomes overly aggressive and broad reaching.

Between interest and penalties and the lien, borrowing money from the government (by not paying the taxes) and then paying the money back over time including penalties and interest is the worst deal you can ever make. It will not work out well for you. Do not use the IRS as a bank.

Do anything you can to pay the IRS off and get yourself out of harm's way, as most delinquent commercial taxpayers do not survive. These are 10 important concepts you must understand, gleaned from years of practice. You must know these facts so you or your inexperienced representative, a professional tax expert, counsel, or accountant do not waste time, blunder, or, worse, cause harm.

> Do anything you can to pay the IRS off and get yourself out of harm's way, as most delinquent commercial taxpayers do not survive.

## Determining the Responsible Party for Tax Debt

When a business fails to pay its 941 payroll tax obligation, as stated earlier, the IRS will determine who is or are the responsible parties. Each individual it identifies will be responsible for the entire amount owed, the entire tax, penalties, and interest. There could be many. This is a critical question often not considered in advance, and when asked too late results in much avoidable damage.

Typically, there is an owner calling the shots, ordering what payments are to be made and when. The owner is usually the one deciding when to pay all the bills, and certainly is the one who decides not to pay the 941 taxes. The owner is the responsible party.

Financial officers, payroll clerks, vice presidents, among others, may be implementing the payroll system and therefore making the tax payments. However, they usually answer to a more senior officer, the owner, on this matter.

Of course, the larger the organization becomes, the more spread out decision making may be, and it is entirely possible that this decision may be determined by a non-owner officer. The second issue, after determining who may be the decision maker, is determining who has signing authority on the checkbooks.

Sometimes there may be multiple signers, or the owner may not sign the checks or may sign checks occasionally, but not the payroll. So signers could include a number of people, all of whom have potential personal responsibility and need to be prepared for an examination. Then there is the treasurer of the corporation, sometimes an honorary title but one with great impact and one that is statutorily responsible by definition. An additional issue involved is the "flavor of the fact pattern." For example, a treasurer, who is the spouse of the owner, and who signs a few checks and makes a few decisions, who benefits from the revenue flow of the business, and who has knowledge that the taxes are *not* being paid, may be held as a responsible party because of the weight of the evidence.

## Here Are the Rules

1. The treasurer can be held responsible because one of the treasurer's responsibilities, statutorily, is to pay the taxes. Thus, the treasurer is a potential responsible party and can be held personally liable for the tax debt.
2. The authorized check signer can be held responsible for unpaid taxes, as this person is required to quit his job when he determines that the taxes are not being paid, effectively eliminating any potential personal responsibility for unpaid taxes.
3. The decision maker who dictates who is paid, even if she is not a signer or does not sign, is held responsible.

Decision-making authority, knowledge, signing authority, and treasurer title, as well as those who receive benefits from the failure to pay, are the major factors that determine who will be held as a responsible party. If deemed responsible, you are equally responsible for 100 percent of the debt due.

Typically, I see a dedicated bookkeeper with signing authority as a convenience to the owner; the bookkeeper may sign most of the checks or at least enough to warrant responsible-party status but is told not to pay the taxes by the owner. It is this person who is on the edge, who could be deemed responsible or not, depending on his or her responses to the IRS questioning. While it is the check signer's responsibility to quit when the taxes are not paid, to remove the possibility of responsible-party status, because that costs the employee his or her paycheck, it seldom happens. The worst situation of all is when the owner's spouse is the bookkeeper and signer. If the spouse is deemed responsible, the family's home is vulnerable and a lien may be placed upon it.

Most of the time the IRS officer is reasonable, and seldom are nonowners included as responsible parties; but on occasion it does happen, and that's a major problem. The owner does not want to see any individual, obviously acting out of loyalty, held responsible, but it can happen. Be aware, plan appropriately and in advance; there is much danger in not paying 941 payroll taxes. In the end, paying or not paying is a judgment call, and bad judgment frequently prevails.

## Understanding the Offer in Compromise

An offer in compromise can be an important and valuable part of a tax resolution program. Does it work? Sometimes.

Simply stated, the offer in compromise proposes a less-than-full resolution of an unpaid tax obligation. Keep in mind, however, that the IRS considers the unpaid interest and penalties as important as the tax itself. The entire obligation—principal, interest, and penalties—is subject to collection. While many believe that the IRS will knock off the penalties or interest if you offer to pay the tax, it just is not so.

> Simply stated, the offer in compromise proposes a less-than-full resolution of an unpaid tax obligation.

First, let's remove one huge misconception: As a rule the IRS does not negotiate.

There are moments when a decision can be insignificantly adjusted, but for the majority of times, the IRS separates decision making, so the offer is handled by a committee and not the revenue officer assigned to work with you for tax collection. There are rules and equations and a system with checks and balances, and so the concept of negotiation is not realistic.

What is in play is understanding how the IRS computes a satisfactory offer, as it has its methods, which must be thoroughly understood to successfully navigate the barriers and succeed in having an offer accepted. These measuring and evaluation devices are public and are typically included in an offer-in-compromise package available from the IRS or online.

The real creativity comes with arranging your financial affairs to best reflect the reality you want to project. This does not mean misstating your assets or liabilities; never do that. It does mean you are entitled to do whatever is in your legal power to pay as little tax as you can, including organizing and presenting your financial position in the best light possible for your needs.

Demonstrating that your offer properly reflects your economic reality and supports your offer in compromise requires skill. While some may say the facts are the facts, the presentation of the facts and the preparation of your financial condition in consideration of disclosing the facts are all part of the process.

There are many reorganizational opportunities you can consider that would have a dramatic effect on the outcome without violating tax liens. For example, protecting one's home is an important aspect of asset planning but must be executed appropriately and with the cooperation of the IRS, but can be done.

One has a few choices to make, which are part of the application process, for example, specifically indicating why the taxpayer is asking for relief and on what grounds. Finally the IRS requires supporting documentation.

Most important is to understand that success comes by complying with the statute, not negotiating against it. If you do comply and present an accurate recitation of your financial condition that supports your workout request, you have a reasonably good chance to succeed.

An offer in compromise, when successful, is a wonderful benefit for the taxpayer. It can take six to 12 months and during that time can be very frustrating as the IRS may ask for the same documentation that you have already provided time and again. The IRS eventually gets it all together and comes to a decision. That's the good news—in the end it can be made to work for you.

So under the proper circumstances an offer in compromise is an excellent tool to reduce your tax debt and resolve the matter. A conclusion can include a lump-sum payoff, a 90-day payout, or even a two-year or longer payout. Remember, however, that the lien remains in place, affecting you and all your assets until the final payment is made.

## Choose Your Poison: Compromise or Payment Program

If you have defaulted on your 941 payroll tax payments, have built up a debt, and are now dealing with the IRS and working it out, there is a reality check you need to address and fully understand so you do not get trapped into a no-win situation.

Here is a real-life example of how it happens.

The IRS deemed the owner-operator of a small business as the responsible party, and so the debt of the business is now the debt of the individual owner. After a fairly vigorous discovery and investigation period where the IRS agent learned all she could through the collection process, including the 433-A and -B forms and other demands for financial documentation, she was pushing the client into an aggressive payback program requiring large weekly payments, enough to satisfy the debt within a few years' time. She "promised" that after a period of paying on this plan, the client could enter into an offer in compromise and reduce the amount owed and that she would help make this happen. It won't happen.

Very simply stated, if the borrower can afford to pay back the debt and demonstrates this ability by entering into an agreement and perform on it for a period of time, why would the IRS accept a discounted payoff? The IRS already knows it can get a full payout with interest and penalties accruing along the way as promised.

Further, the separation between the offer-in-compromise department from the collection agent is extreme, and one has little to do with the other. Thus, she has almost no influence whatsoever.

Her plan was bad advice. Selling a blue-sky offer to entice the taxpayer into a very expensive and brisk payback with a false promise of salvation later on is a cruel ruse. Never enter into a payback agreement and then perform if your intent is to negotiate an offer in compromise. This is the wrong kind of cooperation and works against your best interests—always.

Better to accept reality and stay with the likelihood that you cannot afford to pay back the full debt while paying current 941 taxes and briskly reducing the past obligation. It makes little sense and is likely to result in default again anyway, so what's the point. You have already entered into default and now are primed to do an offer in compromise. So do it. Do not expect you can do both. It's one or the other; pick your poison.

It's not about pleasing the revenue officer so maybe he or she will be nicer to you; it's about being able to afford the workout and resolve the issue while staying in business. That's the challenge. IRS agents are fine with closing you down and liquidating your assets irrespective of what the return will be. Even nothing is OK.

> **IRS agents are fine with closing you down and liquidating your assets irrespective of what the return will be.**

Alternatively, it is unlikely you will be able to afford both the aggressive payback program that the IRS is demanding and the ongoing current payments. It's too much, and paid weekly, it provides you with no room to breathe.

You are bound to fail. Do something else. Qualify for a discounted payoff and then schedule the payments over time and get it done. But the first time you make a payment on IRS's "plan," your workout days are over; it will be straight to liquidation a soon as you default one more time.

You never want a full-payment program unless there are extenuating circumstances that prevent a viable offer in compromise. You can enter into a payment plan for the accepted offer in compromise, however. That's the best plan.

## Don't Wait for the IRS to Attach a Lien

You must always remember, it is your responsibility and duty to yourself and to your business to represent yourself and your business in the light most beneficial to your own needs. Whether you are right or wrong, presumably in default of a required payment, you are still entitled and expected to represent yourself in your own best interests.

This includes arranging your affairs and adjusting your position to your own advantage as much as the law allows. You cannot engage in fraudulent transfers to avoid creditors' rights, but you can still present yourself in the best light possible and support this with appropriately planned and executed adjustments.

However, one area that business owners often do not handle well because it can be confusing to many is when the IRS sends a taxpayer notice that it intends to attach a lien. It is a huge red flag that your property rights are about to change dramatically and for the worse unless you do something about it before the lien attaches.

## Options Before the Lien

Before the lien lands, you should review your position and make certain reasonable and allowable transitions, transfers, sales, and adjustments in your best interests while you can without the IRS being able to review or prevent you. This makes sense, as long as the transfers are for reasonable consideration and support a reasonable business reason or practice.

Yet many in such situations, knowing the lien is coming, frequently opt to wait and do nothing to better their position. Don't wait until the IRS liens attach and then ask for help. By waiting, many safe-keeping maneuvers that could have been accomplished are now impossible or a whole lot harder.

If you decided to sell an asset prior to the lien from the IRS, it is possible to use the proceeds for whatever gainful business purpose you have. Once the lien attaches, you cannot. If you sell an asset under lien, the capital must go directly to the IRS (or whoever has the highest-priority lien position); and bear in mind that the sale can take place only with the IRS's permission, as it must release the lien for the transaction to occur. So once the lien is attached, your ability to arrange your assets in a way most beneficial to you and your company is reduced, hindering your ability to raise and disburse capital for good or important business reasons. The IRS will control all your lien assets, and any sale or liquidation will be solely for the benefit of the IRS or others with priority positions.

> If you decided to sell an asset prior to the lien from the IRS, it is possible to use the proceeds for whatever gainful business purpose you have.

The point is, we must never forget that in any workout with the IRS, SBA, banks, and other creditors, you probably will have some idea about when the lien come, as eventually it will. Even if you have absolutely no idea when a lien may attach, you certainly know if you are in trouble, and confronting these issues sooner rather than later will give you the best vantage point.

When you get the lien warning notice from the IRS, it is your last chance to act before the lien sets its noose around your neck. So as soon as you know you need to respond to the situation, arrange your business and financial affairs accordingly, in the best light for you to survive most effectively with the least damage. That's good business planning sense.

## Why Hiding Assets Doesn't Work

Business owners will do much to protect themselves and their assets when in trouble. Sometimes, it's not a well-thought-out plan and ends up without producing the results desired and also puts them into a worse situation than they were in previously. It can be a step backward instead of a defensive move that makes sense.

**Transferring Assets to a New Company.** Here is an all-too-frequent error. The business owner in trouble creates a new entity, perhaps an LLC, which can be done easily on the Internet in a few minutes. Being the sole owner, she transfers capital, contracts, inventory, whatever she has that is valuable, into this new entity, believing she will protect the assets from harm's way. The owner assumes that the IRS or bank may not find the new entity. Even if it does find it, the assets will be protected because it is a separate entity, which is not guilty of the breaches suffered in the offending company where the assets previously resided. That's the typical plan.

I will not discuss the legal aspects of this issue, as I leave that for you and your lawyer. I will, however, suggest that as a business strategy used to protect your assets from harm, liquidation, seizure, and so forth, this is never a good idea.

If the new entity is deemed an alter ego of yourself and your primary corporation, which owes the money, and if done merely for the purpose of hiding assets to trick the creditor, the newly created company will be deemed the same as the company where the assets came from. They will collapse into one offending entity with no additional protection whatsoever.

So what's the point? Resist this temptation. I see it way too often and must warn you this is a deficient strategy. A transfer of assets has to have a legitimate business purpose and be done at fair market value in order to be provided the full benefits and protection that is offered.

There are many legal requirements that I will leave for you to discuss with your lawyer; however, suffice it to know that the IRS and banks are onto this thinly veiled procedure. You will be liable for the same debts you tried to hide your assets from in the first place. So nothing other than your bad faith will come out of this exercise.

**Fraudulent Transfer.** Another form of the same silliness is called a *fraudulent transfer* and occurs when a businessperson moves assets into his wife's name (or anyone's name) for no consideration, believing he will either hide the asset or preserve it from creditors' attempts to liquidate. Such a transfer can be easily undone by the courts and will result in the asset being returned for liquidation.

Transfers for less than adequate consideration and transfers to immediate family members are all very suspicious and typically do not result in the desired protection. In fact, the IRS code says that any transfer to immediate family members is or can be deemed "fraudulent on its face" irrespective of consideration paid.

Check it out before you do this; there are better ways to achieve what you are trying to accomplish. Talk to your lawyer on this one, before you act.

## Beware the IRS Collection Tools

The IRS has huge power to do many things that will cause you great pain, suffering, loss of property, business opportunity, and, yes, even your home. This we all probably understand, but a closer analysis of some of the IRS collection methods is appropriate to remind you not to ignore the service; there is a better path through cooperation than in avoidance. Just as the IRS code gives the service power to liquidate, the same code gives protection to the taxpayer and provides ways to resolve the issues. They are workable if you know the path and have a guide or a map.

> The IRS has huge power to do many things that will cause you great pain, suffering, loss of property, business opportunity, and, yes, even your home.

However, they have a few tricks you may want to be aware of.

**Protecting Payroll.** At the beginning of this chapter we introduced you to the IRS tactic of levying all your operational accounts. The IRS will remove all funds that are there. Checks you've written against the accounts that are floating at that moment will all bounce. Frequently, the IRS chooses a Friday afternoon to get the payroll account at its highest balance. On Monday morning, if not over the weekend, you will discover it has taken action when your employees tell you they cannot cash their payroll checks.

What you need to know is that the tax code does not permit the IRS to levy and remove cash from your payroll account, but it does it anyway. It does this to make certain you pay attention and cooperate with its efforts to collect. If your payroll account is levied and swept clean, you must call the IRS office handling this matter immediately and demand the payroll money be released. You will have to prove that it was your payroll account that was levied. Once satisfied that it is payroll, the IRS will fax your bank, removing the levy on and unfreezing the payroll account only. That's one emergency off your plate. However, the damage is done, as your employees are out looking for other jobs.

> **What you need to know is that the tax code does not permit the IRS to levy and remove cash from your payroll account, but it does it anyway.**

**Getting Your Attention.** Be aware, that while one part of the strategy is to collect cash, another is to get your attention so that you work out the debt effectively. Some "smart" business owners figure this out and then either attempt to hide money in the payroll account or even use the payroll account as an operating account. This may work for a while, but you will be discovered, which is why you must prove to the IRS that it's current payroll it took (levied) and then the IRS will release the money.

As if that is not damaging enough, now you must find the funds to cover all the bounced checks. The next trick can be fatal or at least very damaging to your ongoing business—this occurs when the agency levies your accounts receivable.

How does the IRS know? You may have provided the information during an interview where an agent ask specifically for you to name the accounts receivables and provide contact information. However, the IRS also has the power to look into your deposit history and determine who has paid you in the recent past. The agency makes the assumption these are ongoing customers who will owe you again, and it levies them all, irrespective of whether they currently owe you anything.

You can only imagine the horror experienced when your best customers call and inform you they are sending the check they owe you to the IRS. They then explain they will not be doing any further business with you for two reasons: First, they are uninterested in having the IRS in their face; second, you are no longer deemed reliable because they fear you will soon be gone. That's the end of your business.

You may recover if your customers are loyal and savvy enough to know the IRS will only send out a request and will do nothing to follow up. Otherwise, it will mean a huge hit on your business status, causing many customers to leave.

## Why You Need Experienced Representation

I have seen a few wrongful acts perpetuated by unscrupulous IRS agents when the taxpayer meets without an experienced specialist knowledgeable about IRS matters. Here are the three most common examples in my experience:

- The agent will occasionally not offer you available alternatives, but will demand the worst conclusion for you, which is the best option for servicing the debt.
- I have seen the results of misguided agents breaking the statutory requirements, misapplying the statute, simply bullying taxpayers into situations that the law did not intend.
- The agent occasionally tries to convince the taxpayer to get rid of the third-party representative, the expert who protects the taxpayer's rights and knows what can and cannot be done.

So here is the rule: Never go into a meeting or say anything or make any commitment or sign any document with the IRS without having an expert guide you. Never.

Like most large organizations, the IRS contains both caring and uncaring people and, occasionally, some who vengefully wield their position. Sometimes, the seemingly nicest agent will take the most aggressive position without your really knowing. Remember, the agent's job is to collect, not advise, and so the advice is unreliable. To understand what's happening and what is the right path requires experience.

Rather than learn while representing yourself, get expert, experienced representation, someone who knows what's happening.

## Beware the IRS Agent, the Wolf in a Lamb's Suit

Most experiences I have had with the IRS are reasonable, and most frequently the agents present themselves in a respectful and helpful manner. On the other hand, I have experienced some agents who do attempt to convince the taxpayer to jettison her third-party expert, the person she has hired to act in her best interests.

Agents typically offer respectful treatment. However, I have seen one exception occur often enough to provide you with a warning. The agent seeks out the taxpayer, who has brought her expert tax guy with her to the first meeting; away from the taxpayer's representative, the agent delivers the kiss of death. It goes as follows:

> You don't want this guy representing you. I am not going to cooperate with him. You will do a lot better with just me. We can work this out together. I will be a lot easier to deal with without him interfering. It's not in your best interest.

I have seen this happen too many times. While friendly and pleasant, the agent designs a plan that no self-respecting tax expert would ever allow, one that requires a payout far more than would most likely have resulted with a third-party expert present. The tax code is complex, and in the hands of an agent against a taxpayer, who is intimidated and wanting the issue to go away, the result is a disastrous plan that deprives the taxpayer of her rights and the best plan possible. In the end, the taxpayer exchanges the potential for a dramatically reduced payout for the IRS agent's very high payout. It's a difficult choice for a taxpayer, and unfortunately, this ploy works all too well. I understand the plight of the taxpayer, who feels the agent is offering a better opportunity to resolve her issues, and that is all she wants to do.

So be aware: If the IRS agent begins to speak to you about the bad decision you have made to allow an expert third-party tax workout guy represent you . . . run for the hills, call your representative, and take cover. Let your representative handle the next discussion and allow him to continue to resolve your issues. This is the only way it will possibly work out well. Beware of the IRS agent cloaked in a lamb's suit; he is really the wolf.

## What to Do About an Overly Aggressive Agent

It happens, a lot. The agent may seem nice, appears to understand your predicament, and sounds as though he wants to help you, but it isn't true. The agent has a job to do and will do it. So let's set the stage and dispel a few myths.

Beware: IRS agents are not there to help you. Do not believe that they have your interests at heart. They do not. I believe, in fact, their goal is to collect all that is owed, quickly, or liquidate the offending taxpayer's business so the taxpayer will not abuse the tax code any further.

- Keeping you in business is not their objective. They are interested in collecting as much as possible; they are usually not committed to keeping your business open just to collect more.
- They will not help you achieve your goals. They will not inform you about options, a better way, or an easier plan.
- Working with them means you will pay the maximum and, more than likely, go out of business still owing a lot of money; and the debt will follow you unless you do something about it.
- They will attempt to make as many people as possible responsible to broaden the personal liability and collection potential.
- They will go after your home and everything you own and your business assets.
- Many agents will simply go for the jugular vein immediately, cutting you no slack, making what you consider unreasonable demands, and putting you out of business in a heartbeat.

Aside from the best advice I can give you, which is to hire an experienced tax professional who knows the IRS and the tax code and can advise you on what to do in your situation, you do have an avenue for relief from an oppressive agent.

When you begin to get the lien and levy notices, you will also get a series of pamphlets. One describes your rights to appeal. It's called a collection due process hearing (CDP). It's a beautiful thing and devised to help the taxpayers get a fair hearing and a reasonable shot at working their problems out without losing their business and everything they have worked their lives to build. Even with a professional on board you may need a CDP to level the playing field and undo the damage already done or being threatened by the agent.

If successful, you will have an independent party from a different office—a person who has fairness at heart—take over the situation and provide you with a fresh review.

If your agent has been heavy-handed, offensive, or simply overbearing, and you feel as though you have not been given a fair chance, then you may file for a CDP. If your rights have been violated in some way, and you want an opportunity to work problems out, yet your agent has not been willing to consider options, you may file for a CDP hearing. The hearing can result in giving you the opportunity to work out your tax obligation while moving your case to another agent or office altogether.

It's a real avenue for help. The review agents must follow the statute, but there is usually a way to resolve an issue without putting you out of business and liquidating your assets.

## Who Will Tell Your Story?

People don't want to deal with the IRS or their banker when in default and owing secured, personally guaranteed debt. Many practice self-destructing avoidance because the situation is so distasteful. Rather than confront and possibly resolve the matter, they prefer to avoid the discussion. "It's too uncomfortable," they say. Everyone in such a situation prefers to communicate through third-party professional representatives, "It's their business, and they know best what to do and what to say."

Besides, you think, "This is really very uncomfortable and intimidating." Fearful in a world you would much prefer to have nothing to do with, you'll escape such confrontations if you can.

You hire a seasoned pro who knows how to handle this situation, usually a lawyer or an accountant, to avoid the uncomfortable confrontation at almost any cost. In fact, you convince yourself that this is the smart way to go, hire a pro and let her do the dirty work. She is better at it, and she will succeed in arranging the best outcome.

One of the more common selling points of such a professional representation relationship is exactly that, removing your need to have direct communication and personal involvement with these distasteful situations.

> **You need to confront your creditor-lender and explain your situation and *then* let the third-party professional clean it up.**

**The Importance of Face Time.** It is important that you include a certain amount of face time in support of your third-party representation. You need to confront your creditor-lender and explain your situation and *then* let the third-party professional clean it up. You can have your representative accompany you to make certain you're not taken advantage of, to mediate, and to help; but you must go at least once to reveal the story and fill the IRS in on what happened. This should come from you.

I have seen the positive results from the debtor confronting his lender or creditor. With an in-person meeting, you can create credibility and demonstrate personal commitment, as well as giving your creditors an opportunity to inspect you to determine the truth of your situation, your story.

It's simple, the truth prevails, and this meeting is a necessary component to the workout. Your IRS agent must believe your story, and if so, the workout will go much faster, easier, with far better results, and with far less loss and expense for you. It is difficult to project the truth successfully through a third party as it appears to the agent you are hiding, and thus credibility drops and cooperation disappears.

**When the Professional Goes Alone.** It's a natural reaction to want to avoid the situation, but it's a failing strategy. Your professional representative also falls into this trap, believing his skill will fill the need and that it's his job to protect you from such uncomfortable confrontations by handling the entire negotiation to deliver a brilliant conclusion. I have seen the workout discussion turn into a disaster as the third-party representative tries to explain why the client will not be present to discuss the issues and the resolution.

Without your direct involvement, using a third-party representative often accomplishes the exact opposite by creating distrust and a belief the client is hiding something. The workout becomes hostile and unproductive, with the secured parties wanting to use their significant power to collect or liquidate, no matter what the results, rather than to cooperate and work out the matter to everyone's best interest. It's all about human nature, theirs and yours.

The creditor wants to hear the story, sense the pain, and believe it's the truth and then will work with the professionals to iron out the details.

The professional can instruct and train and prepare his client about what to best say and what not to say, and such preparation is important, but the client must meet and tell her story and discuss the issues, and then she can retreat behind the strength and power of the representative to successfully conclude, as everyone is satisfied. That's the best strategy.

I have seen the power, intensity and truth, the passion and commitment the client reveals in a meeting, which serves to satisfy the creditor and allows the workout to proceed successfully.

I have also seen the professional attempt to deliver this message and fail miserably, or at least not do the job the client could have done, and prevent a successful workout. Even a client with a quiet, soft-spoken, unassuming, low-energy presentation works. Even a few heartfelt words tell the agent immediately who is sincere and who is not.

Credibility is measured many ways, and once felt, its effect is significant and powerful. Only the debtor can best accomplish this feat, better than any professional representative, be it an attorney, an accountant, or a workout specialist. It's a team approach, and the client must play an important role and then can disappear, leaving the professionals to handle the details.

# Chapter 21

# After the Workout

## Let Go!

**S**ome business owners are too emotionally committed to their business to make the right decision, especially when the right decision is to liquidate the business and close its doors.

The allure of operating a business with no debt is very compelling. Yet a business operating after a debt workout and without making payments on debt may still not be breaking even. Removing the debt load doesn't provide the business with any cash flow. If the business cannot run profitably, why continue?

Some business owners will sit tight, hoping that things will turn around, that business will get better soon and revenues will return. If they simply wait long enough, they will prosper ... especially without any debt.

Other business owners are simply too emotionally attached to their business and don't want to kill their dream.

Still others desire to recapture their large cash investment, which will be lost completely by shutting down the business.

Another common excuse is to stay open to protect jobs, "Good people are depending on the business for their livelihood." The owner feels an obligation to them to keep it going. By the time the owner has these thoughts, the business is failing; the owner is probably not even taking a paycheck, but continues to fight the battle.

The challenge is an effective and responsible evaluation of the business model. If it cannot earn a profit on the current revenue without paying debt service, then the business is simply not worthy of saving. This also includes the owner taking a reasonable paycheck and still making and retaining a profit.

If not, then kill the business, sell the assets, change the model, but do not continue to operate as you are, even if you've removed the debt.

Yes! We can remove the debt and free a business to operate successfully. However, successful operation *after* debt reduction is the real issue. So if you can't do it, get out. If it doesn't work, kill it.

## Stop Doing the Same Ol' Thing

Some companies swimming in unaffordable debt have taken advantage of debt reduction and forgiveness strategies to eliminate or decrease debt so they can survive. Debt workout, however, is only one side of the coin. The other side, which is often ineffectively implemented, is downsizing and sharpening the business model. This is where small business owners commonly make serious mistakes. What usually happens is that they enjoy the benefits of the debt workout strategy and continue to do exactly what they were doing before debt reduction occurred. While they may experience relief for a short while, this behavior sets up another form of disaster. Here is the other side of the coin:

The business owner must reduce payroll dramatically. Not minimally, but significantly. The right amount of employee reduction depends upon the specific business situation. The point is, more often than not, the business owner does not go deep enough.

For the past 10 to 15 years, business has been brisk, with high revenues; growth has been the norm, profits fat and easy to come by. Now competition is fierce, customers are very demanding, and profits are thin. The small business owner must not only downsize but implement strong controls and tight operating procedures. The small business owner must now do a better job at running the business. There is no room for sloppiness or excessive costs. Productivity must go up. Overtime must be eliminated, profits must be monitored, and many other basic business systems must be implemented to assure that the business squeezes out every profit nickel it can.

So the message is, yes, we must reduce the debt; without doing that, there is no hope or opportunity. However, debt reduction isn't enough; you must improve your business operation dramatically. In many instances the business owner is challenged to adjust or even radically change the business model when minor or possibly major changes in sales, operations, and finance are called for. The mandate is to reinvent yourself following debt workout.

Do what works and makes money now, not what you did before. Change your sales methods, production methods, and pricing. Change everything. Undergoing debt reduction and workout, downsizing, sharpening the business operation, and reinventing your business—all four aspects are the success equation.

> Do what works and makes money now, not what you did before. Change your sales methods, production methods, and pricing. Change everything.

## Why Let It Happen Again?

OK, the horse is out of the barn, your notes were called, your business closed and liquidated, and your personal guaranties are now paid off. You lost everything you have worked so hard to build.

What is done is done, but I also know most of you will rebuild. A new business, a new home, restored savings, and you will succeed again. That is the nature of a small business owner—an entrepreneur, a risk taker at heart.

However, you can learn from your experience. You can shut the barn door before the horse gets out this time. But I see small business owners who lost everything rebuild and then do the same things they did last time. They fail to learn how to better protect what is important.

It seems everyone believes it will never happen again. That's not the best bet when so much is at stake and so much has already been lost. It's time to shut the door completely and finally, for once and for all. Here are the rules to live by so you don't repeat the mistakes of the past:

1. If you are the risk taker, leave your spouse out of it, off the books, not involved in the business, and never a guarantor no matter what.
2. Remove your name from the family home. If your spouse divorces you, he or she may get the house anyway, but this way you make

certain your home is never at risk again. Do not believe that just because your spouse is not a guarantor, the bank cannot reach the house through your name. Get your name off the deed. Keep it on the mortgage but off the deed.

3. Similarly, remove your name from your vacation home and other valuable assets.

4. Give your spouse a paycheck with taxes deducted. That way your spouse can build wealth in a separate, individual account. Trust your spouse—this person is your partner. And since you are the risk taker, let your spouse hold your wealth; your spouse will do a better job at protecting it than you will..

5. Put the home into an LLC or a trust, which provides even better protection. Keep your name off as executor or beneficiary; assign those positions to your children.

6. Maintain separate checking and saving accounts.

7. If you can build personal cash, use a 401(k) if possible, not an IRA, since a 401(k) provides much better protection. (If you use an IRA, check your state's protection laws; they vary dramatically.)

8. Have adequate liability, health, and auto insurance.

9. Take a paycheck; why else are you in business? If you cannot, reconsider what and why you are in this business.

10. Build a rainy-day fund. It does rain.

Now you can guaranty anything, take whatever risk you choose, and rest assured that none of your important assets are in harm's way. Following these rules removes you from any ownership position. During your next cycle you will have more options and will be better protected.

## Resuming Business with Vendors

You have implemented a massive workout in which all the debts to unsecured creditors are wiped out and most of the secured creditors, with the possible exception of the first secured lender, partially paid. If only you could now start anew. Well, believe it! I say you can open a new business the next day and do business again with most, if not all, of the same people. Even with those to whom, for the most part, you did not pay a single penny in the end.

"How can this be?" you ask in disbelief.

In a word, it's all about *greed*, the driving force behind most businesses. It's the desire to do more and earn more, even with greater risk than one should accept. Business owners cannot say no to more business.

It's always a business decision. The vendor, lender, or whomever you worked out your debt to, understands the high risk of small business. Most successful business entrepreneurs have crashed and burned a few times in their march to success and stability. They know what happens and how difficult it may be to succeed. They know how easy it is to fail to pay your 941 payroll taxes. Every successful business owner has confronted these issues at one time or another.

If properly handled and communicated during the times the trouble was brewing, doing business after the demise is likely. No one wants to say no to doing business. Everyone will understand that you got jammed and lost that inning. But the game has nine innings, and so you can get up to bat again ... and everyone will let you play, because that is what business is all about: taking risk, winning, and yes, sometimes losing. It's a risk every business accepts and every business owner understands.

Understandably, you may be required to pay cash in advance for a few orders, or COD, until you reestablish confidence and re-create credit. Shortly, you will be back on terms and doing business again, hopefully smarter and better than the last time.

It's human nature to forgive and forget and give someone a second chance. If you did your business respectfully and appropriately, you will be greeted with open arms and tighter terms the next time around.

If there are those who will not do business again, certainly there are more suppliers, and a replacement can be found. If there is a critical supplier you must do business with, a different workout can be engineered, paying back half the cash over a period of time with no interest, a showing of respect, allowing the supplier special treatment, affording the company a chance for recapturing costs, a demonstration of consideration. It's probably a good strategy, if necessary, as it is a drop in the bucket compared with the debt you managed to have discharged.

I have infrequently seen a second business effort be rejected by previous business vendors and service providers.

 # Getting Out on Top

## Selling Short to Turn Foreclosure into Victory

Every day we read about the skyrocketing foreclosure rate. For various reasons, be they economic reversals, interest jumps, lost job, failed business, divorce, or sickness, your bank loan goes into default and you are unable to acquire adequate replacement financing to cover the note. You are confronted with foreclosure as the only result.

Not so. There are options to turn foreclosure into victory. The bottom line is that the resulting return through foreclosure is frequently disastrous for the bank. The auction could yield an inadequate return or, worse yet and frequently, no return at all. Then the bank is stuck with the collateral property and all the ensuing costs and expenses without any return. Bank-owned property severely affects the bank's liquidity ratios and lending ability. There's also the potential that the FDIC could close the bank. This is the bank's nightmare, and it's as big a headache as yours. Therefore, a bank will accept less than the value of the loan, rather than take another property it cannot resell easily or for enough money to warrant the effort and expense.

In view of the significant number of bad loans the banks are experiencing and the large number of failed auctions that force the banks to take over the property, they would much prefer to receive less and recognize the loss. This is called a *short sale*—selling the collateral property for less than the note and having the bank accept the deal with a forgiveness of the shortfall. It requires a convincing presentation of the facts. The bank will not accept this arrangement on a lark; all the pertinent information must be documented and reliable, including appraisals and financial statements. It can be done, but it requires skill and tenacity.

## Kill a Business If It's Not Making Money

Perhaps the greatest waste of assets and time and the cause of way too much personal sacrifice and damage to yourself and family is the protracted running of a failing business. Unless you are still in the start-up phase, if your business is not making you money, it's probably not worth saving. Kill it, quickly!

There is no question that there are astute business owners with a marginal cash flow who can juggle their revenue, duck their creditors, get new vendors, fail to pay 941 payroll taxes, max out credit cards, and then go into default, and yet remain in business tenaciously week after week, year after year, waiting for something to happen to change their luck, meanwhile living in hell.

I have huge respect for such a business owner's commitment. I understand the mantra—I will not give up! I get the belief that tomorrow the big order will come in. I understand you are loyal to your workers who are depending on the paycheck you are generating, even if they cannot cash it until Monday. I get the fact that you are committed to your mission. I understand your ego-driven decisions to hang on and anticipate miraculous growth and development . . . tomorrow. I applaud the attitude but beg for some intelligent analysis.

If the business requires a significant investment to succeed and the capital is unavailable, then success is probably impossible, as a business plan based on a miracle is a deficient plan. You, your employees, your creditors, and your family deserve better; it is a foolhardy person who follows this agenda.

I see so many business owners hanging on, wasting assets, working without taking a check home, sacrificing themselves and their families' well-being . . . for what? If it cannot be done, why pretend it can?

Some businesses require inventory; others require consumer advertising. Some require a tight price point as competition is fierce and thus large volume is required. Others require expensive equipment. Most businesses require growth capital, as payday comes every Friday but revenue may take months to develop and collect.

Many marginal businesses simply require a sales and marketing plan and then a way to implement it. Others carry too much overhead or are pricing too low and are unprofitable. Without the appropriate or necessary resources and strategies, the business is doomed from the first day; it's just a matter of time until the business owner is forced to accept reality, when the phones are shut off, or the tax collector contacts you, or the banker knocks on your door, whichever comes first.

It is perhaps the most difficult decision a business owner has to make, but it remains the most basic. If a business cannot be profitable for reasons beyond the owner's control, and if the business is draining capital and other resources without hope of a turnaround, then it is the businessperson's responsibility to liquidate it and try something else.

Worse yet, you may be wasting valuable assets that could be applied to another business plan that could work. After all, we learn more from failure than from success. So your next rendition may be better than the first because of what you learned.

Many feel that it is a personal failure, a reflection on one's character, capability, and skill. While reflecting on what went wrong is important (so you learn the lessons), the bottom line is relevant; after all, it is business, and you need to stop continued losses and shut down.

Let me state the principle clearly: A smart player knows when to fold his hand and when to make a bet and play. A not-so-smart player holds a losing hand, hoping to bluff his way to victory or pull the inside straight. It may work occasionally in cards, but it seldom works in real-life business.

Kill the nonperforming business that cannot work; it's wasting your time and resources. Before you do, consider the best way to close your business and what to do with the remaining resources.

## Closing Your Business and Allocating Cash

You have spent significant time, expended much money, acquired much debt, and now made the hard decision to end the business. Frequently, it takes time to arrange your affairs and make all the micro decisions required to end one business and start a new life. It's a no-man's ground where you are no longer committed to the original mission. So during the transition there is a period of time that you are still doing business but have an adjusted end vision. This transition is the time when you have critical decisions to make.

What are your obligations regarding the remaining cash and the accounts receivables? In fact, what are your obligations regarding all the assets of the old company?

First, the secured creditors and then the unsecured creditors must be considered. However, within these considerations are you able to divert cash to your own personal needs and requirements? In the moment you decide to end the business, you are free to make certain important decisions.

It's your cash, and presumably it is your decision about what to do with it. If you are closing your company because it is not profitable, then it is unlikely you will have adequate cash to pay off the secured parties; but it's still your cash, and you are entitled to make an assortment of decisions regarding it. Since you will be required to confront your secured lenders who have your personal signature, you must initiate some sort of a workout. But that still does not answer the question of what you may do with the final cash.

There are those who will claim that once you are no longer making business decisions that move your business forward, you are obligated to hand over the cash collateral to the secured parties. This may be so, but we have a transitional moment when you are still doing business but have decided to terminate it.

For all the investment you have made, all the cash you have not taken, all the unpaid hours, there is no reason you cannot allocate adequate reserves to your own accounts to assist you in making this transition safely.

Is this appropriate? I say, "Absolutely yes." You personally owe a debt to your secured creditors, and you will require a workout with them. Are you required to hand over every penny and sell all your possessions to pay the secured debt? They will say yes.

I say no! I believe reasonableness is the benchmark, but the bottom line is that it's your cash and you are entitled to make distribution decisions in your own best interest, including to yourself. At the same time, you need to acknowledge you have a debt to the secured parties that must be dealt with and will not end with the business termination. You are always entitled to a paycheck and to back pay for not receiving one previously. This is reasonable and acceptable to any banker.

This does *not* mean that ordering more inventory, knowing you will not be around to pay for it, and then selling the inventory with the intent of taking the receivables is OK; it isn't. That is wrong, as is racking up charges on your credit cards for personal needs knowing you are unlikely to pay them off. On the other hand, it is a reasonable decision to sell existing inventory and use the cash that comes in to pay yourself as much as you can.

The best decision may be a slow wind-down, with a steady decrease in overhead as you reduce your payroll, cease advertising, sell some assets, and pay yourself well, while you cut costs and reallocate the savings to your own needs.

It's a combination of doing the right thing, avoiding abuse, and taking care of yourself. It is a difficult blending of needs, wants, and responsibilities. It's the right decision to make. You are empowered to allocate the cash and receivables as collected wherever you deem them best spent. This is your right.

Just remember the controlling factor: do not be a hog. You still have to deal with the secured creditors, and that issue does not go away. The unsecured are at risk. You have sacrificed for your business and have invested heavily. It is OK for your business to pay you back within reason.

> Just remember the controlling factor: do not be a hog. You still have to deal with the secured creditors, and that issue does not go away.

## Parts May Be Worth More Than the Whole

In October 2008, Chrysler executives in the know anonymously confirmed that Chrysler was considering selling itself in parts to various other auto manufacturers. It seems as though the executives had determined that the parts of the company were worth more than the whole. This is not a surprise and is something every business owner should consider if faced with an unsupportable business situation, declining sales, and no way out.

First of all, assets can be valued differently to different investors. For example:

- Some may be interested in continuing the original owner's business vision, but only wish to purchase the division that interests them.

The purchasing business may already have a sales force or an administrative division capable of maximizing what the original selling business could not do.

- Other interested buyers may have a unique fit in their product line that can be filled by a particular product the selling business owns but would be duplicating the rest of the business, so they may want to buy only one section.
- A third set of buyers may see a vision for the real estate and want to purchase a division to reach the real estate it is located on. After purchasing, they will scrap the business and develop a better use of the property.
- A buyer may find the inventory worthwhile but not the manufacturing capacity.
- A buyer may find the research and development section valuable and see it as an opportunity to get a whole group of creative engineers or designers, putting them to work on other projects but without the dead weight of the existing company.
- A buyer may want the sales force or the distribution pipeline for similar but different products or even for the same type of product but not the ones the seller was distributing.
- There may be inventions or patents that are desirable to competitors.
- For some investors, the machinery might be more valuable than the entire business. While not valuable to produce unprofitable products, it can be of great value to those who have profitable products to manufacture, especially if the machinery is unique and expensive to develop.
- Some investors want a leveraged buyout of the entire company. They sell unused or excess assets to recapture part or all of the investment so they get what they wanted for a low or no cost at all.

Collectively, the separate parts may be many times more valuable than the whole. This is easy to understand: If the whole is not making any profit, then of what value is it to anyone? But cut it into its valuable pieces, and there may be terrific value to be realized.

We are all familiar with the chop shops we read about and see on TV, garages where stolen cars are chopped into pieces and sold as parts because a $25,000 vehicle whole may be worth $50,000 in parts.

This is the same concept but legal.

We are in a down economy, with many businesses forced to face disastrous declines in revenues. Those investors with cash, if there are any, could be searching for just such an opportunity; and those businesses ready to close their doors, unable to find a buyer for the entire business, could consider the value of selling the pieces. It may be the best alternative for all.

 # Parting Words

## 50 Ways to Succeed ... What Works

There are approximately 30 million small businesses in this country representing approximately 70 percent of all employees. Big business may get the spotlight, but small business is the heartbeat of this country.

Small business is where we do it. Unfortunately, many try to do it alone without help, guidance, or support, isolated, yet committed and focused on their daily tasks.

In summary, I offer you these guidelines for success. Many of these ideas that work I have learned from my clients. Some I have learned from other business owners as we all try to figure out what works and what doesn't.

Many have been covered in this book. This is a summary of the ideas I value most—50 ways to run your business more effectively:

1. Get guidance and direction from your peers; have a board of directors. You will do better than if you go it alone.
2. Numbers are the language of business. Learn to use and understand them; enough with the excuses.
3. Flat management is better than a pyramid organization. Divest authority, grant responsibility, and nurture leadership. Inspect but delegate. Accountability is your control.

4. Teams work best, far better than individual efforts. Create and support teams; help them succeed.

5. Key indicators are crucial to tracking, monitoring, and managing your business successfully. Use them.

6. Systems are critical for success at every level. Write them down and use them.

7. Training to create a career path is critical. Never stop training your employees.

8. Have a business plan before you start a new business or buy an existing one. Make certain you have a cash flow pro forma. Don't launch without enough capital. Wait, raise more, change your plan, or don't do it.

9. Use incentive-based reward systems to increase productivity.

10. Remember: Quality is king.

11. Be careful not to waste money on ineffective advertising. Test before a full launch.

12. Use a website with Web 2.0 to create relationships: a blog, YouTube, Facebook, LinkedIn, Twitter, and so on. Social networking is in.

13. Productivity is the key to profit. Monitor and maintain at a very high level. Eliminate overtime; increase productivity first.

14. Value profit over gross revenue.

15. Discontinue a business when you cannot earn a profit adequate to build reserves and paying you a paycheck.

16. Avoid personal guarantees at all costs.

17. Never allow your spouse to sign anything.

18. Protect your home from business debt. There are many ways to do this, but the best is to take your name off of the title on your home. Organize your assets effectively. Protect them from the risk you take.

19. Make certain you always pay your payroll taxes; use a payroll service to force compliance. Cease operations or make drastic changes if you cannot pay.

20. Repeat business is valuable; nurture those relationships.

21. Word-of-mouth promotion, references, and testimonials are the best form of advertising.

22. Compensate your salespeople by commission, always.

23. Manage through action; set examples by doing.

24. Appreciate your employees, thank them for their effort and loyalty, support them when they make mistakes, and encourage them to

take risks; it will pay you back manyfold.

25. QuickBooks is most often the best answer to effective accounting management systems.

26. Define your market niche and capitalize on it.

27. Ask your employees, customers, and vendors how you are doing and take their advice seriously.

28. Leave your ego (emotion) out of your business decisions.

29. Accept responsibility for your own errors; reward and recognize the successes and achievements of your employees.

30. Successful business is built around high-quality employees; find, keep, train, and build around them.

31. Take vacations often.

32. Keep your word always.

33. Be generous.

34. Have a sales and marketing plan. Review it often and make changes when necessary.

35. Remember that a business is successful because the owner knows how to run a successful business, not because of how good the product or service offered is.

36. Enjoy yourself, laugh; do not take yourself too seriously.

37. Give back; pay forward for those who dug the well for you to drink from.

38. Debt can be dangerous; manage it effectively.

39. As soon as you believe your debt will eventually bury you, do a preemptive workout.

40. Do not allow debt to upend your business or personal life; do a workout.

41. Any debt can be worked out.

42. Always pay your payroll taxes, but if you fail to, that too can be worked out.

43. If your revenues have declined, downsize your operation immediately. Excess payroll will kill you quickly, and then everyone will be out of work.

44. Your banker is the opposition when in default; do not listen to your banker's demands or instructions. Get help.

45. Do not invade your IRA or 401(k) to pay down debt, no matter how insistent your banker is.

46. Do not hesitate to do a workout for fear of credit blemishes; credit ratings can be rehabilitated.

47. Renegotiate everything—leases, vendor pricing, everything. This recession will last a long time. Make adjustments now.

48. Redefine your business equation. The economy has changed, and you must change as well. Reinvent yourself.

49. There are fewer employee issues when you train your employees to be as good as you want them to be.

50. Enjoy your business life. You made the decision to be a small business owner; it can and should be very rewarding. Remember, entrepreneurs are unemployable. You had best make it work.

This is part of what I have learned from my clients, and I expect to learn much more. I thank all my clients for showing me the way to succeed, and I am hopeful you will take these lessons and all the experience in this book and apply the strategies for your small business success.

# Index

## About the Author

Donald Todrin, consultant, solves difficult business problems and builds profitable business organizations. He specializes in resolving complex debt workouts, including defaulted SBA-guaranteed loans and 941 payroll tax defaults, asset protection, and debt reduction. He has implemented 56 (so far) businesses himself, while mastering the science of managing and growing a business. The vast majority of businesses he started have been successful and diverse in industry, size, and structure. As a consultant, he has used his strategies to help hundreds of small business owners, and now, as www.secondwindconsults blog author, thousands have been helped.

Most notable is his lifetime of experience, over 30 years on the firing line negotiating difficult workouts, leading companies through tough turnarounds, bringing them back from the brink of bankruptcy, preserving assets, reducing or eliminating debt, and training executives how to more effectively manage and grow their business.

His academic achievements include:

- A bachelor's degree in economics from the University of Massachusetts, Amherst
- A law degree from Northeastern University
- A master's degree in small business taxation from Boston University

He was a primary participant representing business owners during the Northeast banking crisis in the late 1980s. He delivered over 50 public seminars as well as writing a book entitled *How to Deal with RECOLL, the Resolution Trust, or Your Bank if Your Notes Are Called.*

Don is currently heading up Second Wind Consultants, located at 136 West Street, Northampton, MA 01060, 413-584-2581 (www.secondwindconsultants.com), primarily concentrating on debt workouts and focusing on resolving secured bank debt and SBA guaranteed secured bank loans in default.

His blogs can be read at www.secondwindconsultants.com and www.DonTodrin.com.

He is always available for discussion or consultation.